3-19-04

Spanish

(62-17990)

BARTHOLOMEW GOSNOLD
Discoverer and Planter

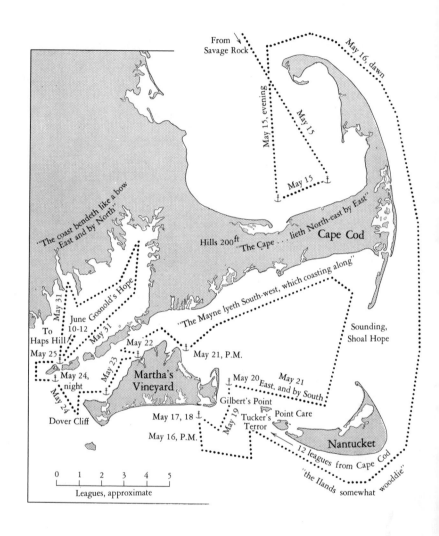

From
Savage Rock

May 16, dawn

May 15, evening

May 15

May 15

"The coast bendeth like a bow
East and by North"

Hills 200ft

"The Cape . . . lieth North-east by East"

Cape Cod

"The Mayne lyeth South-west, which coasting along"

Sounding,
Shoal Hope

June Gosnold's Hope
10-12

May 31

May 31

To
Haps Hill

May 25

May 23

May 22

May 21, P.M.

May 24,
night

May 20

May 21
East, and by South

May 24

Martha's
Vineyard

Dover Cliff

Gilbert's Point

May 17, 18

May 19

Tucker's
Terror

Point Care

Nantucket

May 16, P.M.

12 leagues from Cape Cod

"the Ilands somewhat wooddie"

0   1   2   3   4   5
Leagues, approximate

BARTHOLOMEW GOSNOLD'S COURSE
1602
As described by Gabriel Archer
Schematically indicated by Warner F. Gookin
September, 1948

BARTHOLOMEW GOSNOLD
Discoverer and Planter

New England — 1602, Virginia — 1607

by

WARNER F. GOOKIN, B.D.

with footnotes and a concluding part

by

PHILIP L. BARBOUR

ARCHON BOOKS
Hamden, Connecticut
London, England
1963

Library of Congress Catalog Card Number: 62-19990
Printed in the United States of America

PREFACE

This is the story of Bartholomew Gosnold.

He was a founder of this country. The purpose of this book is to rescue him from obscurity, because Americans have forgotten that Bartholomew Gosnold brought to these shores the first small groups of Englishmen to make good their will to stay. He opened the way for a trickle that became a flood, which turned small colonies into a great nation.

Gosnold lived among his followers, the first colonists of Jamestown, Virginia, less than four months before death claimed him. He lies there in a lost grave, and Americans have given little heed to the record of his contemporaries' naming him "the first mover" of that plantation. Nor do many remember that prior to his Virginia venture Gosnold settled briefly on that part of our coast now known as New England, in the hope of planting there a small English trading colony — seven years before Henry Hudson discovered Manhattan for the Dutch, twelve years before Captain John Smith explored "New England," and eighteen years before the Pilgrims settled themselves at Plymouth.

Scattered scraps of information that have gone into the making of this book have for the first time been assembled within a single set of covers in this year of grace nineteen hundred and fifty-two, three centuries and a half after Gosnold's initial visit to America. The information has come from varied sources. Some of it is as old as the oldest printed books about America; much of it is a new contribution to our understanding of Gosnold, recently gleaned from the parish records of old English churches, from wills, and from other documentary sources used in genealogical research. In particular, I count myself favored of fortune, in that one correspondent after another, men trained in their respective fields, have sent me unrelated pieces of information which I have been able to fit together, as one does a picture puzzle, into an entirely new portrait of Bartholomew Gosnold and his environment.

The professional historian will occasionally find me using

surmises not supported as yet by that direct documentary evidence which I hope may be found. In most of these instances my defense is that the pieces of the puzzle fit together — and that, in itself, constitutes the evidence that they have been correctly correlated with the demonstrable facts.

This must not be understood to be a definitive work on Gosnold. It is offered to the public, particularly to the American public, as their introduction to a stranger who hitherto, even to historians, has been hardly more than a name.

It is a rash thing I undertake, to write a book about a founder of America, in a field which has been minutely examined by the best of historians ever since the writing of history became an exact science. My excuse is that, whereas many ponderous works of reference say that nothing is known of Gosnold's origin and background, I have happened to find, with the help of my English correspondents (to whom all credit is due), the key to an understanding of Bartholomew Gosnold's brief but brilliant career.

It all started quite innocently on my part, with no particular planning or forethought. I found myself somewhat prematurely retired. It appeared to me that a pleasant avocation for my declining years might be a bit of research, of the scientific sort in which I had had some training in my university days both in this country and in Germany, into the question of why the island on which I lived had been named Martha's Vineyard. There had been published twenty years previously the bare fact that Bartholomew Gosnold had a daughter named Martha who, according to a church record in England, had been duly baptized about five years before he named the island; beyond this there was nothing known of her maternal ancestry or of the reasons for giving her that name.

After much casting about, an inquiry directed almost by chance to an understanding official in the country of Essex, England, brought me the evidence that Bartholomew Gosnold had married Mary Golding, and that she was the daughter of Martha Golding and granddaughter of Sir Andrew Judde. With the reading of this report there came to me the recollection that the greatest of all merchant adventurers of his day, Sir Thomas Smythe, was also a grandchild of Sir Andrew, and therefore a first-cousin of Bartholomew's wife.

To speak figuratively, Bartholomew Gosnold by his marriage had become a princeling of a regal House of Merchant Adventurers. Bartholomew Gosnold, therefore, is no longer to be pictured in our works of reference as an unknown, but as a member of the family group led by the great Merchant Prince, Sir Thomas Smythe, who founded the famous East India Company and became for its first twelve years the presiding Treasurer of the Virginia Company of London — a family which included in its ramifications many another notable merchant and famous mariner.

Learned gentlemen, both American and British, authorities in the field of early voyages to America, to whom I first communicated these discoveries, informed me that I had made a discovery which would shed new light on an obscure area of this nation's beginnings. They urged me to publish these findings, which I have done heretofore in historical journals, and now propose to put into this book. In the last few years I have searched as diligently as was possible for me in my circumstances for any possible further bit of information bearing even indirectly on Bartholomew Gosnold and his work. Not the least of my hopes is that scholars more competent than I am will find new material to correct and amplify what I have written. . . . [Left incomplete.]

I must acknowledge encouragement and help received from scholars, editors, librarians, archivists, friends and neighbors. . . . [The word "then" as used below refers to the year in which he drew up the list — presumably 1952. The editor presents the list as it was left (but with one or two omissions filled in) as comprising those to whom he would have wished an acknowledgment to be made.]

Dr. Fulmer Mood, then of the University of Texas.

Dr. David B. Quinn, then of the University of Wales.

Dr. Samuel Eliot Morison, of Harvard University.

Dr. Douglas Adair, then editor of the *William and Mary Quarterly*.

Dr. Arthur Adams, then editor of the *New England Historical and Genealogical Register*.

Rev. Clayton Torrence, then editor of the *Virginia Magazine of History and Biography*.

Dr. Lawrence C. Wroth, then librarian of the John Carter Brown Library.

The Staff of the John Carter Brown Library.

Dr. Walter Muir Whitehill, of the Boston Athenaeum.

Mr. Irvine Gray, then Record Officer, Shire Hall, Gloucester, England.

Mr. F. G. Emmison, County Archivist of Essex.

Mr. L. H. Haydon Whitehead, Record Searcher and Genealogist, Long Melford, Suffolk.

Miss Lilian J. Redstone, then County Archivist, Woodbridge, Suffolk.

Mr. Charles Partridge, dean of Suffolk archivists, Stowmarket, Suffolk.

Mr. Francis A. Foster, friend and neighbor, "whose avocation is genealogical research", of West Tisbury, Massachusetts.

Mr. Alexander O. Vietor, Curator of Maps, Yale University Library.

Mr. Leander McCormick-Goodhart, then a summer resident of Martha's Vineyard, retired diplomat.

Mr. Percy Chase Miller, a personal friend [now deceased].

Mr. Gerald Chittenden, then President of the Dukes County Historical Society, Edgartown, Martha's Vineyard.

Whatever mistakes I may have made in fact or in interpretation are of course my own responsibility.

Warner F. Gookin [1952?]

EDITOR'S NOTE

The author of this work, the Reverend Warner F. Gookin, dedicated his last years to a definitive study of one of the unsung heroes of England's early expansion — Captain Bartholomew Gosnold. Most unfortunately, Mr. Gookin did not live to see the task completed, and for several years his unfinished manuscript lay in the Library of the Dukes County Historical Society in Edgartown, Martha's Vineyard, awaiting completion and annotation. Tasks of this sort do not find ready volunteers.

By a curious accident, late September 1959 found the editor in Martha's Vineyard looking for potential light on another subject — Captain John Smith, friend and associate of Gosnold's in the Virginia Venture. Further curious accidents led to mention of the manuscript and eventually to an agreement between the Society and the editor that he would do everything within his power to prepare it for publication. Many contretemps have delayed the realization of this agreement, but in delaying it have perhaps benefitted the result. To polish and complete another writer's work is thankless; to re-gather dispersed background material and locate unspecified sources, all but futile. Yet the importance of Mr. Gookin's exposition of Bartholomew Gosnold's proper place in the history of English colonization has so overshadowed qualms and demands on patience alike that the editor has almost been elevated to co-authorship. It is to be hoped that this anomalous method of writing biography may prove more successful than he dares expect.

This hope is expressed not from the point of view of justification or reward for either the original author or the posthumous arranger. It is expressed in the name of the subject, Captain Gosnold, whose services toward the lasting establishment of English-speaking America have heretofore been buried in an anonymous grave. This is Mr. Gookin's great work: that he had the patience and the insight — the intuition, if you will — to bring

Gosnold into the light of history again, after three and a half centuries of twilight that darkened into oblivion.

Gosnold was not the first mover of American colonization in England. He was not the first colonizer. He was neither a distinguished political figure nor a hero who single-handedly brought about some cataclysmic change. Yet where Sir Humphrey Gilbert and Sir Walter Ralegh, Captain Edward Hayes and Richard Hakluyt, and a handful of other entrepreneurs and colonialists had failed, spectacularly failed, Gosnold in an inconspicuous, almost humdrum, way set in motion the machinery that was finally to affect world history through the establishment of this country.

Gosnold stands depicted as a persistent salesman and devoted propagandist, as a practical mariner and a courageous soldier. What others had planned, he made possible — less as a leader than as a man with a will, with a dedicated purpose in life. In short, Gosnold was Pathfinder for New England and Pioneer in Virginia. Those who came later crowned his work with success.

Neglected if not forgotten by history, Gosnold's name was yet for all time written on the hidden stones on which our State is built. Warner F. Gookin is to be thanked for bringing it once more before our eyes.

The editor, in his own right, avails himself of the opportunity to acknowledge his great indebtedness to Professor David B. Quinn, now of the University of Liverpool, for repeated "consultation" by air-mail, and to thank the following for their help:

Mr. Francis A. Foster, mentioned by Mr. Gookin,

Mrs. Benjamin C. Mayhew, Secretary of the Dukes County Historical Society, who has been tireless in her efforts to supply pertinent information,

Mr. Dudley T. Easby, Jr., Secretary of the Metropolitan Museum of Art, New York City,

The Staff of the New York Public Library, particularly in the

Reserve Room, the Map Room, and the American History and "Genealogical" Rooms, and

Mr. and Mrs. Adrian Lamb, of New Canaan and New York City, for their repeated hospitality in the latter, whereby work at the Library was made pleasurable, as well as profitable.

Philip L. Barbour

Newtown, Connecticut

Jamestown, Virginia

And amongest other of worthy memory in this plantation, you shall understand that CAPTAIN GOSNOLL, a brave soldier and very ingenious, spent much money, and adventured his person, and drew in many others, at the beginning of this plantation.

JOHN STOW, *The annales of England* [1614]

PART I

Bartholomew Gosnold
Scion of the Gosnolds of Otley in Suffolk.
His Birth and Youth

Chapter I

NORUMBEGA

In the year 1582 English lads of the generation of eleven-year-old Bartholomew Gosnold could read for the first time a true tale of the North American Indians. It was told in a sixty-year-old document translated by the Reverend Richard Hakluyt for his first printed collection of mariners' narratives of voyages to America. This document was a letter, written by one Giovanni da Verrazzano, an Italian from Florence in the service of King Francis I of France. In it, Verrazzano gave the King an account of a voyage up the coast of North America. Highly colored and somewhat fanciful, this was designed to stir the imagination of the King rather than to give specific geographical information. Nevertheless, it contained the first useful account of a place recognizable as located in the region we know as New England.[1]

From Verrazzano's "Letter" one learned that the explorer's vessel, entering a large harbor, had been welcomed by natives of the land, who approached the ship in twenty small boats. Trifling gifts of small bells and glass beads enticed these people to board the great vessel. Among them were two Kings, one older and one younger, both clad in deerskins, and ornamented with chains of many-hued stones.

Verrazzano describes his Indian visitors as the goodliest and fairest natives they had found on the voyage. "They exceed us in bignes," he wrote: "they are of the colour of brasse, some of them incline more to whitenesse; others are of yellow colour, of comely visage, with long and blacke haire, which they are very careful to trim and decke up; they are blacke and quicke eyed, and of sweete and pleasant countenance . . ." And he added that during his two-weeks' stay great numbers of these people came often to the ship, their faces "all bepainted with divers colours, shewing us that it was a signe of joy."

Among their ornaments were plates of wrought copper which they esteemed more than gold. The rich red of copper appealed to them; the pale yellow of gold made it seem to them the basest of metals. They showed no interest whatever in silk or embroidered fabrics. The utility of articles of iron and steel was beyond their comprehension. Glass baubles, azure and red, were treasures to them.

The voyagers journeyed fifteen or more miles into the interior and saw treeless plains twenty-five leagues broad, fit for planting. They entered a thick wood of oak, cypress, and other trees bearing varieties of nuts and fruit. They saw deer and other fur-bearing animals, which these people took with nets or shot with their bows and arrows.

There were numerous other details to interest boys of Bartholomew's age. They read that the Indians' arrows were tipped, not with iron but with points of flint, jasper-stone, or hard marble, and that with other sharp stone tools they cut down huge trees to make their boats of one whole piece of wood, hollowing them out with wonderful art. The largest of these hollowed logs could carry ten or twelve men.

The houses of these people were made with half-rounds of trees set in a circle ten or twelve paces in circumference and covered with mats of straw "wrought cunningly together, which save them from the wind and raine." There was no order in the arrangement of these separate lodges. Taking off the mats, they moved these houses according to their convenience and the season. They planted "pulse" [peas, beans, etc.], but lived mostly by hunting and fishing.

Verrazzano found these Indians kindly and hospitable, generous in supplying the voyagers with stores of food for their ship. They were the same people who, over a century later, were to give asylum to Roger Williams when he fled to the Narragansett region from the face of his persecutors. And thus Verrazzano gave Englishmen their first glimpse of *Norumbega*, the land that was to become New England. Bartholomew Gosnold, who read Verrazzano's letter, grew up to be the first Englishman to search

4

for this place, discovering instead another bay — Buzzards Bay — only a few miles east of the one visited by Verrazzano three-quarters of a century before him.

The land, said Verrazzano in conclusion, was in the parallel of Rome, forty-one degrees and two-thirds; "the mouth of the Haven lieth open to the South half a league broad."[2] Within, he added, it extended twelve leagues, increasing in breadth to form a gulf twenty leagues in compass. In this gulf were five small islands full of trees. There were hills on both sides of the southern entrance, with many rivers flowing into the sea. In the midst of the entrance there was a natural rock of freestone suitable for fortification, to which Verrazzano might have added had he been in a flippant mood, "try and find it."

For the readers of this publication of 1582, called *Divers Voyages, touching the discoverie of America,* Hakluyt printed in the margin opposite Verrazzano's account of the kingdom at 41° 40′ N., this note: "The Countrey of Sir H. G. voyage." Even so young a reader as Bartholomew would understand that the initials were those of Sir Humphrey Gilbert, for all England was talking of this Knight's plans for a great expedition to *Norumbega.*[3] The family tutor would occasionally suspend, we imagine, the parsing of Latin in the manorial schoolroom at Otley (where the walls were frescoed with scenes from the classics) to repeat for the small group of Gosnold scions the latest report of England's progress toward empire.

It was high time that England had colonies of her own in America. Sir Francis Drake had recently been assaulting and pillaging Spanish colonies and Spanish ships in Central and South America, to the tune of 600,000 pounds on a single voyage — but after all he was, in modern slang, a hijacker, victimizing the Spanish racketeers themselves of their ill-gotten gains. How much better for England to have her own American plantations amongst Indians who regarded gold as a worthless metal, whence, by trade and development of the land's natural resources, wealth would be brought continuously to England![4] But the merchants of the guilds, supporters of the established trade routes through the northern seas and the Mediterranean, ever willing to fit out a vessel for piracy and plundering in the tropical Atlantic, were not ready to invest the large sums needed to maintain a colony until it became productive of wealth.

Sir Humphrey Gilbert had obtained in 1578 a patent from the Queen broadly giving him the right to establish a colony in North America at any place not already in the possession of another Christian nation, meaning, of course, that he was to avoid localities preempted by France in the north and Spain in the south. His maritime activities in the first years under this patent are not recorded in such a way as to make them comprehensible in purpose or in accomplishment. In 1582, however, Gilbert began to appeal to knights and gentry who for one reason or another were interested in a new life beyond the seas. He conveyed to them by assignment rights to about ten million acres in exchange for their financial support of his expedition. These acres were located on or near the Dee River, according to Gilbert's agreement with Sir George Peckham, but this river is not shown on Dee's own map.[5]

Rumors of these things must have made even the landed gentry of Otley, Suffolk, perk up their ears, for to every country gentleman the easy acquisition of more land and forests was the best of all reasons for colonization overseas. After interminable delays, word finally came that Sir Humphrey had sailed on June 11, 1583, with five vessels. This was followed immediately by the disquieting news that one of them, fitted out by Sir Walter Ralegh, Gilbert's younger half-brother, had been forced to turn back by a sick or hungry crew on the second day out.

The expedition, it was explained, had sailed to Newfoundland because of the lateness of the start, to replenish its supplies from the well-stocked fishermen assembled there before sailing on south to Norumbega. Late in the summer another one of the fleet, the *Swallow*, was reported back in England, having returned with some of the sick and fearful, under the command of Captain William Winter. How amazed young Bartholomew Gosnold would have been had he been shown, by some occult art, that twelve years later he was to become by marriage a near relative of this Captain Winter. Even less could Gosnold know that Gilbert's visionary adventure was shaping his own destiny.

The *Golden Hind* (named for Sir Francis Drake's famous ship, then on exhibition in the Thames hard by the palace at Greenwich), owned and commanded by Captain Edward Hayes, returned late in September, the sole survivor of Gilbert's fleet, with a tale of disasters.

Gilbert had attended to certain matters of government in Newfoundland on behalf of the Queen, then, as planned, had sailed south with his three remaining ships fully provisioned. Something went wrong with the sailing directions. The *Delight*, a 120-ton vessel, with the bulk of the supplies on board, went ashore a hundred leagues short of their destination, a total loss with the entire crew, as was supposed, of ninety-six men. (Unbeknownst to the captains of the other ships, sixteen men had escaped in a pinnace. After suffering extreme hardship, they finally reached the southern shores of Newfoundland and were ultimately returned to England, to tell their story of the shipwreck.)

It was useless for the expedition to press on, with only Gilbert's ten-ton frigate, the *Squirrel*, and Hayes' forty-ton *Golden Hind*. Orders had been given for a return to England. Sir Humphrey had insisted on sailing in his own little frigate, with the squirrel of his coat-of-arms proudly displayed on the prow. Somewhere near the Azores the *Squirrel* had been in the lead at night, when a great storm struck. Anxious watchers on the *Golden Hind* had seen the masthead light of the *Squirrel* disappear. Nevermore was there sight or word of the gallant frigate or of her reckless commander.

These were the beginnings of the birth pains of New England. Two decades were to pass before Bartholomew Gosnold, grown to full maturity, undertook to do what Sir Humphrey Gilbert had failed to do. He succeeded in landing settlers, although but for a brief stay, in the region described by Verrazzano.

The full story of Gilbert's voyage was written by Captain Edward Hayes for Richard Hakluyt. Bartholomew had reached his eighteenth year, and was half-way through his university studies, when Hayes' narrative appeared in 1589 in the work entitled *Principall Navigations, Voiages and Discoveries of the English nation.*[6] In it, and in the succeeding edition of 1598-1600, Hakluyt also reprinted Verrazzano's *Letter*. Gosnold called this work familiarly the "Booke of Discoveries" when he had occasion later to refer his father to it for a description of the Indians of Norumbega.[7]

Two other works advocating a trans-Atlantic settlement in the temperate zone were printed in 1583 as the result of Gilbert's activity. One was by Christopher Carleill, who had hoped with the aid of his step-father, the Secretary of State, Sir Francis Walsingham, to rival Gilbert's voyage, but with better financial backing.[8] Bartholomew Gosnold undoubtedly had a copy of this work thrust into his hands by his vigorous young mother-in-law, Martha Golding. Martha had been an aunt of sorts to Carleill, that is, Martha's "brother[-in-law]", John Barne, was Carleill's uncle.[9] It is probable that Martha would want her new son-in-law to follow in the footsteps of her late "nephew", of her own age, who died two years before Bartholomew Gosnold married into the Golding family.

The other publication of 1583 was by Sir George Peckham, Gilbert's chief assignee. Hakluyt, as well as Hayes, seems to have contributed to this pamphlet, called *True Report*, since the following quotation, at least, shows Peckham echoing Hakluyt. In his words appears the first clear account of the ocean highway from England to New England.

> For after once we are departed the coast of England, wee may passe straightway thither, without danger of being driven into any the countries of our enemies, or doubtfull friends: for commonly one winde serveth to bring us thither, which seldome faileth from the middle of Januarie to the middle of May, a benefit which the mariners make great account of, for it is a pleasure that they have in a few or none of other journeyes. Also the passage is short, for we may goe thither in thirtie or fortie dayes at the most, having but an indifferent winde, and returne continually in

8

twentie or foure and twentie dayes at the most. And in the same our journey, by reason it is in the Ocean, and quite out of the way from the intercourse of other countreyes, we may safely trade and traffique without peril of piracy: neither shall our ships, people, or goods there, be subject to arrest or molestation of any Pagan potentate, Turkish tyrant, yea, or Christian prince, which heretofore sometimes upon slender occasion in other parts have stayed our ships and merchandizes, whereby great numbers of our countreymen have been utterly undone, divers put to ransome, yea, and some lost their lives: a thing so fresh in memorie as it needeth no proofe, and is well worthy of consideration.

Besides, in this voyage we doe not crosse the burnt line [equator, or torrid zone], whereby commonly both beverage and victuall are corrupted, and mens health very much impayred, neither doe we passe the frozen seas, which yeelde sundry extreme dangers: but have a temperate climate at all times of the yeere, to serve our turnes [needs].[10]

This was the course which Bartholomew Gosnold chose to follow in 1602.

CHAPTER II

SCION OF THE GOSNOLDS

Referring to Bartholomew Gosnold's slightly older contemporary, William Shakespeare, A. L. Rowse finds the explanation of the latter's inexhaustible vitality in the period in which he lived. That age must be taken into consideration in unfolding the story of Gosnold's life.

> The Elizabethan Age was so much the most intense and electric experience of a young people suddenly coming to maturity, with new worlds opening out before them, not only across the seas but in the mind. It is incredible what intensity of experience was crowded into those two decades at the end of Elizabeth's reign: . . . in that short span, [the English people] gave evidence of all that they had it in them to achieve in the centuries to come.[1]

In those two decades Bartholomew Gosnold had his impressionable adolescence, obtained his classical and legal education, and established himself as the head of a family.

Stability of character is one of the expected fruits of a lineage long established in security. This Bartholomew had: he was one of the fifth generation[2] of a family seated at Netherhall Manor in Otley, Suffolk, proudly bearing arms the origin of which seems lost in the mists of antiquity. Since those who were entitled to arms felt obliged to know something about them[3], Bartholomew in his youth must have been told of John Gosnold, the progenitor of the Otley Gosnolds, and his son John, who built or rebuilt the manor house in the reign of Henry VII, and who built so well that the timbered structure stands to this day. Only the moat, once filled with water, is now in part filled in — a flower garden.

Bartholomew was undoubtedly told even more about his great-grandfather, Robert Gosnold the elder, second lord of

Netherhall manor, who was born a very few years before Columbus discovered Guanahaní, and who lived to bequeath in his will of 1572 a nest-egg of twenty pounds to his latest great-grandson, Bartholomew, then about a year old.[4] During his long life as patriarch of the family, Robert Gosnold the elder had shared in the prosperity of the era by acquiring numerous properties — manors, farms, leased lands and meadows — which provided the wealth of the Gosnolds. By then, in fact, Henry VIII, by despoiling the monasteries of their lands and making them available to the country gentry, had indirectly made the family all the richer.

There were other distinguished Gosnolds, not direct ancestors, about whom Bartholomew surely would have heard. One of these was his grand-uncle, John Gosnold, an eminent Member of Parliament in the reign of Edward VI, and Solicitor General for a term. In this capacity, John had had a hand in the plan to place Lady Jane Grey on the throne on the death of young King Edward. John died without leaving an heir, fortunately before Queen Mary had a chance to chop off his head for such disloyalty.

Grand-uncle John's two sisters would also have been extolled before young Bartholomew, for they had married two brothers of the Golding family, first cousins of the Elizabethan author and translator, Arthur Golding, and of his half-sister Margery, second wife of the very noble sixteenth Earl of Oxford and mother of Edward Vere, the seventeenth Earl, who succeeded his father before Bartholomew Gosnold was born.

Bartholomew's grandfather and grandmother Gosnold, Robert and his wife Mary Vesey, died long before Bartholomew was born, leaving five sons and eight daughters. This younger Robert leaves little mark in history, and the many cousins provided by so large a family with two or three notable exceptions seem to have had no part in Bartholomew's career. Of his grandmother it may be said that she was an aunt of Abram Vesey, who married into the Winthrop family of Groton. In later years this connection interested the Puritan Governor of Massachusetts not

11

at all. The Gosnolds were notable defenders of monarchy and episcopacy.[5]

As we approach Bartholomew's own life, the number of near relatives whom he would have heard mentioned, and in later cases personally known, naturally increases. To repeat, Bartholomew had eight aunts. One of these, Dorothy, married Sir John Gilbert, of Finborough Hall, Suffolk, son of a London goldsmith. Sir John and Lady Dorothy had three daughters, all of whom married knights. The second daughter, Elizabeth, married Sir Roger North of Mildenhall, Suffolk, a son of Sir Henry North, who "taking early to arms was, 25 Elizabeth [1583], in that expedition to Norembega under Sir Humphrey Gilbert."[6]

Bartholomew's uncle, Robert, the third of that name, became lord of Netherhall Manor on his grandfather's death in 1572, his father having predeceased him. He was then about forty and in the midst of a distinguished career. But long before that separate entries in the published records of the University of Cambridge reveal that Robert Gosnold and two "impubes" brothers [that is, they had not yet reached puberty], Anthony and John by name, were matriculated on the same day, Michaelmas, 1550, "sizars from Jesus [College]". The picture of Robert probably aged sixteen, going up to the great University with his two little brothers tagging along is a charming one. (The term "sizars" meant that the three lads were granted an allowance from the college to enable them to study. In return, they were expected to do some sort of service. This is not surprising, since they were three of thirteen children, and their father had not come into any inheritance from the still-flourishing Robert Gosnold the elder.)

This Robert, whom for convenience' sake we may denominate Robert III (the Gosnold family presents the rather unusual succession of seven Roberts, eldest-son of eldest-son, born within a range of less than 150 years,) was admitted to Gray's Inn to study law in 1553, and his brother Anthony followed him there a year later. Robert was still in London in 1559, for in that year he inherited from his father a bed "which he hath in London" the possession of a bed in those days being a prerogative of at least some wealth and to be mentioned formally in wills.[7] About this time he married exceptionally well, taking as his wife Ursula Naunton, a granddaughter of the illustrious Sir Anthony Wingfield, Knight of the Garter, and his wife, Elizabeth Vere, sister of John Vere, fourteenth Earl of Oxford, upon whose death the title passed to a second cousin — the father of the Vere who married Margery Golding.[8]

In 1561 Robert was appointed a Justice of the Peace for Suffolk, an honorable appointment for the preservation of the peace in the county and the discharge of other magisterial functions. A portrait of him, dated about 1610, portrays him as an elderly gentleman — he was perhaps seventy-five — of commanding character and proud mien. His influence on his great-nephew was, we may assume, very great.

Robert Gosnold III died in 1615, outliving most of his sons and nephews, including his heir, Robert (IV), and that gentleman's nephews, Bartholomew and Anthony, who had died in Virginia. Of his two surviving sons, he seems to have preferred the elder, Anthony "of Swilland", so called to distinguish him from the other Anthonys who surrounded the old man. Another Anthony, son of Robert (IV) and the youngest of the Anthonys, had gone to Virginia with Bartholomew and was still there when Robert III died in 1615, and Robert's grief at the loss of Bartholomew and the other Anthony (his brother) is reflected in the injunction that grandson Anthony was to have one hundred pounds provided he returned from Virginia within a year. Nevertheless, Anthony refused to desert his post — apparently that of someone's employee — for at least six years longer.[9]

Bartholomew's father, another Anthony and the brother of Robert III, is seen as closely associated with Robert in most of the documents that have been preserved. As a younger son, he of course had no share in the entailed manor and its dependencies. But his grandfather Robert Gosnold the elder had dealt generously with him in bequests of land. Indeed, both brothers, following the custom of the time, had much more likely

13

studied law in order to manage their large estates than with any thought to becoming barristers. Both, however, seem to have practised law in London for a few years, Anthony no doubt sharing his brother's chambers. Anthony probably returned to Suffolk about 1580, if not before, to take possession of the land willed him by his grandfather to be his in that year.[10]

From Otley a highway today leads down the valley to Woodbridge, passing through Clopton about two miles from Otley and between Burgh and Grundisburgh a mile or so farther along. Through this valley from Otley to Grundisburgh flows a narrow stream called the Finn, which ultimately finds its way to the broad estuary of the River Deben a mile and a half below Woodbridge. Somewhere in this valley, within four or five miles of Otley, Anthony Gosnold had his chief holdings; he is known in the documents as Anthony Gosnold of Clopton and Grundisburgh. This region in the southeastern part of the County of Suffolk is said to have changed little in the last three centuries. It is described as a pleasant countryside, criss-crossed with many lanes. Its rolling hills and heath and small fields are given over entirely to agriculture. Woodbridge, three miles from Grundisburgh, served as its port for the shipment of grains and produce in small vessels to London.

Anthony Gosnold seems to have done nearly as well for himself by marriage as his brother Robert. About 1570 he took to himself as wife Dorothy Bacon, a granddaughter of Thomas Bacon of Hessett. Thomas Bacon was a cousin of Lord Keeper Sir Nicholas Bacon, but of what degree it has been impossible to determine. Thomas Bacon in his will of 1547 names Sir Nicholas his attorney and overseer of his will — an appointment which usually implies a close relationship. An uncle of Dorothy Bacon (grand-uncle of her son Bartholomew) in 1559 likewise named, as overseer of his will, "Sir Nicholas Bacon, the Right Honourable Lord Keeper of the Great Seal of England."[11] It seems quite likely, therefore, that the sons of Sir Nicholas Bacon, well-known in history, were aware that a kinswoman of theirs had married Anthony Gosnold and borne a son Bartholomew.

14

As the sons of Anthony Gosnold approached maturity, the father seems to have gone about the business of establishing himself as a major landowner. In 1584 he bought from his friend Lionel Talmache some thirty acres of woodland, including timber trees, at a cost of £390. This was presumably to provide himself with lumber for the rebuilding or restoring of ancient manor houses. In 1589, there were prepared three elaborate surveys, one of the Manor of Burgh, one of the Manor of Cleves (described as partly in Grundisburgh and partly in Burgh), and one of the Manor of Grundisburgh Hall. No lord of the manor is named in these surveys, but other documents indicate that without any doubt Anthony Gosnold began at this time payments looking forward to the acquisition of these manors — one of them, Grundisburgh Hall, apparently in partnership with his cousin William York.

From several documents, too fragmentary to tell the whole story, it appears that Anthony and Bartholomew Gosnold in 1589 paid the sum of £320 to certain parties who had a claim on the manors of Burgh and Cleves.[12] The subsequent history of these manors is so obscure that it is difficult to tell much about them. No one knows precisely where they stood, how long they stood, or what specific areas they covered.

Unfortunately the transactions in the purchase of these manors got Anthony Gosnold into serious financial difficulties, involving his brother Robert as well, in the last decade of the century. One creditor who the Gosnolds thought had made a friendly loan without mention of interest became annoyed at the end of five years because he had received neither interest nor principal; he averred that Anthony had paid the amount over to his brother, but that it had gotten no farther. On his creditor's insistence, Anthony was imprisoned in 1600 in the King's Bench Prison in Southwark "as a result of borrowing more money to pay the interest."[13] Robert then petitioned the Court of Chancery to have the whole case reviewed. Evidently there was something more to be said on the Gosnold side of it, but there information ends.

15

In the course of time, all difficulties — financial and otherwise — seemed to be overcome. A Court Book of the Manor of Cleves beginning the Court General of "Anthony Gosnold, gentleman, lord of said manor", records a court held by him (for the settlement of differences between tenants, and between himself and the tenants) on April 11, 1608, followed by others held in his name by Lionel Edgar, steward, up to October 26, 1609.[14] But from this record, we learn that Anthony Gosnold held his last court. It is an ill omen, for about this same time Robert Gosnold appears briefly as lord of the manor at Grundisburgh. Within three years all of Anthony Gosnold's manors had passed into the hands of a family named Clenche.

Anthony Gosnold had two sons. According to established custom, one of the manors, Cleves, presumably the largest, had been destined for the eldest son and heir, while Burgh Hall was for the younger. From scraps of information it is to be inferred that Anthony Gosnold dropped out of the scene in 1609, perhaps shortly after October 26. The cause may not be far to seek, for within two weeks of that date a ship had arrived in London with news of the death of his second son in Virginia in January of that year.[15] With his eldest son already dead, this snuffing out of the male line of his branch of the family may well have caused the death of septuagenarian Anthony himself, perhaps so suddenly that he made no will — at least, none has been found.

Anthony Gosnold's other children, besides the two sons whose deaths belong to the story of Jamestown, Virginia, were all girls. With one exception, little is known of them. The exception is Bartholomew's sister Elizabeth Gosnold. Elizabeth married Thomas Tilney, of Shelly Hall, near Hadleigh, Suffolk. He was a descendant of the Tilney who was great-grandfather to Anne Boleyn; despite the remoteness of the connection Queen Elizabeth had recognized it by making a royal visitation to Shelly Hall in 1561. Her memory was a long one and doubtless she knew that Thomas Tilney was a kinsman, although a distant one. His bride of the year 1599, born Elizabeth Gosnold, may possibly have been presented at Court.

16

Records relating to Bartholomew Gosnold himself are scanty. He probably completed his education, as his father and uncle had done, by studying law — else the reference to New Inn would be meaningless. Four and a half years had elapsed since his matriculation at Cambridge, allowing time for him to have taken his bachelor's degree. Two parish registers even title him *Magister*, but in the incomplete records of the University there is nothing beyond his entry in 1587.[16] Three more blank years follow the 1592 reference. Then Bartholomew Gosnold married, an event calling for a chapter of its own. But to close this obscure chapter of Bartholomew's life it is not beside the point to evoke a scene or two from the countryside in which he lived, for the call of the great world beyond his rural valley came to Bartholomew Gosnold while he was still a youth. That call possibly came from nearby Woodbridge, on the broad estuary of the Deben, only an afternoon's canter down the country lane. In the words of the eminent Suffolk antiquarian, Charles Partridge of Suffolk:

> [Woodbridge] is a delightful little town, one of the prettiest little market towns in England nestling on the slopes of what in Suffolk must be called a hilly district. The sun always seems to shine on it and the gleaming Deben to love it for its beauty.
> It seems almost incredible that in "the old days" warships were built at its [now] quiet quays. Yet . . . the old town must have been well in touch with the wider world.[17]

Twice as far away, and to the southwest, was Ipswich, a much larger town and port. Birthplace of Cardinal Wolsey, "this Ipswich fellow",[18] here was a lively port, suitable for trade with the Continent, where ships were built and sailcloth made. There at Ipswich, too, we may be sure, young Bartholomew dreamed dreams that were to take him to the New World.

17

CHAPTER III

NEIGHBORS AND COUSINS

The Gosnolds of the generation into which Bartholomew was born moved socially in the upper circle of Suffolk county families. These families played no known part in Gosnold's later adventurings. In fact, it may be said that Bartholomew married above them,[1] into a group which by participation in maritime "merchant adventures" and common trade had become leaders in England's national affairs and builders of the British Empire. Yet, as a part of Bartholomew's early environment, these important personages in county Suffolk must be mentioned.

There were the Wingfields. Several of the grandchildren of Sir Anthony Wingfield, K.G., whose given name was freely used in the Gosnold family, lived in manors in the vicinity of Otley. A Henry Wingfield, possibly Sir Anthony's grandson, as a token of his familiarity with the Gosnolds, "inscribed" his name on a window-pane in the hall of the manor-house at Otley — a choice item to be noted by an antiquarian two centuries or so later.[2] To repeat, Bartholomew's aunt, Ursula Gosnold, was a granddaughter of Sir Anthony's, and so a cousin to all of the near and distant neighbors belonging to that family.

Aunt Ursula supplies a splendid example of how far family ties could be recognized in Bartholomew's day, a family-feeling difficult to realize in the present day. Ursula was the daughter of Elizabeth Wingfield, five generations down from the first (Mowbray) Duke of Norfolk, and William Naunton. She was an aunt, therefore, not only of Bartholomew and a number of other Gosnolds, through her husband, but also of Naunton nieces and nephews, including the well-known Sir Robert Naunton, a politician who later became Secretary of State. Sir Robert's will, dated long after Bartholomew's death, mentions "cousin"

Winifred Gosnold, who was actually no relation at all in a modern sense, but the widow of John Gosnold, son of Sir Robert's aunt Ursula and her husband, Robert (III) Gosnold — a perspicuous illustration of the acceptance of marriage-relationships in that age as the practical equivalent of blood-relationships.[3]

Then there was the Talmache family of Letheringham, some five miles from Otley, in which the eldest sons for generations were successively named Lionel. That they were friends of the Gosnolds in Bartholomew's day is shown by the scribbled name "Edward Gosnold" in the manuscript of Chaucer's *Canterbury Tales* in the Talmache library. It seems that this was some childish prank and that the Edward in question was Bartholomew's youngest uncle. Later, his oldest uncle, Robert III, had a row with the Lionel Talmache of 1599 about a meadow in Helmingham (only two miles from Otley and where the scribbled-in manuscript was.) This dispute was settled by the Sir Anthony Wingfield of Letheringham of that generation. And finally, still later, Robert Gosnold (V) in his day married Ann Talmache, who thus became the sister-in-law of "the younger" Anthony Gosnold of Virginia — he who refused to go back to England for the £100 left him by grandfather Robert (III).[4]

The little town of Coddenham, six miles west of Otley, provides more than a little that is of interest to this story. Edmund, a brother of Robert Gosnold the elder, had settled there and acquired, together with his nephew, John Gosnold the Solicitor General, the Manor of Vesseys, otherwise called "the Priory or the 'Manor of Coddenham Vicarage'." Edmund's only son died young and Bartholomew's uncle John, while still very young, removed to Coddenham to take the place of the deceased son. Uncle John was a failure in life and the Manor passed to Edmund's son-in-law, Christopher Ungle, who in turn passed it on to his son, William. In 1580 William Ungle lost it somehow to another member of the family. These Ungles of Coddenham were, of course, cousins in the third or fourth degree to Bartholomew Gosnold. They are mentioned because it seems quite possible that the William Unger ["laborer"] whose name appears among the first lot of Jamestown colonists may in fact have been a William Ungle of Coddenham with his name mis-spelled.[5]

The story about Bartholomew's uncle, John Gosnold of Coddenham, is this. In the days when "the public peace" seemed to require the extermination of Protestants by axe and flame, two young men from Coddenham were employed "in the palace." Somehow these two, presumably John Gosnold and one George Loosen, learned that a fellow servant, Thomas Spurdance, was a Protestant — conceivably an indiscreet one. They told this to "Mr. Gosnal" — probably Edmund — in Coddenham, who seems to have reported it to the ecclesiastical authorities. Not too many years later an account of Spurdance's trial and execution by burning at the stake appeared in John Foxe's *Book of Martyrs*.[6]

An early recorder of the Suffolk scene makes this comment: "It was the observations of old men in Coddenham that lived till my time that since Gosnold and Loosen persecuted that martyr Thomas Spurdance (mentioned by Mr. Foxe) their families did never thrive. Loosen sold his whole estate by parcels to severall men, and died full of lice. Mr. Gosnold a great man in estate decayed by little and little and left a very small pittance to his children. His eldest sone Capt. [Robert] Gosnold (whose mother was sister to Mr. Andrew Tinnellmarsh [Kinwellmarsh]) was at one time Governor of Landguard fort [Suffolk] in the time of King Charles."[7]

Our interest in this tale is because of Captain Robert, son of old John Gosnold and a first cousin of Bartholomew. Having no inheritance, Robert turned soldier in time to be involved in the Essex revolt and be thrown into the Marshalsea Prison in 1601. Then, shortly after the accession of King James, when Captain Robert should have progressed under the favor of the new monarch, he got into difficulties again — difficulties of quite a different sort.

According to one of the papers in the case, Captain Gosnold was "a great commander in the Isle of Wight, in the King's pay." Several depositions about the affair were made by persons concerned with it, and were preserved among the state papers. But as usual it is somewhat difficult to reconstruct the story from the published abstracts of these affidavits.

The most lucid runs as follows: "Ryche, his wife, and Captain Christopher Levens, being in company with Captain Gosnold, Mr. Bowyer Worsely, and others at Mr. Denyse's, the new book of statutes of the last parliament was called for and Gosnold made trifles of many of them, namely of that against conjurers and against the marriage of two wives. Gosnold also used the following speeches to Ryche's wife: 'He never before had heard any woman speak so well of the King as she had done;' — 'the King is a good hunter and he kills bucks, but he is good to does, and he grows weak in the back, his date is almost out;' and 'His back is weak and he is going on his last half year.'"

In another deposition, it appears that "Katheren Ryche did rise suddenly from the table saying, 'Marry, God bless the King, I hope he shall live amongst us these forty years,' after which she went discontented to her chamber."

The discontented lady seems to have been rather free with her kisses at this lively party, for her husband, Captain Barnabe Ryche[8], in still another deposition advances this argument: "She never saw Gosnold before that day or since; yet at divers times when she came out of her chamber to sit down, she entertained both Gosnold and Worsely with each of them a kiss. Here was then no show of quarrel yet. Now afterward if, finding herself discontented with Gosnold for his traitorous demeanor towards the King, she denied him another kiss for a farewell, is her testimony thereof the worse because she had shown her dutiful affection to her prince?"

Mr. Denyse, the host of the gathering, is reported in one of these depositions as having expressed the opinion that Gosnold was a "counterfeit papist, and ill-affected to the King."

All this was of course serious indeed, and Gosnold was put behind bars, so to speak, for a while. Yet he suffered no permanent hurt, since there is record, five years later, of his appointment to an important military post, the first of several — the normal promotions of a military officer enjoying the favor of

King James. Nevertheless, the affair — which lasted from September until at least December, 1604, and kept Gosnold under restraint until after July 1, 1606 — must have been embarrassing to his cousin Bartholomew, because that was precisely the year and a half or so when Bartholomew was seeking means of approach to the King, that there might be obtained from his Majesty a charter for a company to settle in what is today called Virginia.[9]

The general neighborhood of Coddenham contributes another bit to knowledge of Bartholomew Gosnold's associations of quite a different sort. On the first relief, or supply, ship sent out to Jamestown late in 1607 there went a Matthew Scrivener, apparently unannounced and long a "mystery figure" in the narratives of the Jamestown settlement for the reason that he was sent as a new member of the local council, and yet was a very young man. The explanation lies in a Coddenham association; for Ralph Scrivener, Matthew's father, owned three manors there. Obviously young Matthew was a friend of the three Gosnolds who had gone to Virginia in December, 1606, and followed them at the earliest opportunity, recognized as a new leader by the London Council.[10]

Ralph Scrivener, the father, is described as of Ipswich and Belstead, three miles away. In an instrument of 1598 it appears that Robert Gosnold III conceded to Ralph Scrivener and others the right to sell certain properties in Otley.[11] In 1607, Ralph Scrivener died and his property, including the three Coddenham manors, passed into the ownership of his elder son John. The date of his father's death probably determined somehow the time of Matthew's departure for Virginia, where he lost his life in the accident which took the life also of Anthony Gosnold, Bartholomew's younger brother, and all the other occupants of a small boat, which apparently capsized across the river from Jamestown in January, 1609.[12]

Here, as on many preceding occasions in the life of Bartholomew Gosnold, Richard Hakluyt enters into the picture. Three years later that reverend geographer bought from John Scrivener the manor of Bridge Place in Coddenham, in partnership with his son Edmund, to be an investment for the latter. As he trod the village street in Coddenham in that year of 1612 Hakluyt's heart must have been heavy with personal grief for the three young men who had known the place so well and who now lay dead in Virginia — Bartholomew Gosnold, Anthony Gosnold, and Matthew Scrivener.

In 1599, Robert Golding, Bartholomew's father-in-law, together with another lawyer from Bury St. Edmunds named John Mallowes, bought a quarter-share in another Coddenham manor called the manor of "Deanys." How long he held this is not known, but there is notice of Edward Bacon, of Shrubland Hall, buying the "right" of the same share, and dying in 1618.[13] Since Edward Bacon was knighted in 1603, this indicates that Golding did not hold the property for long. (He was a son of Sir Nicholas Bacon, and therefore a kinsman of Bartholomew's mother.)

Probably the most useful of Bartholomew's cousins was John, third son of his uncle Robert (III). John was about three years older than Bartholomew, and presumably the two, along with their brothers, were educated together in the schoolroom of the manor at Otley. It is of course possible that this assumption, along with a resultant friendship between the two, is a mistaken one. Bartholomew may have considered John an insufferable sprig, fit only for a life of servitude at court, and John may have thought of his younger cousin as a boorish fellow better off in foreign parts.

One likes to believe, however, that adolescent companionship and the bond of blood kinship made John Gosnold a friend at court in the days of Bartholomew's need. For John, as a Gentleman Usher in the last years of Elizabeth's and throughout James's reign, could have had many an opportunity to put in a good word for Bartholomew and his colonization schemes with the gentlemen and nobles in the royal antechambers. Then, too, John's wife, Winifred Windsor, was a lady of unquestioned distinction — her mother was a third cousin of Queen Elizabeth

23

and of James V of Scotland, King James's grandfather.[14] Mistress Gosnold, as well as her husband, could and may have done much for Bartholomew's causes.

When we remember that John Gosnold died merely an "esquire" and his wife merely an esquire's wife it is worth stopping to observe the magniloquence with which John's widow described his station in life and her own ancient lineage. For on the monument she erected to his memory in the church at Otley, she gave nearly as much space to her own descent as she did to the virtues of her late husband. This is the only Gosnold monument which escaped the ravages of Puritans when they went through the churches, destroying every effigy or memorial with "popish" wording in its inscription. So, with honor to John Gosnold and in deference to his widow's wish that all be known, it is printed in full:

> Here resteth interred the body of John Gosnold Esqr. 3d sonne of Robert Gosnold of Otley Esqr. and Ursula his Wife, borne of the right antient and worthy families of Naunton and Wingfield of Letheringham. He spent his tender years in good studies at Oxford and his talents were not hidden, his riper years he spent in Court where he served in the place of Gentleman Usher in ordinary the Maies of Q. Elizabeth and K. James 26 yeares and was after a gentleman of the privy chamber in ordinarie to K. Charles.
>
> He married Winifred ye daughter of Walter Windsor Esqr. and son of William Lo: Windsor and of Margarett his Wife daughter of Sr. Geffery Poole Knight, sonne of Sr. Richard Poole Kt. and the Lady Margarett Countesse of Salisbury his Wife, daughter of the right noble Prince George Duke of Clarence Brother to K. Edward the fourth of England, etc.
>
> He departed this Life the 17th of February Anno Dni 1628 aged 60 yeares, who had issue by his said Wife 5 sonnes and 3 daughters, to whose memory his sadd Wife caused this inscription to be erected.[15]

In accordance with the custom of the time, John Gosnold had paid for this office of Gentleman Usher the round sum of £500, which was advanced by his father, Robert Gosnold (III). John did not make enough out of the job to repay his father, but was forgiven the debt in the latter's will.[16] Besides the cash payment there was of course influence brought to bear to secure the appointment. As no date is available for John's marriage to

Winifred, it is a question whether he got the job because of his wife's influence, or whether he got his wife as the result of securing a court appointment. It is quite possible that the marriage was arranged by Lady Dorothy Stafford, a first cousin of Winifred Windsor's mother, and John's place at court was secured at the same time through Lady Stafford's influence. The time has come, therefore, to make an acquaintance with Lady Stafford.

Before proceeding to that pleasant task, however, it should be remarked that King James found John Gosnold a useful person to have around. Although there is little information about this for the first twenty years of James's reign, the surviving records show that on November 10, 1623, King James directed Attorney General Sir Thomas Coventry "to prepare a grant to Mr. Gosnold, the King's servant (and to another deserving gentleman) of the whole benefit of a concealed escheat." Mr. Gosnold, accordingly, was to share in an estate to which the King had title in the absence of legal heirs.[17]

CHAPTER IV

LADY STAFFORD AND HAKLUYT

Lady Dorothy Stafford deserves at least a passing mention by historians who tell the story of the settlement of America. This lady, long since forgotten, was Queen Elizabeth's right-hand woman. The title "Mistress of the Robes" has been used to place her, but it is quite inadequate as a description of her function at Court, for which actually no term exists. She might, however, have been described as a foster-aunt.

Queen Elizabeth could not have had more than the dimmest of recollections of her mother, if any at all, for the unfortunate Anne Boleyn was beheaded when the princess was two years and eight months old. Anne's sister, Mary, married to Sir William Stafford, took her place, even if not officially, until her death when Elizabeth was ten. Sir William remained her uncle, and when he took to himself another wife, his cousin Lady Dorothy Stafford, Lady Dorothy became as it were a substitute for Princess Elizabeth's aunt.

Few details are known of the true relationship between Sir William and Lady Stafford and the young princess except that Lady Stafford was called upon to take her place at Court when Elizabeth ascended the throne, a place such as an aunt might have been accorded. And in that relationship of foster-aunt she remained until the Queen's death. Sir William had died in exile during Mary's reign — they had both fled to Geneva — and Lady Stafford did not marry again. She remained a widow throughout the long period of her attendance on the Queen, whom she survived by one year. In 1604 she died and was buried in St. Margaret's, Westminster, with a memorial tablet showing a painted representation of Lady Dorothy with her six children. Of these, one son (of whom we are to hear more) became the English Ambassador at Paris, and a daughter was the first wife of

26

Sir John Scott, who after her death married a sister of Sir Thomas Smythe who was, of course, first cousin of Bartholomew Gosnold's wife. Sir John Scott was named one of the King's Council of the Virginia Company of London in March, 1607, while Bartholomew Gosnold was on his way to Virginia, financed by that same Company.

A few trenchant, if perhaps apocryphal, remarks have been found which give glimpses of the more difficult side of Lady Stafford's life. Once when negotiations were under way concerning a proposed marriage of Queen Elizabeth to the brother of the King of France, the latter sent a message saying that if her demands were too exacting, France might join with Spain and put Mary Stuart on the throne. The story has it that "This thoroughly alarmed the queen, who kept Lady Stafford awake all night with her lamentations, and was in high fever in the morning" — although "indignation" might seem to have been more in keeping with Elizabeth's character. Then it is said that when Elizabeth's willingness to fulfil the marriage agreement was questioned, she broke into strong language, as was her habit, and called curses down upon her own head if she did not instantly marry the French Duke after his brother granted her demands. Calling Cecil as witness to her words, she renewed her vows, swearing "her wonted oath", and Cecil "whispered to Lady Stafford as he left the chamber, that if the Queen did not fulfil her words this time, God would surely send her to Hell for such blasphemy."[1]

At a somewhat later period, a gentleman happened to remark in a letter, "The Queen has of late used the fair Mrs. Bridges with words and blows of anger; and she, with Mrs. Russell, were put out of the Coffer Chamber. They lay three nights at my Lady Stafford's, but are now returned again to their wonted waiting (on the Queen)." (Mrs. Bridges had offended the Queen by accepting the attentions of the Earl of Essex.)[2]

In a happier mood, the Queen appointed Lady Stafford's son Edward as ambassador to France, knighting him forthwith.

Sir Edward had married Lady Douglas Sheffield, a charming widow wronged by the Queen's beloved, the Earl of Leicester. There was a wedding, cried the lady; there wasn't, retorted the earl. So Edward Stafford married her, putting her safely beyond the earl's reach, which doubtless pleased Elizabeth, ever driven into frantic rages when one of her favorite courtiers was found to have a paramour.

Sir Edward Stafford took to Paris with him the Reverend Richard Hakluyt to serve as his chaplain and "secretary." This clergyman, second to no one in furthering the colonization of the North American continent, had already acquired a certain amount of fame in England, although only about thirty-one at the time of his appointment. He had won notice for his intensive study of geography and cosmography at Oxford and as the editor of the *Divers Voyages,* published about a year before the embassy left for Paris in the fall of 1583.[3] In providing this position for Hakluyt, Sir Edward Stafford, certainly unaware of all that was to come of it, set forward the settlement of America, for every encouragement given to Hakluyt's studies helped to push England's search for the world's wealth westward across the Atlantic. "We are half persuaded", wrote the chivalrous courtier and poet, Sir Philip Sidney, to Sir Edward on July 21, 1584, "to enter into the journey of Sir Humphrey Gilbert very eagerly; whereunto your Mr. Hakluyt has served for a very good trumpet."[4]

For several critical years, Hakluyt was at this vantage point in Paris, a listening post for the study of French maritime activities and for the investigation of the strength and purposes of the Spanish in the New World. Needless to say, Hakluyt made good use of his opportunities. Beginning with the fond — and ambitious — mother using her position at Court to get an appointment for her son and the son's choice of Hakluyt for the chief secretaryship there gradually came a broadening of Hakluyt's knowledge which led to the writing of his greatest work.

Soon after — two years or so after Hakluyt's final return to England — the young university student Bartholomew Gosnold was drawn, there is good reason to believe, into Hakluyt's orbit, through another chain of circumstances set in motion by the same Lady Dorothy Stafford. While the evidence for an early association of young Gosnold with the geographer is entirely circumstantial, it seems when gathered together quite convincing, particularly as on sound documentary evidence we know that Gosnold and Hakluyt were associated in obtaining from King James the charter for the incorporation of the first Virginia Company in 1606. If it be true that Gosnold's activities in the field of colonization were inspired and guided by Richard Hakluyt, then Gosnold emerges from the obscurity of a lone and unexplained adventurer and takes his rightful place in history as a disciple of England's master mind in the island kingdom's transition to world empire.

Hakluyt's close association with the ladies of Sir Edward's family is well documented. Lady Douglass Stafford, the ambassador's wife, had been born a Howard, a younger sister of Charles Howard, Lord Howard of Effingham, Lord High Admiral. Master Richard Hakluyt was more than a little mindful of this relationship, making reference in his dedication of a book of that period to "our famous hero, Charles Howard, second Neptune of the ocean, and brother-in-law of Edward Stafford, our most prudent Ambassador to his most Christian Majesty."[5] In a later dedication to Howard himself, Hakluyt found occasion to say, "The bounden duty which I owe to your most dear sister, the Lady Sheffield, my singular good lady and honorable mistress, admonished me to be mindful of the renowned family of the Howards."[6] These connections are to be remembered in considering what success Sir Walter Ralegh might have had in his proposal of 1602 that the Lord High Admiral confiscate Bartholomew Gosnold's cargo if the elder Lady Stafford and Richard Hakluyt had not been friends of the Gosnolds as well as of the Howards.

In 1584 there occurred an important event in which Lady Dorothy Stafford surely participated. That summer Richard Hakluyt was recalled from his post at the side of her son, the ambassador in Paris, to confer with Sir Walter Ralegh. Out of this meeting came the *Discourse of Western Planting*, written, as Hakluyt says in the preface, "At the request and direction of the Right Worshipful Mr. Walter Ralegh now Knight", and delivered to the Queen herself.[7]

The greater part of the *Discourse* is a detailed study of Spain's conquest and occupation of tropical America, together with a running discussion of how best to break this power of Spain in the western Atlantic — Spain's West India. The general nature of Hakluyt's proposals may be seen in this sentence from the fifth chapter. "The planting of two or three strong forts upon some good havens between Florida and Cape Breton [Nova Scotia] would be a matter in short space of greater damage as well to his fleet as to his Western Indies, for we should not only oftentimes endanger his fleet in the return thereof [therefrom], but also in few years put him in hazard in losing some part of Nova Hispania."[8] Hakluyt also conceived that these vantage points would enable the English to prey upon the vessels of the Spanish fishing fleet, that went yearly up the coast to the fishing grounds near Newfoundland.

This must all have been very pleasing to Ralegh, for belligerency toward Spain was inherent in Ralegh's colonizing activities, as well as in his covetous desire for the wealth to be gained from them. In his twelfth chapter, however, Richard Hakluyt began to advocate an approach to the American coast which was quite different from that followed by Ralegh in sending out the Grenville and later expeditions. Ralegh's idea was to send his fleets in force south of the Tropic of Cancer, enduring the burning heat of the Caribbean that the fleet on its way to the American coast — which came to be called the Virginia coast — might pause amongst the Spanish-owned islands to despoil them, and to do battle with any Spanish ships which might be encountered. This made the voyage to Virginia one that consumed at least three or four months, requiring the ships to replenish their supplies of wood and water on the way.

Hakluyt in the *Discourse of Western Planting*, beginning in Chapter 12, proposed quite a different approach: "In this voyage, we may see by the globe that we are not to pass the burnt zone [the tropics] or to pass through the frozen seas, but in a temperate climate . . . and it requireth not, as long voyages do, the taking in of fresh water by the way in divers places, by reason it may be sailed in five or six weeks."[9] By this Hakluyt meant of course that colonizing expeditions ought to sail directly across the north Atlantic to that part of the coast between Florida and Cape Breton where they intended to start a settlement. This route would not be an invitation to conflict by the fleets transporting men and supplies to America, but rather an avoidance of it. It may perhaps be thought of as Hakluyt's diplomatic policy, as contrasted with Ralegh's desire to engage the Spaniards in combat wherever and whenever possible.

In his twentieth chapter, Hakluyt returned to the theme, saying: "The passage cutteth not near the trade of any prince nor near any of their countries or territories, and is a safe passage, and not easy to be annoyed by prince or potentate whatsoever."[10] And in this last chapter he returned to speak of Norumbega as the place he had in mind for the planting of colonies: the land north of the 40th parallel "which is called by its inhabitants Norumbega."[11]

The *Discourse* was not printed during Hakluyt's lifetime for obvious reasons. Among other things, it contained too frank a revelation of what England's purposes ought to be. There was also the minor point that Ralegh may not have been pleased by its strong insistence on a direct crossing. In fact, Hakluyt chose in the next years, 1586-1587, to flatter Ralegh in the dedications of three works published in that period. Yet the published *Discourse* is immensely valuable as a revelation of the great geographer's mind and aims in the "planting" of America.

If it is right to assume that Bartholomew Gosnold was under Hakluyt's influence when he made his decision to sail directly across the ocean to the regions described by Verrazzano, then this document holds the answer to the question why Gosnold made choice of Sir Humphrey Gilbert's destination as his own.

What had happened behind the scenes is not specifically

31

known, but it must be added that during his audience with the Queen, possibly after and because of his presentation of the *Discourse,* Elizabeth granted "to Richard Hakluyt . . . that canonry or prebend within the cathedral church of the Holy Trinity, Bristol, which shall the first become vacant, with all its appertaining emoluments, to hold for life. . . ." The date was October 5, 1584. Sometime between then and the end of 1586 Richard Hakluyt was admitted and he became the recipient of a goodly income for the rest of his days, with no duties requiring his residence in Bristol.[12]

In 1575 Queen Elizabeth had presented to "Lady Dorothy Stafford, a widow", the manor and park of Wetheringsett.[13] This was one of the many manors which had fallen into the hands of Henry VIII, the Queen's father, who had leased it for a long period of years. Queen Elizabeth in her day "took the Manor away from the See of Ely for a pension." None deserved this grant more than the long-suffering Lady Dorothy. Before relinquishing her rights to the advowson, Queen Elizabeth in 1575 appointed to the benefice, as rector of Wetheringsett, one Richard Huggard.

In the course of the years, grown old and cantankerous, the Rev. Mr. Huggard became troublesome to his neighbors and to Lady Stafford's tenants. Twice in 1587 and 1588, within three years before he died, he was haled before the courts of the neighboring Manor of Brockford and fined, once for pasturing on the common where he had no right, and again for extending a dike onto the land of a freeholder.

In 1587 he had complained to a church court that Lady Dorothy Stafford's tenants had not been paying their tithes. Lady Stafford engaged the services of Anthony Gosnold, Bartholomew's father, to protect her tenants' interests. The attorney, following the custom of the time, had the property demised to himself, so that he might appear before the Court of Chancery as complainant, taking it out of the "Court Christian" for review in the court appointed to protect property rights.

The squabble is an amusing one as it is reported in the

court's proceedings.[14] The original Bill of Complaint is missing, but in the abstract of Huggard's defence it appears that he denied having received tithes amounting to six shillings eight pence (half a "mark", in legal parlance) yearly. In fact, during the twelve years of his incumbency, he had received no money whatsoever. He admitted that he had in some years been given a buck and a doe from the park in part payment of the tithe, but in some years there was a buck only or a doe only, and in years of scarcity neither. He did not think that he should be impeached in the Chancery Court for having taken the matter to the Court Christian, the ecclesiastical court, as was his right. He knew of no document relieving the Lodge and Park of all tithes, except six shillings eight pence, and in any case, he had received no money at all. He denied particularly that he was covetous or contentious, as he said was untruly and slanderously surmised in the bill of complaint.

In his rejoinder Anthony Gosnold maintained that from time out of mind there had been paid to the rector six shillings eight pence and no more, upon request, in a single payment as tithes for all the premises. He maintained that certain deeds, instruments and writings containing an agreement made between the parson and the tenants of the premises, came into the custody of the defendant, but were missing. He averred also that he could prove that no deer were given to the rector in place of tithes.

The records do not say how the case was decided, but in 1590 Mr. Huggard died, and was buried, according to the parish register, in the churchyard at Wetheringsett. Probably few tears were shed. Lady Dorothy Stafford immediately appointed the Rev. Richard Hakluyt to the rectorship.

It is a foregone conclusion that Anthony Gosnold, whose home was about ten miles from Wetheringsett, would be called upon to explain the troubles with Huggard to the new rector and to assist in the location or replacement of the missing documents, that there might be no misunderstanding about the tithes in the future. It is to be assumed further, with only slight possi-

33

bility of error, that the chance which brought Anthony Gosnold into the affairs of the church at Wetheringsett, also brought his son Bartholomew into contact with the great master of geography while Bartholomew was still a student in the University. In fact it is impossible to read the source material of Bartholomew Gosnold's activities without meeting Richard Hakluyt at every step of the way.[15]

The probability of an early acquaintanceship between Hakluyt and Bartholomew Gosnold is increased if one considers three persons to be found in the court of Queen Elizabeth several years before the end of her reign. There is Lady Dorothy Stafford, who had become a friend and patroness of Richard Hakluyt, and who had employed Anthony Gosnold in legal matters at Wetheringsett. There is John Gosnold, Anthony's nephew and Bartholomew's cousin, who became a Gentleman Usher to the Queen and thus came in contact with Lady Stafford. And there is John's wife, Winifred, a daughter of Lady Stafford's own cousin. (Lady Stafford, like Winifred, was a descendant of Sir Richard Pole and his wife, the Lady Margaret, Countess of Salisbury.)

Even if Bartholomew was not taken to Wetheringsett by his father on a visit to Hakluyt in 1590 or soon after, as is probable, then before the end of the decade this court group must have brought together the geographer and the young man who was to be a leader in two notable voyages. An assumption that this did not happen is in this case less tenable than the inference that Gosnold was under the influence of Hakluyt for some years before Gosnold's voyage to Norumbega in 1602.

In the quiet study of the rectory at Wetheringsett, within easy riding distance of Bartholomew's home, during the ten years after his appointment in 1590, Hakluyt concluded his vast work of 1,600,000 words in three volumes, entitled *The Principal Navigations, Voiages, Traffiques and Discoveries of the English Nation, made by Sea or over-land, to the remote and farthest distant quarters of the Earth, at any time within the compasse of these 1500. yeeres: Devided into three severall Volumes, accord-*

34

ing to the positions of the Regions, whereunto they were directed.
The three volumes appeared in 1598, 1599, and 1600.

This was the undigested raw material of geography — the chaos out of which a new science was to be created — a compendium of ancient documents and works of Hakluyt's own day, painstakingly copied, many of them in their original tongues as well as in translation.

The Rev. Richard Hakluyt as a youth had been shown by his older cousin, another Richard Hakluyt, a lawyer and an authority on England's overseas trade, that there was no higher objective in the ministry of the Lord than to study the works of the Lord and his wonders in the deep, as they were seen by those who go down to the sea in ships and occupy the great waters. The reverend geographer's work therefore was done in a deeply religious mood. He inflamed his countrymen with a desire to extend the frontiers of England to the shores of America, vying belatedly with Spain. Indeed, in 1606 Hakluyt himself all but sailed with the fleet bound for Virginia, of which Bartholomew Gosnold was Vice-Admiral. He was no longer young, however. The call of the sea was by then too faint.[16]

CHAPTER V

THE JUDDE FAMILY

For her wedding, young Mary Golding journeyed with her parents, Robert and Martha Golding, from their home in Bury St. Edmunds, Suffolk, fifty-four miles toward London, to the home of her grandmother, Dame Mary Judde,[1] a widow of many years, who lived luxuriously at Latton, near Epping, Essex. The bridegroom, duly named in the Latton Parish Register for 1595, was Bartholomew Gosnold. Mary Gosnold's bridal chamber may well have been that designated in the old lady's will a few years later as "the Queen's Chamber."

Mary Judde, in marital adventures extending over half a century, had been united in holy wedlock successively to three wealthy London merchants, two of them widowers with children of their own by a previous marriage. When she died in 1601 she was possessed therefore of a numerous family and of considerable fortune, invested largely in household furnishings, although there was something over £2,000 to be distributed in cash bequests (undoubtedly equivalent to at least $150,000 today). From the persons mentioned in her will, with their known relatives, it is evident that great-grandson Bartholomew had joined a bewildering array of personages, some well remembered, others still living.[2]

This matriarch, Dame Mary Judde, with an allure for wealthy widowers, began life as Mary Mathew, of Colchester, Essex. She was entitled, she thought, to the arms of her forebears, which were in fact confirmed unto her shortly after she inherited her share of the Judde fortune. Her first husband was Thomas Langton of London, who left her with several marriageable daughters. One of these, Mary, married Sir William Winter, Surveyor of the Navy, and brought into the world a large family, including several sons who became well-known mariners —

Nicholas Winter, Edward Winter (later knighted), and Captain William Winter. Lady Mary Winter died in 1575 and the children, at any rate the younger ones, presumably passed into the custody of their grandmother, as Mary Judde in her will claims all of the surviving ones as her own "sons" and "daughters". Since Mary Winter was a half-sister of another daughter of Mary Judde's who in turn became the mother of Mary Golding, Bartholomew Gosnold acquired all these Winter grandchildren of Dame Mary's as "cousins", by marriage.

Jane, another of Dame Mary's daughters by her first marriage, married John Barne, who thus became an uncle of Bartholomew's wife. He had interesting family connections of his own. His brother, Sir George Barne, a London merchant, served a term as Lord Mayor. A sister married first Alexander Carleill, giving John Barne as nephew the famous naval commander, Christopher Carleill. Secondly she married Francis Walsingham, at the time a leading Member of Parliament, who was to become Queen Elizabeth's Secretary of State. Another of John Barne's sisters married Sir John Rivers, who also had served a term as Lord Mayor of London, and who was the father of Captain John Rivers, a well-known mariner.

In a list of those who sailed with Drake on his expedition of 1585-1586, in the course of which he rescued the discouraged colonists of the first group sent to "southern Virginia" (today's Commonwealth of Virginia and adjacent North Carolina), appear the names of these connections of the Judde family into which Bartholomew married about ten years later: Christopher Carleill and an Alexander Carleill, probably a nephew; Edward and Nicholas Winter, sons of the Surveyor of the Navy; and John Rivers. As lieutenant under Christopher Carleill we also find the name of Thomas Gates (knighted in 1596), who appears somewhat mysteriously as an incorporator in the first Virginia Charter of 1606, which was granted after Bartholomew Gosnold had spent a year, perhaps two, in promoting the cause.[3]

On February 7, 1552, Mary Langton, nee Mathew, became the third wife of Sir Andrew Judde. This marriage took place, a chronicle of the period reveals[4], only five weeks after the decease of Thomas Langton of the Skinners' Company. In due time she bore Sir Andrew a daughter named Martha, the only child of the marriage.

By his first wife, Mary Mirfyn, Sir Andrew had had a daughter named Alice, who grew up to marry Thomas Smythe, commonly called "Mr. Customer Smythe" from his position as collector of customs duties for Queen Elizabeth, which, incidentally, permitted him to amass a huge fortune quite legitimately. The third son of Alice and Mr. "Customer" Smythe, also named Thomas, became a wealthier gentleman than his father and was knighted in 1603 — undoubtedly in that order. This son, having made a fortune in Russian furs[5], took the lead in the formation and direction of the East India Company, chartered by Elizabeth in 1600. He also took the lead, it is believed, in the absence of definite records, in the formation and direction of the first Virginia Company of London. He held office in the Virginia Company as the presiding Treasurer for its first twelve years. This Company succeeded in settling a colony at Jamestown, Virginia, from which grew the United States.[6]

Little Martha Judde was born into the world to be half-sister not only of Lady Winter and Mistress John Barne, but also of Alice Smythe. Martha could have had only the vaguest of recollections of her father, Sir Andrew Judde, who died before she had completed her sixth year; but surely she often stood before his memorial in St. Helen's Church, Bishopsgate, studying this record of her famous father's achievements:

> To Russia and Muscova
> To Spayne Gynny withoute fable
> Traveld he by land and sea
> Both Mayre of London and Staple
> The Commenwelthe he norished
> So worthelie in all his daies
> That ech state full well him loved
> To his perpetuall prayes.
>
> Three wyves he had one was Mary
> Four sunes one mayde had he by her

Annys had none by him truly
By Dame Mary had one dowghter
Thus in the month of September
A thousande fyve hundred fyftey
And eyght died this worthie Staplar
Worshipynge his posterytye.[7]

The third marriage of Dame Mary Judde — who retained to the end of her days the name of the most famous of her three husbands — was to James Altham, another London merchant, alderman, and sheriff. For "contemptuous disobedyence" of a court order of the aldermen, he was dismissed from that office in 1561[8] and retired to Latton, where he bought not only the great Manor but also most of the village. This marriage brought into Dame Mary's family circle a new set of step-children, all mothered by James Altham's first wife, daughter of the London haberdasher, Thomas Blanke. Altham died in 1583, leaving his widow to enjoy for eighteen years her share of the fortunes of her three husbands.

Dame Mary's will of 1601 is a wondrous affair of five large, closely written pages as copied for probate.[9] It distributes the contents of some sixteen parlors and chambers. The chief beneficiaries were an unidentified Wolley family (probably that of one of her daughters), the Golding family, and the Barne family. The Winters, the Althams, and others, were minor beneficiaries.

There were eight large bedsteads with their featherbeds and furnishings, and two little hanging beds. Mary Gosnold got one of the latter with its furnishings and all the household effects in the room that was known as Robert Golding's chamber. For all the beneficiaries there were lists reading like inventories, of what each was to receive, every item of fabric being mentioned individually, or, in the case of napkins, given by the dozen. The grand total of the fabric articles, linens, damasks, Turkish covers, and others, by a rough count came to some 424 items; but that was not all, since the hangings and furnishings of the beds were not separately itemized. Distributed also were sundry pieces of parlor furniture and some 120 pieces of plate, silver-gilt and silver. There were two sets of "Apostle" spoons

— the usual present of sponsors at baptisms — twelve each. Jewelry consisting of a gold chain and six rings, with diamonds, emeralds, rubies, and turquoise, were given to favorite daughters and granddaughters.

Martha was given, in addition to her long list of furnishings, her mother's coach with a pair of stallions and all their accessories, including "a quilt of yellow and blue sarcinet" and a (cloth of) silver pillow with Dame Mary's arms on it. To Martha also was left a nest of gilt goblets with a cover, "which were Mr. Andrew Judds."

By this will, apparently, the great manor house was denuded of its furnishings, or "moveables", which were the personal property of Dame Mary Judde — according to the custom of the times. However, as the Althams undoubtedly had the income from the lucrative lands about, and one of the sons, Sir James, became a Baron of the Exchequer, probably its refurnishing was not a troublesome matter financially.

In the long list of servants and clergymen to receive bequests appear the names of Mr. Chatterton, Master of Emanuel College in Cambridge, who was to preach the funeral sermon, and of a Mr. Dunn, minister at Latton. The two thousand pounds in cash were evidently distributed among the more needy of the beneficiaries; the Goldings were not included among these.

The Smythe grandchildren of Sir Andrew Judde, step-grandchildren of the testator, are not mentioned in this will, neither for that matter had Sir Andrew mentioned them in his. This branch of the family was possibly too saturated with wealth either to need or to appreciate bequests from the Juddes.[10]

There is scant information to be had about Robert Golding, Bartholomew Gosnold's father-in-law. He is named by Dame Mary as her son-in-law, the husband of her daughter Martha, and was to be an executor of the will. In the latter part of his life, from 1580 until his death in 1610, Robert seems to have been a prominent and active citizen of Bury St. Edmunds, apparently a lawyer. He served as recorder for the town of Eye — he may have been a son of John and Christian Golding of

Eye, whose wills mention a son Robert, a minor, not further identified. It is somewhat more than just possible that this Robert Golding was the lawyer of the Inner Temple who was appointed "Reader" or honorary lecturer in 1579 and twice in 1588, and who became Treasurer of the Inner Temple, for the term 1589-1590 — appointments usually crowning a brilliant career of a lawyer sufficiently wealthy to bear the expense of entertaining in the manner expected of the holder of these honors. If Martha's husband was this lawyer of the Inner Temple, it means that at the age of about thirty-eight he married a girl half his age — a happy outcome, perhaps, of a long association with the Judde family as Dame Mary's legal adviser.[11]

This seems the more likely when the question is raised as to what circumstances led to the marriage of Anthony Gosnold's son to the daughter of Robert Golding. The best guess is that Gosnold and Golding were associated somehow, perhaps merely as friends, in the practice of law. Robert Golding of the Inner Temple entered upon his studies in the same years which found Anthony Gosnold studying law at Gray's Inn. The two obviously began their practice of the profession at about the same time. Anthony Gosnold married late in life, his older son Bartholomew having been born only a year or two before Mary Golding. It would seem, therefore, that the two fathers had parallel and probably closely associated careers. If the identification of Robert Golding is correct, then the two were born within a year of one another, were at Cambridge together, studied law in the same years, married within a year of one another, and died only a year apart.[12]

But however the marriage of her daughter was brought about, Martha Golding was predisposed toward a son-in-law who would sail the seas in the search of wealth. She had grown up in the society of merchant adventurers at their highest level. Although only five or six years Sir Thomas Smythe's senior, she was — as has been pointed out — his aunt, and he was a man who has been called the Cecil Rhodes, or alternatively the J. Pierpont Morgan of his day.[13] Sir Thomas's sister, Martha

41

Golding's niece, also has a claim to attention, since she became the second wife (succeeding Lady Stafford's daughter) of Sir John Scott, one of Sir Thomas's associates and a leader in the first Virginia Company of London. Merchants who became Lord Mayors of London were indeed a commonplace in the family album of Martha Golding.

On the sea-going side, she was the aunt of the three sons of her older half-sister, Mary Winter, all of them naval officers. The eldest was Master Nicholas Winter. Next came Captain Edward Winter, later knighted, who married the daughter of the Earl of Worcester (and granddaughter of the Earl of Huntington) — the lady for whom a room was always reserved in Dame Mary Judde's household. Lastly there was Captain William Winter, who sailed as far as Newfoundland with Sir Humphrey Gilbert and who was still living at the time of Bartholomew Gosnold's voyage to Norumbega.

This was an age when couples joined together by God might not be put asunder by man. Marriages "made in heaven" created relationships as valid as blood ties. Brothers-in-law and sisters-in-law thus became "brothers" and "sisters". Martha Golding, accordingly, by what might today seem an unwarranted extension of "in-law" relationships, was an aunt of sorts to Captain Christopher Carleill and to Captain John Rivers, as well as aunt by birth of the sea-faring Winters. The Drake expedition in which members of her family participated was undertaken when Martha's daughter Mary was in her early teens. Who can doubt that glamorous tales of these adventures in the family circle prepared little Mary for a life as the wife of an adventurer such as Bartholomew Gosnold turned out to be!

To this day, a large verdant island off the southern coast of Massachusetts, discovered by Bartholomew Gosnold in 1602, is named Martha's Vineyard. For nearly three centuries and a half no one has known why Bartholomew gave it this name. Little Martha of the Judde family in the course of years became a grandmother, and her name was given to Bartholomew's first-born child, Martha Gosnold. In her honor, therefore, Bartholomew named this island, the first on the American coast to be given the name of one of Queen Elizabeth's subjects. The name is a banner flung aloft by Bartholomew Gosnold to proclaim to his own and to following generations that all of America was to be taken over by England's merchant adventurers. Martha Golding, daughter of the adventuring City of London, with her ancestry, kinsmen and associations, represented for him the forces in England that were to create a new nation; and it was her name, having become that of his own child, that he wished to perpetuate in the New World.[14]

CHAPTER VI

BURY ST. EDMUNDS

One of the noble abbeys demolished in the reign of Henry VIII was that of Bury St. Edmunds, Suffolk. At the site of the ruins there arose a new town to which was drawn the gentry of the outlying manors of Suffolk, Norfolk, and Cambridge, to live together in a pleasant community. By the last decades of Queen Elizabeth's reign, it had doubtless acquired the characteristics ascribed to it by Daniel Defoe early in the eighteenth century. "It is a town famed for its pleasant situation and wholesome air," he wrote. "This must be attributed to the skill of the monks of those times who chose so beautiful a situation."[1]

It was in this town that Robert and Martha Golding settled some time before their daughter Martha was born to them and baptized at St. Mary's Church on September 21, 1580. On September 7, 1592, there was buried from St. James' Church, John, the son of "Robert Goldyinge." In 1583, the signature of "Robert Goldyinge" appears with that of others of the Guildhall Feoffees (a board of trustees for the holding of town property) on an order concerning almshouses. He was still, or again, a member of this board two years before his death, as the minute-book notes that "Mr. Goldynge" was present at a meeting of April 8, 1608. In the proceedings of the Chancery Court for the reign of Elizabeth I there is a case recorded in which the town of Bury St. Edmunds, represented by Robert Golding, Esq., and others as plaintiffs, sued to recover certain properties belonging to the town's Free Grammar School, founded by King Edward VI. In 1599, as has been mentioned, "Robert Goldynge" was associated with another lawyer of the town in the purchase of a share of a manor at Coddingham.[2]

It was evidently in the town house of his wife's parents at Bury that Bartholomew Gosnold made his home. The baptisms

44

of all but one of his children are entered in the parish register
of St. James' Church.

> April 24, 1597, Martha Gosnold
> October 20, 1600, Robert Gosnold
> August 2, 1602, Susan Gosnold
> December 16, 1603, Bartholomew Gosnold
> December 11, 1605, Paul Gosnold
> February 5, 1607, Martha Gosnold.

A child born and baptized elsewhere was named Mary.
She is mentioned in the will of her grandmother in 1614 and in
a later will as Bartholomew's oldest (surviving) daughter. She
was probably born early in 1599.

The first-born Martha had obviously died before a second
Martha was given the name in February, 1607 — that is, before
her ninth year. There is in the same parish register the entry
of a burial on December 2, 1598, of one "Martha Gosnold, gent."
It has been assumed, questionably, that this records the death of
Bartholomew's first child. It is at least unusual, although not
impossible, for an infant of less than twenty months to be designated as a gentlewoman. But the more important question is
this: if the first-born Martha was over three years dead in 1602,
why was the next baby girl to be born named Susan, instead of
Martha? It would seem to be within the range of possibility
that the Martha Golding baptized in 1580 married a Gosnold,
quite likely Bartholomew's brother Anthony, at the age of eighteen, and died shortly after her wedding, on December 2, 1598.
Unfortunately there are no further records to clarify the matter;
it seems quite unlikely, however, that Bartholomew would have
given the name "Martha" to the island of his discovery in America
if his first-born child, to whom he had first given the name, had
died before that event.[3]

The interval of three and one-half years between the recorded baptisms of his first and second children calls for further
explanation, which can only be guesswork. It is noticeable that

in 1602 and again in 1606 Bartholomew sailed away on expeditions, leaving his wife to bear him a child in his absence. He may have done the same thing late in 1596, or early in 1597, for this is the only interval in which Bartholomew might have had an apprenticeship at sea.

It ought to be said, however, that it is by no means certain that Gosnold needed any such apprenticeship for his voyage of 1602. Gentlemen of that period seem to have gone to sea in command of ships somewhat as a modern yacht owner takes his vessel out, leaving the business of navigation and the handling of the ship entirely to a sailing master. The function of a captain in that case would be limited to telling the sailing master where he would like to be taken with his settlers or his troops, as the case might be.[4] "Captains" Ratcliffe, Martin, and Archer, for instance, returned to Virginia in command of ships of the third supply under Lord Delaware's deputy, Sir Thomas Gates. John Smith sarcastically writes of them that they were "graced by the title of *Captaines of the passengers.*" One cannot imagine that the argumentative lawyer, Gabriel Archer, knew anything about navigation or the handling of a ship.[5]

If, however, Bartholomew Gosnold did have any training at sea, he possibly obtained it by enlisting under the Earl of Essex in some subordinate capacity in the fleet of the Azores expedition of 1597. The slight indications that this might be so lie in the acquaintance of Gosnold with officers of the expedition: the Earl of Southampton, who backed his voyage of 1602, and Sir Thomas Gates and Sir George Somers, who were among those whom Bartholomew persuaded to sign the petition to the King for the Virginia Charter. The Earl of Essex himself, as a son-in-law of Sir Francis Walsingham, probably knew that the Secretary of State in his younger days had married into the same Barne family with which the Judde family was connected; at any rate, the Earl of Essex is known to have been a friend of Sir Thomas Smythe, Bartholomew's first-cousin by marriage. Bartholomew therefore could easily have secured an appointment under the Earl.[6]

A simpler explanation of the three-and-one-half year interval between the baptisms recorded at Bury St. Edmunds may be merely that Bartholomew during these years took his family to a house of his father's in Grundisburgh. There are no parish registers extant for Grundisburgh, Clopton, and Otley in these years. Consequently it may be that Mary Gosnold, and perhaps another, unrecorded, child were born in Grundisburgh (where Bartholomew and his father are known to have had property at one time), and the record of their baptisms lost. This alternative, however, leaves no interval for Bartholomew to have been at sea for any length of time before he sailed to Norumbega in 1602.

It is needless to suggest that Bartholomew and his wife lived in the ordinary, comfortable manner of the lesser gentry, although little is known specifically. Their sons' names do not appear in the rolls of the Free Grammar School of Bury St. Edmunds; it is quite likely they had private tutors, or they may have gone to board at school away from home. Paul eventually matriculated at Cambridge University and entered the ministry, where he suffered in mid-career at the hands of the Puritans. He published a sermon "preached . . . the ninth day of August, 1644," defending monarchy and episcopacy.[7] After Bartholomew's death, Mary Gosnold's second husband, Jasper Sharpe, mentioned in his will that he spent all of her money and a great deal of his own on the upbringing of Bartholomew's children.

Giving historical imagination the reins, however, we may, as a part of the family scene at Bury, picture Martha Golding driving up to London in her inherited coach, with its prancing stallions and the Judde coat-of-arms, to call on her nephew, Sir Thomas Smythe, in his counting-house. There we can imagine that she would, with firmness, require nephew Thomas to give her son-in-law Bartholomew all the backing possible to make him an adventurer to America of high standing — and we can imagine Sir Thomas obligingly complying.

The measure of Martha Golding's devotion to the husband and children of her daughter Mary is found in her will of 1614. It is a brief and charming document, and is given here, some-

47

what out of its chronological place, to complete the picture of the household at Bury St. Edmunds.

In the name of god amen the laste daye of November in the yeare of our Lord god one thousande six hundred and Fourtene I Martha Goldynge of Bury S Ede in the county of Sufk widowe being sicke in body yet of ye best mynde and memory (thanks be given to almighty god) doe ordayne and make this my psent laste will and Testament, revokinge all former wills by me heretofore made in manner and forme following, that is to saye: Firste I comend my soule into the merciful hands of almighty god, my maker and redeemer and my body to be buryed in christian buryall at the discretion of my executrix hereunder named. Item my will and meaneinge is that my executrix and superviser hereunder named shall within one yeare right after my decease sell to the best advantage and benefytt that she can my gold cheyne and brasiletts and all the beddinge hangings, beste coverlett, quilte, and all the furnyture in my beste chamber, my turky carpet and the livery cupboard clothe suitable to yt, all my gilte and pcell gilte [gilt-lined] plate and all my damaske and diaper Lynnen [pure white with a pattern, nothing to do with babies] lyeing together in one chiste. And the money thereof comeing (together with one hundred pounds wh lyeth by me in golde) my will and meaninge is shall be equally devyded amongst my grandchildren, that is to saye: Robt Gosnold, Bartholomew Gosnolde, Paule Gosnolde, Mary Gosnold, Susan Gosnold and Martha Gosnolde, pt and pt lyke. And to have the same as they shall attayne their severall ages of one and twenty yeares. Itm I give and bequeathe to the saide Mary Gosnold my grandchild six silver spoones and sixe gold buttons. Itm I give and bequeathe to the saide Susan Gosnold six silver spoones and sixe gold buttons. Itm I give and bequeathe to the saide Martha Gosnold sixe silver spoones and sixe golde buttons with a lytle Jewell. Itm I give and bequeathe to John Anthony my servante Fourty shillings in money and a mourning cloake. Itm I give to Barbara Copsey my servante fyve shillings. Itm I give to John Eagle tenn shillings. All the reste of my goods and chattells as well moveable as ymmoveable of what nature or quality soev therewith of ready money, plate, Jewells, utensills and furnyture of householde whatsoever (not before gyven and bequeathed) I give and bequeath them to my loveing daughter Mary Gosnolde, widowe, whom I doe ordayne and make my sole executrix of this my last will and Testament. And I doe hereby nominate and appointe my servante Thomas Claydon to be superviser hereof, and doe give him for his paynes a mourneinge cloake. In witness whereof I the saide Martha Goldynge have to every leafe of this my laste will beinge in number two put to my hande and seale the daye and yeare first above wrytten.

Subscribed sealed and published by the saide Martha Goldinge for her last will and Testament in the presence of Willyam Partridge.[8]

PART II

Bartholomew Gosnold, Adventurer,
Who Found the Places Called
Cape Cod, Martha's Vineyard, and Elizabeth's Isle
In the North Part of Virginia
1602

CHAPTER VII

A VOYAGE INTENDED

The Muse of History is capricious. She has printed large nd often *A Description of New England,* written by Captain ohn Smith ten years after he himself had been told about this orthern part of "Virginia" by Bartholomew Gosnold, Gabriel ,rcher, and others of his intimates in the Jamestown colony. et quite inexcusably, this mythical custodian of ancient docu- ients has permitted a prior work on the same subject to fade om men's memories.[1]

The prior work, called *A Treatise,* written by Captain .dward Hayes, is a succinct and reasonably accurate account f the flora and fauna of the coast between the fortieth and forty-)urth degrees of latitude, the region afterwards named "New ngland" by Captain John Smith. It was not, like Captain Smith's *)escription,* a report of a voyage to these parts, but a compilation f the known and assumed facts which had been collected by .ichard Hakluyt for the use of Sir Humphrey Gilbert's proposed xpedition to the region — known at the time as Norumbega. [ayes had, therefore, no information about the geographical spects of the coast or its inhabitants, but was solely concerned .ith its resources or "commodities", with particular reference) the economic needs of England, and the desirability of the .nd as a place where English colonies might be planted.

The significance of Hayes' *Treatise* derives from the fact 1at it was used as a prospectus, or plan, of the voyage under- ,ken by Bartholomew Gosnold in 1602, although it was not rinted until three months after Gosnold's return to England, nd then as an appendix to the work called, in short, John Brere-)n's *A Brief and True Relation of the Discoverie of the North art of Virginia.*[2] The *Treatise* was obviously intended to be an

51

introduction or explanation of Gosnold's objectives on the voyage which Brereton describes in his narrative.

Captain Hayes is best remembered as captain of the *Golden Hind* — one of the ships in Sir Humphrey Gilbert's expedition of 1583 — and as the chronicler of that expedition. The *Golden Hind* was the only ship to return safely to England of the three that made the disastrous attempt to coast southward to Norumbega from Newfoundland. The loss of his largest ship, with most of the supplies for the expedition on board, had compelled Gilbert to abandon his project, somewhere off the coast of Nova Scotia.

On a fair September day[3], when Gilbert's small frigate and Hayes' *Golden Hind* lay not far apart, before starting their return voyage, Gilbert was able to board the *Golden Hind* to confer with Hayes. His words were in the nature of a last will and testament, for, as has already been related, his little ship, the *Squirrel,* with all on board, was bound to eternity.

Gilbert's final word to Captain Hayes was that he "assigned the Captaine & Master of the Golden Hind, unto the South discovery, and reserved unto himselfe the North, affirming that this voyage had wonne his heart from the South, and that he was now become a Northerne man altogether." He announced that he planned to undertake another voyage to Newfoundland in the following spring. This directive laid upon Hayes the responsibility for finding the lands in Norumbega that Gilbert, with the assurance of a land-speculator selling sight unseen, had assigned to his supporters. Long after the original assignees had lost their rights, Hayes turned over to Bartholomew Gosnold the privilege of making the "South discovery."

Immediately upon his return to England in 1583, Hayes reported to Sir George Peckham, chief assignee of land in Norumbega by indenture from Sir Humphrey Gilbert. Peckham and his son had been given "fifteen hundred thousand acres of ground" — twice the area of the modern state of Rhode Island. This was to be located at Peckham's discretion on the west side of "that river or port called by Master John Dee, Dee River, which river

y the directions of John Verrazanus, a Florentine, lyeth in
titude 42° and hath his mouth lying open to the south half a
ague broad, or thereabout, and entering within the said bay
etween the east and the north increaseth his breadth and con-
nueth twelve leagues or thereabouts, and containeth in itself
ve small islands newly named the Cinque Isles."[4] This was the
eart of the supposed "gold country" described by Verrazzano,
hich became Gosnold's "purposed place", at 41° 40′ N. on the
merican coast.

Sir George Peckham had in hand the draft of a tract men-
oned in the first chapter of this study. It was a verbose docu-
ient, replete with citations from the classics and arguments
tting forth the desirability of English colonization in Norum-
ega. Peckham hastily reorganized his material, adding as his
rst chapter a report on Gilbert's expedition obtained from a
ight honest and discreet gentleman", Master Edward Hayes.
Jithin a matter of weeks, Peckham's manuscript was in the
ands of a printer, to be published under the title *A True Re-
orte*.[5]

The need of haste was evident, because Gilbert's rights
nder his patent, passed on to his assignee, were to lapse in June,
584, if no settlement had been made by that time. This gave
eckham only a few months to organize an expedition, to start
rly in the spring following the publication of his book. Nothing
ame of the efforts to promote such an expedition, and Captain
ayes could not perform the task laid upon him by Sir Humphrey.

Peckham, for some obscure reason — perhaps Spain — was
omewhat coy in his *True Reporte* about revealing the location
f the vast acreage assigned to him. He remarked that he did
ot make the latitude of it public "because I do certainly under-
and that some of those which have the managing of this matter
now it as well or better than I myself, and do mean to reveal
e same when cause shall require to such persons whom it shall
oncern and to no other." Eventually, as one of those managing
e matter, Captain Edward Hayes, quite probably passed the
equired information on to Bartholomew Gosnold, as the latter

sailed directly for Peckham's assigned lands in the latitude given by Verrazzano.

The *Dee River* mentioned in Peckham's indenture appears on Dr. Dee's map, but without the name.[6] On it is situated the town of Norumbega, supposedly the Indian capital of a large province. The river is drawn as a mighty one, formed by the confluence of two large streams flowing down from mountains. Although it is shown as emptying into the west side of the head of Narragansett Bay, it is doubtless the Taunton River, which is navigable some thirty miles up from Fall River, on a northeastern branch of the Bay, and which has a tributary more or less like the one shown on Dr. Dee's map. John Winthrop, Jr., of Connecticut, wrote of this river to his father in 1636, saying, "A ship of 500 tons may go up to about ten or twelve miles." In a smaller vessel he had sailed far beyond that point to the head of navigation, at a place called by the Indians "Titicut".[7] But where Dr. Dee got his knowledge of this river is a mystery.[8]

About this time, late in 1583 or early in 1584, Hayes wrote a long and satisfying account of Gilbert's expedition at the request of Richard Hakluyt, who published it in his *Principal Navigations* of 1589.[9]

In the wild years after the destruction of the Spanish Armada — in 1589 and 1590 — when English ships unhindered were sweeping the Atlantic in search of enemies to plunder Captain Hayes was haled before the High Court of Admiralty to answer three counts of piracy on the high seas, an English, a Dutch, and an Irish ship being involved. We do not know either Hayes' defense or the issue of the cases; but in 1596, and after, Hayes enjoyed the confidence of Sir Robert Cecil, Secretary of State, of the Earl of Essex, of high officials in Ireland and finally of King James himself. Obviously Hayes had not blemished his record.[10]

In a letter from Edward Hayes to Sir Robert Cecil, dated May 15, 1596, Hayes showed interest in a project which other letters indicate was a proposal of copper coinage for Ireland. Anticipating a rejection of his plan, it seems, Hayes wrote of himself as "now an olde professed Sea man and zealous towards the voyage of Guiana. Whearyn . . . I am veary willyng to follow Sir Walter Raulegh with the best meanes I can procure."[11] But Hayes made no voyage to Guiana. From 1599 on, to the end of his life, he was actively engaged in Irish affairs. In this interval, therefore, between his vague dream of a Guiana project in 1596 and the beginning of his employment in Ireland in 1599, must be placed his revival of interest in a voyage to the "northern part of Virginia", and the writing of his *Treatise*.

A passage in the *Treatise* sharply criticizing Sir Walter Ralegh for his failures in the "southern part of Virginia" lends some support to this dating. The words are found in Hayes' argument for his own plan, which reads in part as follows:

[Upon the] coasts of *Newfound-land* is the greatest fishing of the world; whither doe yeerely repair about 400 sailes of ships, for no other commoditie than Fish and Whaleoiles.[12]

[But once we have transported some few people, there will also be profit by trading with the Savages and our merchants will be encouraged to invest. Then] the supply shall easily and continually be sent by ships, which yeerely goe from hence unto the *Newfound-land* and [back to] us; and the intercourse & exchange we shall have with all nations repairing hither, shall store us with aboundance of all things for our necessities and delightes. Which reasons if they had beene foreseene of them that planted in the South part of *Virginia* (which is a place destitute of good harbours, and farre from all trade) no doubt but if they had settled neerer unto this frequented trade in the *Newfound-land,* they had by this time been a flourishing State, and plentifull in all things.[13]

These words obviously were written more than a few years after Ralegh's unsuccessful efforts, begun in 1585, to bring about the colonization of "the South part of Virginia."

The first paragraph of Hayes' *Treatise* deserves to be quoted in full, not only for its expressed intention to start a colony in the temperate zone, but also for its quaint meteorological concepts:

The voyage which we intend, is to plant Christian people and religion upon the Northwest countries of America [i.e., northwest of the Atlantic], in places temperat and well agreeing with our constitution, which though the

same doe lie betweene 40. and 44. degrees of latitude, under the Parale
of *Italy* and *France,* yet are not they so hot; by reason that the suns hea
is qualified in his course over the Ocean, before he arriveth upon the coast
of *America,* attracting much vapour from the sea: which mitigation of h
heat, we take for a benefit to us that intend to inhabit there; because und
the Climate of 40 degrees, the same would be too vehement els for ou
bodies to endure.[14]

Elsewhere, Hayes wrote of "those lands which we inten
to inhabit", mentions those who will be "trading with us at ou
intended place", and throughout, by the use of the first perso
plural, indicated plainly that he himself was to be the leade
— or at least a member — of the colony. It appears, howeve
from the evidence of Brereton's *Relation,* that the leadership c
the expedition passed to Bartholomew Gosnold, perhaps becaus
there was insufficient financial support in sight before the Ea
of Southampton came to Gosnold's aid. Meanwhile, Hayes ha
entered (1599) upon permanent employment in Ireland, obv
ously preferring an assured position to the chances and dangers o
an attempted settlement in America at his advanced age.[15]

The steps by which this leadership devolved on Gosnol
must remain a matter of conjecture. Captain Edward Hayes wa
well-known to the Judde-Winter family, into which Bartholomev
had, so to speak, married in 1595. Hayes and Captain Williar
Winter (first-cousin of Bartholomew's wife) had been fellov
captains on the Gilbert expedition of 1583. Long before that, i
1567, when Hayes was a youth of perhaps seventeen, his fathe
also Edward, a Liverpool merchant, was mentioned as the beare
of a letter to Captain William Winter's father and another nava
man, both described as "Queen's officers of Admiralty in Lor
don." This points to early contacts between the Hayes an
Winter families. But it is more interesting to find a letter writte
December 21, 1601, by Edward Hayes the younger and hi
"kinsman", Thomas Hayes, to Secretary Cecil from "Clerkenwe
Close, at Lady Scott's house." So far as is known, Lady Scot
can be none other than the wife of Sir John Scott — his secon
wife, whom he married in or about 1599. She was a sister c
Sir Thomas Smythe, first-cousin of Bartholomew's wife, on th

other side of the involved family-tree. These notes make it certain that Captain Hayes was acquainted with Bartholomew Gosnold's "in-laws", and probably with Bartholomew himself.[16]

There can be little doubt also that Richard Hakluyt, who may well have known Gosnold as well as he knew Hayes, had a hand in the arrangement by which Gosnold undertook in 1602 the voyage originally planned by Hayes. Prolonged study of all the pertinent circumstantial evidence will almost certainly lead to the conclusion that both the Gosnold voyage of 1602 and the Salterne-Pring voyage of 1603 were planned by the alert geographer to open up for settlement and trade the Norumbega that had intrigued him in his younger days. It is to be remembered that in his *Discourse of Western Planting*, presented to Queen Elizabeth in 1584, Hakluyt had much to say about the desirability of Norumbega as a place for English colonization. In 1602 and 1603 he had two young protegés, Gosnold and Salterne, at hand to make the initial voyages.

More or less by chance is Hakluyt's connection with the Salterne-Pring voyage of 1603 known: the narrative of that voyage, with its information about Hakluyt's share in it, came into the possession of the Rev. Samuel Purchas after Hakluyt's death and was published in *Purchas His Pilgrimes*.[17] On the other hand, the publication of the documents connected with Gosnold's voyage was evidently in Hakluyt's own hands; there was one other to tell of Hakluyt's connection with the enterprise, and he did not choose to do so. Nevertheless, his guiding hand is seen behind Gosnold's voyage, as will become clearer.

It seems altogether probable, therefore, that it was Hakluyt who persuaded Bartholomew Gosnold to adopt as his own the plan for a voyage worked out by the old "professed Sea man", Captain Edward Hayes. The evidence that Gosnold did just this is found not only in the fact that the *Treatise* was united in publication with Brereton's *Relation*, but also in a comparison of some of the essential points made by Hayes with the reports made by Brereton and Archer. These may be most conveniently arranged in a series of numbered paragraphs, as follows:[18]

57

1. Hayes wrote, "The course unto these countries is through the ocean . . . to be made; apt for most winds that blow, to be performed commonly in thirty or thirty five days." Gosnold's direct crossing actually took about seven weeks; but Brereton was careful to report, "We were longer in our passage than we expected, which happened that for our bark being weak, we were loath to press her with much sail."

2. Hayes wrote, "So as the only difficulty now is in our first preparation to transport some few people at the beginning." The narratives of the voyage report that Gosnold intended to establish a settlement, perhaps more accurately a trading station, beginning with twenty men. The sincerity of Gosnold's effort has been questioned, on the ground that this small number indicated a certain unwillingness to envisage realities in the planting of a colony. But the historians who make this criticism are obviously unaware that Gosnold was following what at the time seemed to be the best of advice; and they are certainly forgetful of the fact that Captain John Smith, after two and a half years' experience in Virginia, purposed in 1614 to effect a settlement in the same region ("Norumbega") with sixteen men and boys.[19]

3. Hayes wrote, "The charges whereof shall be defrayed by our first return of fish and some commodities of sassafras, hides, skins and furs." The main item in Gosnold's return cargo was sassafras. At three shillings the pound, the long ton stowed below on the ship was reckoned to be worth £336 sterling. Some furs were obtained from the Indians, but probably not many, as it was not the season for taking furs. The hold of the ship was filled with cedar logs, also mentioned by Hayes as a desirable and valuable commodity.

4. Hayes wrote, "Neither is it our intent to provoke but to cherish and win [the savages] unto Christianity by fair means; yet not to trust them too far, but to provide against all accidents." It is evident from both Brereton and Archer that Gosnold's company treated the natives with courtesy and consideration; their petty thievery is mentioned as an excusable trait in untutored

savages. At the same time it is obvious that Gosnold refrained from landing on shores thronged with Indians. The explorers found on a remote island a lake with a plot of ground an acre in extent in the center of it. Here the prospective settlers built their "fort" in seclusion, with the lake forming a natural moat about it, maintaining guards lest they be caught unaware. They arrived and left, however, at peace with the local inhabitants.

5. Hayes wrote, "The cliffs upon the coast and mountains everywhere show great likelihood of minerals. A very rich mine of copper is found, whereof I have seen proof; and the place described." Both Archer and Brereton indicated plainly that they were on the lookout for minerals. Archer mentioned "many glittering stones, somewhat heavy," brought up on the lead while sounding off the coast of Maine; he also remarked at "Savage Rock", where but a brief stay was made, that the cliffs were all rocky "and of shining stones which might have persuaded us to a longer stay there." Brereton reported of the island named Martha's Vineyard that the "seaside [is] all covered with stones, many of them glistering and shining like mineral stones." Both narrators described fully the copper ornaments worn by the natives. Brereton told how he learned by sign language that the copper for these ornaments came from mines on the mainland.

6. Hayes remarked, "There be fair quarries of stone, of beautiful colors for buildings." Brereton reported "this island [Martha's Vineyard], as also all the rest of these islands, are full of all sorts of stones for building."

7. Hayes mentioned trees that would make masts for the greatest ships of the world. Brereton reported an island full of high timbered oaks and cedars "straight and tall."

8. Hayes wrote, "The soil is exceeding strong, by reason that it was never manured." Both narrators reported a successful experiment in planting, showing that English seed would sprout to a height of nine inches or more in two weeks.

9. Hayes wrote, "Fish, namely cods, which as we incline more unto the south, are more large and vendible . . ." Brereton and Archer confirm this by their reports on cod fishing at Cape Cod and at Martha's Vineyard. Hayes mentioned other sorts of fish, "more plentiful than in any parts of the known world." Brereton wrote that the schools of fish that they daily saw were "wonderful."

10. Hayes wrote, "The ground bringeth forth without industry, peas . . . grapes . . ." Brereton wrote of a great "store" of peas "which grow in certain plots all the island over," and of vines "that we could not go for treading upon them."

Hayes concluded his *Treatise* with a discussion of the widespread hope that there was a river in the temperate zone which would afford passage through the continent to the South Sea — still so called, although Magellan had long since named it the *Pacific*. When Gosnold explored the head of the bay now known as Buzzards Bay, he found the outlets of two small streams. Of these Archer wrote, "this land is beautified with two main rivers that (as we judge) may haply become good harbors and conduct us to the hopes men so greedily do thirst after."

There are many other commodities mentioned in the narratives, too numerous to be listed here, which seem to have been selected for notice by way of direct report on the fulfilment of Hayes' expectations.

This brief comparison leaves no reasonable doubt that Gosnold used Hayes' work — a description of the region that Sir Humphrey Gilbert sailed to "discover" — as a guide-book to his own "purposed place." In this sense, Hayes undoubtedly bridged the gap between Gilbert and Bartholomew Gosnold, passing on to the latter the task of finding in the temperate zone the lands Gilbert had set apart for settlement.

An Edward Heyes of Liverpool, gentleman, left a will dated November 7, 1598, and proved October 12, 1602. This was the will of the father of Captain Edward Hayes, to whom he left a gold signet-ring, and nothing else. The chief bequest in the will was a long gold chain, which the testator's "lord and master" gave him when he waited on him at Court. This chain was given to John Egerton of Egerton, about whose connection with Hayes nothing is known, while the residue, after other bequests, went to the testator's wife.

The Edward Hayes who appears in the Burgess Rolls of Liverpool and in West Derby Hundred in 1600 is certainly the elder Edward. The Mr. Hayes of Liverpool listed among the subscribers to an expedition planned by Sir Humphrey Gilbert in 1578, on the other hand, is almost certainly the younger one. The Thomas Hayes already mentioned is known only as a "kinsman."

Edward Hayes, in addition to the project for copper coinage for Ireland in 1596 had a scheme for copper coinage in England which he unsuccessfully brought up with Lord Burghley for the better part of two decades, after which he pursued each successive Lord Treasurer until 1613 with no better luck. Other schemes he had, too, many of which fell through. Still, four years of intensive effort ended in his obtaining a handsome pension of £100 a year shortly after the accession of James I in 1603. This was his reward until the end of his life for help in carrying out the debasement of the English silver coinage. A "public service" it was called.

Apart from America, Hayes was full of schemes of various kinds up to his death. On June 20, 1610, a petition is recorded for reviving an old decayed forest in York, belonging to the Duchy of Lancaster, which Captains Thomas and Edward Hayes would lease.

No documents concerning Edward Hayes appear in the records after 1613, from which it is probably to be inferred that he died about 1614. He cannot have been much older than Ralegh, that greater but still unsuccessful colonialist, so it may be reckoned that he was perhaps thirty-three when he made his memorable voyage with Ralegh's half-brother, Sir Humphrey Gilbert. That would have made him fifty-two or thereabouts when he turned over to Bartholomew Gosnold his plans for a "north Virginia" (New England) settlement.[20]

61

Chapter VIII

THE EARL OF SOUTHAMPTON

Henry Wriothesley was a youth of high intelligence, but inclined to be impetuous and heady. His friends and mentors found it necessary to spend a great deal of time in getting him out of trouble. Through the death of his father in 1581, Henry became the third Earl of Southampton when he was eight years old. He was straightway made a ward of the Crown and placed in the "close custody" of William Cecil, Lord Burghley, the strong man among Queen Elizabeth's Ministers and Master of her Wards. The relationship was probably a bit trying for both of them.[1]

When Henry was twelve he was sent off to the University of Cambridge, where he took his degree at the age of sixteen, the age when many boys of his generation were about to enter the University. He travelled abroad to complete his education, until he was presented at Court in his seventeenth year.

One of the happiest results of old Lord Burghley's guardianship of the young Earl was that the lad was brought into intimate contact with Lord Burghley's son, Robert Cecil. Robert had brains — more than enough to offset the deformity caused by a very early fall from his nurse's arms[2] — and what is more, he had a pleasing personality, a gentle and patient manner. We can picture Robert Cecil, barely twenty-one, welcoming the eight-year-old Earl to his father's household, and becoming very fond of the lad. This was fortunate for Henry, because in the course of the years Robert attained a position which enabled him to restrain the Queen's rage when Henry's impetuosity involved him in grievous offenses against the Crown.[3]

A typical and well-known anecdote about the young Earl, then aged twenty-four, tells of a gambling game in which he, Sir Walter Ralegh, and another gentleman participated, playing in the Presence Chamber of the Queen after the Queen had retired for the night. Unable to sleep, she sent one of her squires to ask the gentlemen to desist and depart. They paid no heed to him. The squire then threatened to call the guard, and Sir Walter Ralegh got up and left, breaking up the game. The next day the Earl met this squire between the tennis-courts and the garden and, in a flare of temper, struck the man. The squire retaliated by pulling out some of the young Earl's shoulder-length hair. When Queen Elizabeth heard of the incident she thanked the squire and briefly banished the Earl from Court.[4]

This happened just before Southampton left for Paris with his friend Cecil, by then knighted and Secretary of State, who had been entrusted with the delicate mission of representing the Queen in pending negotiations for peace between France and Spain. The Earl at the time had been having an affair with one of the Queen's Maids of Honor. While he was in Paris, he heard that she had borne him a son, and he hurried back to marry her — without the Queen's permission. He then returned to Paris, hoping that the Queen would not hear about his presence in London and the reason for it. The Queen, however, could not but learn the whole story. She sent for Southampton and had him committed to the Fleet Prison for a few days for behaving himself "to the dishonour" of her Court.

Southampton had been a devoted admirer and follower from his fifteenth year of Robert Devereux, Earl of Essex, seven years his senior. He was constantly at Essex's side. By the time he was twenty-three he obtained command of the *Garland*, one of the ships of Essex's expedition to the Azores. Two years later, in 1599, Essex appointed him Lord General of the Horse in Ireland — against the Queen's express command. Southampton was not yet twenty-six.

The tragic story of Essex's revolt against the Queen two years thereafter is too well-known to need retelling here. Suffice it to say that he dragged Southampton into the mess as his chief co-conspirator. Both were tried, condemned to death, and sent to the Tower. Essex was executed, but Robert Cecil persuaded the Queen, despite Southampton's "record", to commute the sentence to life-imprisonment.

While he was in the Tower Southampton conceived the idea of bettering his financial fortunes through a considerable investment in the voyage planned by Bartholomew Gosnold — a voyage intended to start a settlement among Indians who, according to Verrazzano, were plentifully supplied with gold.[5]

This phase of the story is told in language typical of the times by a contemporary named William Strachey, writing about 1611-1612. After discoursing on Sir Walter Ralegh's failures in colonization, Strachey had this to say:

> [The colony] lay neglected, untill yt pleased god at length to move againe the heart of a great and right noble Earle amongest us.
> 'Candidus, et talos a vertice pulcher ad imos'
> ["Shining, yea handsome from head to toe" Horace] Henrye Earle of South- ampton to take yt in consideracion and seriously advise how to recreat and dippe yt anew into spirrit and life, who therefore (yt being so the will of the eternall wisdome, and so lett all Christian and Charitable hearts believe in compassion to this people) begonne to make new enquiries and much scrutiny after the Country to examyne the former proceedings to- gither with the Lawfulnes and pious end thereof, and then having well weyed the greatnes and goodnes of the Cause, he lardgly contrybuted to the furnishing out of a shippe to be Comaunded by Captayne Bartlemew Gosnoll and Capt Bartlemew Gilbert and accompanied with divers other Gentlemen, to discover a convenient place for a new Colony to be sent thither who accordingly in March anno 1602. from Falmouth in a Bark of Dartmouth called the Concord sett forward holding a Course for the North-parte of Virginia.[6]

William Strachey was a "second-generation gentleman" (like his contemporary, William Shakespeare, whose *Tempest* was based on a Strachey letter) who went out to join the colony at Jamestown, Virginia, arriving there after being wrecked on the reefs of Bermuda in May, 1610. He served for a year as Secre- tary and Recorder of the colony, succeeding Gosnold's friend Archer, who died during the winter 1609-1610, as Recorder.[7] Be- tween the fall of 1611 and the end of 1612, Strachey prepared the manuscript, but it remained incomplete and unpublished when he died in 1621.[8]

Strachey had no compunction about using the wording of

other men's reports as his own, but there is no reason to doubt the authenticity of his statement about the part played by the Earl of Southampton in the sending forth of Gosnold's voyage. In the first place, Strachey had opportunity in Virginia to talk with young Anthony Gosnold, the son of Bartholomew's first-cousin, and probably with others closely associated with Gosnold — perhaps even with some who had been with Gosnold on the 1602 expedition. In the second place, Strachey made three known copies of his manuscript, each dedicated to a different person, which undoubtedly were seen by people who could easily confirm or deny the facts during Southampton's lifetime. In the third place, Strachey's chapter on Gosnold's voyage used, in large part, the wording of Brereton's *Relation* — in other words, Strachey had in his hands that printed work of 1602, which, on its title page and in its dedication, mentioned only Sir Walter Ralegh, with no reference whatever to the Earl. Nevertheless, in the last copy of his manuscript, presented to Sir Francis Bacon in 1618, the chapter on Gosnold has this heading: "The success of the good ship called the Concord, set forth by the Earl of Southampton, and commanded by Capt. Bartholomew Gosnoll, for discovery upon a right line, falling about Sachadehoc."[9]

There can be no doubt that Strachey intended this chapter heading to be a supplement to the information found in Brereton's *Relation*. A reasonable inference would seem to be that Southampton's name had been omitted in the publication of 1602 because he was then under condemnation as a traitor, imprisoned in the Tower under sentence of death.

At this point another of those startling coincidences that have come to light in the study of the small world of Bartholomew Gosnold's environment must be noted. During the year in which the Earl of Southampton, a prisoner, was apparently making up his mind "to set forth" the expedition of Bartholomew Gosnold, Gosnold's cousin-by-marriage, Thomas Smythe, was also in the Tower, accused of complicity in the same "revolt." (Essex had obviously relied on him for assistance, as one of the two sheriffs of London.) Smythe was soon exonerated, but it is quite possible that he and the Earl, fifteen years his junior, met and talked inside the Tower walls. Smythe's financial resources were not affected by his brief imprisonment — Southampton's were. The possibility exists that Gosnold's 1602 voyage came of meetings between Smythe and Southampton. If so, the link must have been the Earl of Essex.

At the time of Essex's mad act, Smythe was Sheriff of London. Essex is reported to have been under the impression that Smythe would provide him with a thousand men to help him carry through his plot. The Sheriff, however, was much too sensible a man to do anything of the sort. Instead, he tried to persuade the Earl to surrender himself to the Lord Mayor of London. When this was proven, Smythe was released.

Why did Essex expect such help? There were business connections of a sort, but Smythe had resisted Essex's attempts to insinuate "distinguished friends" into purely mercantile matters — that is, Smythe and his associates, for he was not yet the magnate he later became.[10] More likely the tie was a slim family connection, through marriages. In one way, Essex's wife was a daughter of Sir Francis Walsingham by his *second* marriage, and Sir Francis, by his *first* marriage was a brother-in-law of Smythe's aunt. In another way, Essex's stepfather was Sir Christopher Blount and Thomas Smythe's third wife was a Sarah Blount. Sir Christopher was sufficiently involved in the "revolt" to be beheaded on Tower Hill also. Nevertheless, nothing may be proved by this. There is not enough documentary evidence, and a blood-relationship between Sarah and Sir Christopher is uncertain. There is, however, considerable reason for postulating some sort of tie between Smythe and Essex, and by virtue of that, some sort of tie between Smythe and the young Earl of Southampton whose idol was Essex.

Granted, on admittedly slight grounds, that the Earl and Sheriff Smythe had opportunity and reason to confer during their imprisonment, the matter of improving Southampton's position would surely have come up — Smythe's release being clearly a matter of letting the law take its course. Putting the cart in front of the horse for the moment, the result was that the Earl, inveterate gambler that he was, resolved to gamble on an expedition in search of wealth or fame in America. Then, it may be suspected, Smythe told the Earl about Bartholomew Gosnold, who was to be in charge of an expedition originally promoted by Captain Edward Hayes — or who might be put in charge, if such an expedition got beyond the planning stage. Furthermore, Richard Hakluyt (here it is recalled that Southampton was far from illiterate!), whose geographical counsel had aided Thomas Smythe in his newly organized East India Company, was also interested in Gosnold's voyage to America. Somehow, for somebody's benefit, it seemed fitting that the Earl of Southampton should be associated with the overseas project, still very much *sub rosa,* involving Gosnold.

Even discounting Smythe's participation in the planning of Gosnold's voyage, Southampton's circumstances undoubtedly constrained him to lay the whole matter before his mentor and savior, Sir Robert Cecil. Further, the Rev. Richard Hakluyt was at the time Cecil's Chaplain, as well as his intimate adviser on geography and English overseas expansion. Cecil, indeed, must have given his unofficial approval, otherwise the Earl would not have dared to go ahead with the project.

On the title page of that small book called Brereton's *Relation,* printed immediately after the return of the voyagers, is the statement that Sir Walter Ralegh had given permission for the expedition, which may or may not be true. In the short dedication to Sir Walter, Brereton intimated that because of his high station, a report on the voyage was due him; but nothing was said to indicate in any way that Ralegh had anything to do with "setting forth" the voyage.

The omission of any reference to the Earl of Southampton is understandable, as it would have been most impolitic to reveal to the public this praiseworthy activity on the part of the prisoner in the Tower. But when Strachey wrote his account ten years later, the situation was reversed. Southampton was a free man, enjoying high favors from King James. It was Sir Walter Ralegh who was in the Tower then. Strachey found no reason, therefore, to magnify Sir Walter's part in Gosnold's expedition, even assuming — which is highly doubtful — that he had any part whatsoever, or had even given him permission to go. (It must be remembered that Sir Walter had certain rights in North America.)

If it is true, as it appears, that Southampton (although openly conforming with the Church of England) harbored only the friendliest feelings for the "old Faith",[11] it may be that Southampton's interest in Gosnold's project was motivated by the hope of a colony in which persecuted Catholics might find refuge. On the whole, however, it seems more likely that he was moved by the expectation of an immediate return of gold from the region described by Verrazzano, which was to be Gosnold's destination. To make this clear, it seems desirable to run ahead of this story, and beyond its scope as a study of Gosnold, to tell about the Earl's later adventures.

Shortly after King James' accession to the throne of England, he not only released Southampton from the Tower, but appointed him Governor of the Isle of Wight for life. About ten years later, having deferred action for reasons entirely unknown to us, Southampton decided to have a further investigation made of the island discovered by Bartholomew Gosnold. He fitted out a ship of the Isle of Wight commanded by a Captain Edward Harlow and sent it out, according to a very brief report made by Captain John Smith, to search for this island supposed to be somewhere about Cape Cod.[12]

It would appear that the Earl had harbored a doubt all these years as to whether Gosnold had made a thorough search for gold, as expected of him. It is also evident that the Earl had not been furnished with precise sailing directions for reaching the island named Martha's Vineyard by Gosnold, which Brereton had described as being four miles in compass. Harlow found no such island — which is not surprising, because there is every reason to believe that Brereton's report had purposely been made

68

misleading. But Harlow did, somehow, get into Nantucket Sound, where he found a large island which the Indians called "Capawack". This was in fact the island that Gosnold had named Martha's Vineyard.[13]

Harlow's only accomplishment was to capture Indians at various places, whom he took, with one exception, back to England for interrogation. Among them was one named Epenow, made prisoner at Capawack. After the voyagers returned to England, Epenow was taken to London. The story is told both by Sir Ferdinando Gorges and, more briefly, by Captain John Smith. In the words of Smith, Epenow was "a man of so great a stature, he was shewed up and downe *London* for money as a wonder."[14] Gorges himself interrogated Epenow as well as other Indians, but his account appears to be confused.[15] In any event, by 1613 or 1614 all Plymouth and other West Country men associated with Gorges knew that Capawack and Martha's Vineyard were the same island.

The persistent questioning of Epenow had finally given this native an idea as to how to get himself taken back home. He told his captors that there was indeed gold on his home island, Capawack — Martha's Vineyard — which he would gladly show them if they would return him to his own place. He would not reveal where, however, until he was actually on his own soil. At last the gold to be had in the region south of Cape Cod was within Southampton's grasp! For the third time, the Earl decided to risk his money in a gamble to get gold.

With the help of Sir Ferdinando Gorges, Southampton fitted out a ship under the command of a Captain Hobson and sent him, in the words of John Smith, "in search for a Mine of Gold about an Ile called Capawuck, South-wards from the Shoules of Cape *James*" — Smith had renamed Cape Cod to win some slight favor from the King. The ship was provided with a small troop of soldiers from the Isle of Wight.

When the ship anchored in the harbor at Capawack, some time in June, 1614, the people of Epenow's tribe came out to the ship to engage in what seemed to be the usual friendly bartering. Taking advantage of this, Epenow, although firmly held by several English guards, was able to arrange with his people for his escape. On the following day the natives again came out in their canoes. As they approached the ship, Epenow broke away and leaped overboard. The Englishmen were immediately assailed with showers of arrows and their return fire was ineffectual. The ship was forced to give up the battle, departed in haste, and returned to England with nothing to show for the large expenditure except the wounds of the members of the expedition. This ended Southampton's attempts to get gold from Gosnold's Martha's Vineyard.

Meanwhile, in 1605, a broad farce called *Eastward Hoe* had been written and played in London, ridiculing those who sailed to America for gold. One character says: "Who would not sell away competent certainties to purchase, with any danger, excellent uncertainties? Your true knight venturer ever does it."[16] In a later scene, the expectation of easily-found wealth across the ocean is caricatured in the following passage, a parody in part of a fanciful report made by David Ingram in 1582:

> I tell thee, gold is more plentiful there than copper is with us; and for as much red copper as I can bring, I'll have thrice the weight in gold. Why, many, all their dripping-pans and their chamber-pots are pure gold; and all the chains with which they chain up their streets are massy gold; all the prisoners they take are fettered in gold . . .[17]

Chapter IX

GENTLEMEN OF THE VOYAGE

One of the fruits of college life is the fervor it instills in youths, transplanted from their homes, to seek a new security in a larger environment, by forming new friendships. These bonds of adolescent comradeship are frequently carried into mature life as links with tried and trusted friends to whom appeal may be made in time of need. It is not surprising, therefore, that when Bartholomew Gosnold made his decision to be the first Englishman to sail directly to Norumbega or New England across the ill-charted waters of the North Atlantic, he called to his side two who had been his associates at the University of Cambridge: John Brereton and Gabriel Archer.

Both Brereton and Archer wrote narratives of the voyage, which on comparison — each sometimes confirming, sometimes suplementing, the other — furnish an integrated whole, a detailed account of all that Gosnold saw and experienced, together with each writer's own impression of the new lands discovered. Unfortunately neither of them had anything to say about the occasion for the voyage or its aftermath.

Beginning with these two recorders of the voyage, it is appropriate here to introduce the half-dozen members of Gosnold's company whose names are known. John Brereton was the third son of a prosperous Norwich mercer, holder of the high office of sheriff in that city, then the second largest in England. A year or so younger than Bartholomew Gosnold, Brereton continued his studies at Cambridge until he attained his Master of Arts degree in 1596, and then entered the ministry. His first appointment was to the curacy of Lawshall, a village six miles south of Bartholomew's home in Bury St. Edmunds.

It is altogether probable that Richard Hakluyt, whose parish at Wetheringsett was less than twenty miles by country lanes from Lawshall, knew this young curate, meeting him at whatever gatherings were held in those years for the clergy of the diocese or archdeaconry. Hakluyt, with the missionary zeal expressed to the Queen in the opening chapter of his *Discourse of Western Planting*, would seize on every opportunity to tell his brother clergy, particularly the more youthful of them, that colonization among the savages of America would lead to "the gaining of the souls of millions of those wretched people, the reducing of them from darkness to light, from falsehood to truth, from dumb idols to the living God, from the deep pit of Hell to the highest of Heavens."[1]

Brereton wrote of the voyage as one accustomed to the making of fine phrases and well-rounded sentences. He could write the resounding words, "We found ourselves embayed with a mighty headland", and was able to dismiss a bewildering bit of navigation with the crisp comment, "We sailed round about this headland, almost all the points of the compass." His style has the smoothness of a present-day copy writer extolling the delights of a new real-estate development, or of a health-resort. Of a place on the mainland, he wrote, "We stood awhile like men ravished at the beauty and delicacy of this sweet soil."[2]

His *Briefe and true Relation of the Discoverie of the North part of Virginia*, "Written by M. John Brereton, one of the voyage", appeared as a tract forming part of a twenty-four page pamphlet which included also a paragraph on the voyage of Samuel Mace (sent out in that same year by Sir Walter Ralegh to search for the people of the lost colony of 1587) and the *Treatise* of "M. Edward Hayes, containing important inducements for the planting in those parts. . . ."

This first edition was published in October, 1602, three months after the return of the expedition. A second edition followed quickly — doubled in size by the addition of five brief documents the origin of which will be discussed later. It is a historical misfortune that no copy of either edition appears to have reached, or survived in, America, and the first American historian to make a study of Bartholomew Gosnold's voyage did not have access to a copy. This was Jeremy Belknap, who in 1798 published an account of Gosnold's course among the islands south of Cape Cod based entirely on Archer's Relation (available in Purchas' *Pilgrimes*), a study containing errors of interpretation which could have been avoided had Belknap known Brereton's supplementary data. Several of Belknap's misconceptions have come down in works of history to the present day and will be difficult to displace.[3]

Turning now to the next companion, Gabriel Archer was admitted to Gray's Inn after leaving Cambridge and there studied law. He has been identified in the records of this seat of learning as "of Mountnessing, Essex, Gentleman."[4] That he was trained as a lawyer is confirmed by his recorded activities in the Jamestown colony, where he became more famous than he was as the obscure author of a *Relation* of Gosnold's voyage.[5]

Archer's account of what happened in 1602 is mainly a straightforward day-by-day journal of the voyage. One might think that he had made use of the official log of the *Concord* (not extant, if it ever existed), except that he had little or nothing to say about occurrences in which he did not personally participate. For instance, when the ship was anchored in the southern part of Cape Cod Bay, Archer stayed on board to fish, while a landing party went ashore. Archer mentioned this landing, but information as to what happened on shore comes entirely from John Brereton. Again, when Gosnold made his first landing on Martha's Vineyard, the incident is related only by Brereton; Archer had evidently again stayed on board the ship, and therefore had nothing to tell of the landing party's stroll about the place. On the other hand, when Archer stayed at the "fort" (which served also as a habitation), while Gosnold went cruising around Buzzards Bay, Archer's story tells of the shore-party's privations and their worry about the delayed return of the ship, but nothing of Gosnold's experiences while away from the island.

Archer had a wry sense of humor, expressed in his penchant

for giving quaint names to places. He named a little islet where a canoe was found "Hill's Hap", obviously because someone named Hill had the "hap" (luck) to find the canoe there. Then he found it amusing to reverse the name when another islet was found consisting of a hill crowned with a growth of tall cedars. This islet he called "Hap's Hill." Archer devised several more names of this sort, none of which were mentioned by Brereton, who named only the chief islands discovered, Martha's Vineyard and Elizabeth's Isle.[6]

Archer's lively interest in everything that he observed in the course of the voyage, and his usually clear reporting, give on the whole the most useful information for a study of Gosnold's course and discoveries. The measurements reported in the narrative, and the relative position of places are remarkably accurate when properly lined up on a modern chart. Those historians who have impugned Archer's accuracy have done so because of errors in their own basic assumptions, making it appear that Archer was giving measurements for places far removed from those he actually had in mind.

It should be noted here, nevertheless, that both the narratives are characterized by strange and obvious omissions, without doubt the result of editorial work done in London when the two narratives were being prepared for publication. The intent of the omissions or deletions was plainly to prevent later voyagers from following Gosnold to his Martha's Vineyard.[7]

The three most important physical features inexplicably missing from the narratives are these:

(1) Nantucket Sound, which the explorers must have seen from "the highest hills" they climbed on Cape Cod.
(2) The dangerous shoals east of Cape Cod, through which they must have passed as they "trended the coast southerly".
(3) The large island now known as Martha's Vineyard (twenty-five miles long, with high hills), which the explorers must have passed on their way from Cape Cod to Buzzards Bay.

74

These and other incidental omissions make it almost impossible for the uninstructed reader of the narratives to obtain a clear picture of Gosnold's discovery of Martha's Vineyard and its Sounds.

Archer's manuscript, evidently prepared for publication in 1602, was not printed then. It finally came into the hands of Samuel Purchas, Hakluyt's successor in the publication of mariners' narratives — he acquired many from Hakluyt's heirs — who published it in 1625. In 1625, also, less than a hundred folio pages farther on, a brief letter written by Archer on August 31, 1609, was published by Purchas. The former is Archer's first appearance in print, the latter his last. In a marginal note, Purchas relates that Archer died during the following winter, the "starving time" of 1609-1610, when the Virginia colony was almost wiped out.[8]

There is reason to believe that Archer's 1602 manuscript, or a copy of it, was used a year or so after he died, and in any event before mid-March, 1611, in the making of a map for King James. The original of this map is not extant, but somehow don Alonso de Velasco, Spanish Ambassador at King James' Court, had it redrawn for his own use. This version of it, now commonly called the Velasco Map, was found in the archives at Simancas, Spain, in the 1880's.[9]

Each section of the "Virginia" coast on this map was drawn according to reports of the English explorers who visited that particular region. That Gosnold's discoveries were drawn solely as Gabriel Archer described them in his *Relation* is evident from the map's peculiarities. The word "penguin" is placed across the arm of Cape Cod (between modern Sandwich, Hyannis, and Falmouth) to show where birds of this species, the great auk, were shot by the expedition — an incident related only by Archer. The island named "Elizabeth's Ile" shows an "Increeke" or "sandie cove", and is much larger than that named "Marthay's Viniard", in closer accord with Archer's description than with the facts.

A most curious feature of the map is that the cartographer drew two great indentations in the shore of the mainland —

great bays or sounds — where there should be only one, that which is now known as Buzzards Bay. This is plainly the cartographer's attempt to portray the two sounds mentioned by Archer in a phrase ("from Sound to Sound") which is not supported elsewhere in the narrative. Actually, Archer may have had in mind Vineyard Sound, lying between the long string of the Elizabeth Islands, as they are known today, and the equally long shore of Martha's Vineyard; but as both the true size of the Vineyard and the plurality of "Elizabeth's Ile", and the existence of the sound, had not been accurately known (or had been expunged from the first part of Archer's narrative), the map-maker did the best he could with the phrase implying the existence of two sounds. These and other interesting features show that the cartographer had the use of Archer's *Relation*, but no other source of information about Gosnold's discoveries.[10]

Another interesting member of Gosnold's company was Robert Salterne of Bristol, not mentioned in either of the narratives of Gosnold's voyage, but named by John Smith and Samuel Purchas in their chronicle of a voyage made a year later under Captain Martin Pring (a young mariner, born a matter of months after John Smith, on his first command). Smith's account is patently a condensation of the fuller document printed in *Purchas His Pilgrimes*, which states that Master Richard Hakluyt, "after divers meetings and due consultation", persuaded the merchants of Bristol, where he was Prebendary of the Cathedral, to "set forth a Voyage for the farther Discoverie of the North part of Virginia." Hakluyt then visited Sir Walter Ralegh to obtain permission for the voyage — Ralegh "had a most ample Patent of all those parts from Queene Elizabeth" — and took with him a John Angell "and Master Robert Salterne (which had beene in the said Discoverie the yeere before with Captaine Bartholomew Gosnold)."[11]

Pring and Salterne in two small ships, made, like Gosnold, a landfall off the coast of Maine, in 1603. But they then coasted south inshore, instead of cutting across the "great gulf" of Massachusetts Bay as Gosnold had done. Passing to the south side of oston Harbor, and still following the shore, they came to a arbor where they found sassafras in abundance. This was the lace later called New Plymouth by Captain John Smith, and :ill later occupied by the Pilgrims. Smith, in his brief version f the Salterne story which purports to be by Salterne himself, 'rote that Salterne served as Pring's pilot. Fortunately, it was ot necessary for Salterne to pilot the ships over the Nantucket hoals and to the islands south of Cape Cod.

The name Robert Salterne of Bristol recalls the fact that in 583 Richard Hakluyt had been sent to Bristol by the Secretary f State, Sir Francis Walsingham, to enlist the support of the herchant adventurers of Bristol for an expedition to be sent long with or following Sir Humphrey Gilbert, under the comhand of Walsingham's son-in-law, Captain Christopher Carleill. Iakluyt's dealings at that time were with Master William Salerne, "deputy of the merchant adventurers." Hakluyt was sucessful in his pleas, and Master Salterne produced promises of he necessary vessels and cash, although he was never called ipon to fulfil them.[12]

Clearly young Robert Salterne must have been a near relaive of the deputy, that is, either a son or a nephew, or possibly grandson — we know he was still alive in 1625.[13] Hakluyt had probably watched this youth grow up in the course of his occaional visits to Bristol as Prebendary. It may also be taken for ranted that it was Hakluyt who placed Robert Salterne on board Gosnold's ship, and sent him out again the next year inder Pring.

Samuel Purchas in a marginal note to Pring's *Relation* elates that Robert Salterne became a clergyman and was a hinister of a church at the time Purchas consulted him with 'eference to Pring's voyage. Possibly the Rev. John Brereton as vell as the Rev. Richard Hakluyt had something to do with balterne's decision to enter the ministry. Possibly also Bartholohew Gosnold himself was not without influence on the young han, as Gosnold was eulogized after his death as a "worthy and eligious gentleman."[14]

77

In contrast to lawyers Gosnold and Archer, clergyman Brereton and subsequent-clergyman Salterne, Captain Bartholomew Gilbert stands out strikingly. Captain Gilbert appears on the title page of Brereton's *Relation* as a captain ranking equally with Captain Bartholomew Gosnold. But if Gosnold was the "hero" of the piece, the villain was certainly Gilbert. Archer, no saint himself, mentions Gilbert disparagingly. Others undoubtedly called him a rascal.

The first thing to be said about Captain Bartholomew Gilbert is that, contrary to some previous opinion, he was not a relative of the half-brothers, Sir Humphrey Gilbert and Sir Walter Ralegh. Extensive search of the pedigrees of Sir Humphrey's family shows that there was no Bartholomew Gilbert amongst them. Also, the famous letter of Sir Walter Ralegh about the cargo of the *Concord* shows that Bartholomew Gilbert was introduced to him as a complete stranger. He was certainly given no recognition as a kinsman of one of Ralegh's half-brothers.[15]

In Ralegh's letter, Gilbert is identified as he "that had the great diamonde." The allusion is to an old scandal. As the papers in the case are quite unknown to students of Gosnold's voyage, it seems appropriate to present the gist of them, along with verbatim extracts. First there is a document endorsed by Sir Robert Cecil, Secretary of State, as from "Mr. Ashley": "Information of the fraudulent transactions of Rowland Branford, Bartholomew Gilbert, How, and others, relative to the sale of certain diamonds and other jewels obtained by them from Josias Hooper, mariner, and others, which jewels were taken at sea and bought for little, and offered to the Queen at a high price."

Another document from Sir Anthony Ashley to Sir Robert Cecil, dated December 23, 1597, reported: "Since the writing of our letters this day delivered your honor I have by good chance taken hold of Bartholomew Gilbert, who was wonderfully appalled upon the questions which I administered unto him and hath betrayed some further matter than was known before. Howbeit he refuseth to answer particularly to the matter f the great diamond by reason of his bond to his partners, How nd [Terrell], but prayeth he may be spared till the bond be ad in by commandment of her Majesty or otherwise. Then he romiseth not only to disclose everything yet unknown conerning the great diamond, but other matters also as yet little hought on. I have him at the present in my house till your urther directions. It is needful that some others that cannot yet e come by, be presently sent for by warrant, especially one Villiam Wyles of Ratcliffe, mariner."

In a letter dated May 6, 1598, Sir Anthony Ashley wrote Cecil: "Now that your honor is disburdened of your importunate negotiations I pray your ear to what has fared touching the diamond and my poor self. Upon sundry examinations at last t falleth out that Terrell, one of the parties pretending interest herein, never laid out one penny, but that most part of the 00 pounds was disbursed by B. Gilbert and the rest by [How] . . The Queen being herewith justly indignant, commanded hem to Marshalsea; but upon submission has released them."[16]

It was quite the custom in those days for high officials of he state to send out privateering expeditions for their own rofit, which is perhaps why no mention is made of whom the ommon seaman Josias Hooper defrauded by concealing jewels on his person. As for Gilbert's part in the diamond scandal, he robably evaded long imprisonment by surrendering all rights o the jewels — and it may be guessed that they came without rice into the hands of Queen Elizabeth, or of her Treasurer.

The second count in the indictment against Captain Barholomew Gilbert is that culpably, through parsimony and peraps because of sinister motives, as the commissary officer of Gosnold's expedition he failed to supply enough food for the ntended settlement. The gentle Brereton reports that Gosnold found himself faced with a situation where he was to remain n a settlement with but twelve men "and they but meanly rovided." The forthright and censorious Gabriel Archer, in rather involved language, hints that Captain Gilbert intended to sell the cargo on his return to England for his own benefit and not to return with a further supply, leaving the settlers to be come another lost Virginia colony. Gosnold himself, after the safe return of the voyagers to England, wrote to his father in bitterness but without personal recrimination: "When we came to an anchor before Portsmouth, which was some four days after we made the land, we had not one cake of bread, nor any drink but a little vinegar left."[17]

The third bit of evidence showing Gilbert's unprincipled character came to light when Sir Walter Ralegh purposed to ask for the prosecution of the voyagers on a charge of evading customs duties, when they brought their valuable cargo back to England, allegedly without Ralegh's permission. Gilbert promptly offered to become a customs "informer", promising to tell the appointed officials where his recent companions on the voyage had taken the valuable bags of sassafras.

Bartholomew Gilbert died horribly the next year on voyage to "the south part" of Virginia (that is, Virginia as known today), sent out by Ralegh, when Indians overwhelmed a landing party ashore for wood and water and killed all but one of them. Ordinarily such parties were not attacked by Indians unless the Englishmen through foolhardiness exposed themselves in weakness, or showed signs of fear and cowardice. Gilbert possibly brought his fate upon himself.[18]

Nothing in the records suggests Bartholomew Gosnold's reasons for the selection of Bartholomew Gilbert as his co captain. No personal point of contact has been found, either through family relationship or other connections. The best guess seems to be that Captain Gilbert came, as it were, with the ship The old *Concord* had probably been turned over to Captain Gilbert to run on shares, Gilbert to find a profit wherever he could, and few questions asked; therefore, Gosnold in chartering the *Concord* had to take Gilbert because Gilbert was already in command of the vessel. It seems reasonably clear that Gilbert was to sail the ship back to England, returning immediately to the new settlement with fresh supplies and probably with more colonists. There was perhaps divine providence in the turn of events which relieved Gosnold of further dependance upon the good will and assumed integrity of Bartholomew Gilbert.

Another member of Gosnold's company whose name is known was one Master Robert Meriton, mentioned along with the list of "commodities" published with Brereton's *Relation* as "the finder of our sassafras in these parts." Meriton was presumably a botanist-pharmacist taken along for the specific purpose of identifying plants useful as the source of drugs. In a document written by the older Richard Hakluyt, the lawyer, published in the appendix of the second edition of Brereton's *Relation*,[19] there is a long list of persons with particular skills to be taken along on an expedition planning to make a settlement, in which second place is accorded to "men skillful in all kinds of drugs."

One man of the greatest importance among the ship's company is mentioned but once — where Archer notes that no current was perceived by "William Strete the master" in the open sea one hundred leagues west of the Azores. A ship's sailing-master was necessarily an experienced seaman, responsible for the practical navigation of the vessel. If this William Strete was a comparatively young man, it is possible that he was the same as the "William Streets, mariner," who on November 16, 1626, took part in a conveyance in the Virginia colony as agent for Daniel Gookin, rewarding a retiring manager of Gookin's plantation at Newport News.

There were thirty-two persons in all on board the *Concord*. Twelve of these including eight seamen, Archer reported, had intended from the beginning to return to England when the ship was sailed home by Captain Gilbert and Master William Strete. Twenty, including Bartholomew Gosnold, had intended to stay as settlers.

Besides the six already named, the names of two others of the company are known because they were the butts of Archer's little jokes in the naming of places. There was a man named Tucker, who was so vociferous in proclaiming his fears on an occasion when the ship almost grounded that Archer

81

named the place Tucker's Terror. Also, to repeat, there was presumably a man named Hill, who had the luck to find a canoe on a little island, leading Archer to suggest Hill's Hap as an appropriate name for the place.[20]

It would doubtless add to the sum of knowledge about Gosnold if the names of more of the "gentlemen of the voyage" could be learned. A number of them may have accompanied Gosnold to Jamestown four years later and died with him there.[21]

CHAPTER X

ANCHORS AWEIGH

On Friday, March 26, 1602, Bartholomew Gosnold stood on the high poop of the *Concord* in the harbor of Falmouth, Cornwall, ready to start for America. Eighteen and a half years before, Edward Hayes had limped into port there, bringing the sorrowful news of the defeat of Sir Humphrey Gilbert's colonial plans. Younger by a decade than Sir Humphrey had been when he set out, Gosnold also thought to plant a colony, where Hayes had laid the plans. He was part of the development of England's colonial planning, and he too suffered a kind of defeat. Yet Gosnold, sailing westward, did show the way to the unknown North part of Virginia." The voyage on which he was about to embark, almost surreptitiously, and from an inconspicuous port, proved to be the turning point in the planting of Anglo-Saxon America.

It would be idle to guess what thoughts ran through Gosnold's mind as he stood there — they might have been of the fabulous fortunes of old Sir Andrew Judde and Thomas Smythe; or of his father and uncle, three hundred miles away in Suffolk, with his brothers and sisters and cousins; or of the handsome Earl of Southampton, whose fire was all but out, smothered by the ashes of the Queen's scorn, yet kept aglow by that difficult little man, Sir Robert Cecil; or of Master Hakluyt and Captain Edward Hayes, most responsible of all, perhaps, for the very planks on which he stood. Certainly, Gosnold must have thought of Mary, his wife, and of Robert, his son, and Martha, his daughter. But this is all dreaming. What surely happened was much shouting and running about: "Get your sails to the yards; make ready; men into the tops; men upon the yards!" And then,

"What! 's the anchor away?" — "Yea, yea!" — "Let fall your fore-sail! Who's at the helm there? Coil your cable! . . ." It was not easy to get a ship away. Little time for dreaming.[1]

The *Concord*, like others of its time sailing the deep waters was according to any present-day standards a dangerously small vessel. The ship, being somewhat undermanned, had only eight seaman, who with Captain Gilbert, the sailing-master William Strete, and two others unidentified, were to have been the entire complement of the vessel on its homeward trip. She was there-fore probably comparable in size with the smaller of the two vessels which sailed with Martin Pring on Gosnold's course to America the following year, a twenty-six-ton vessel according to Pring's narrative, having a complement in all of thirteen men and a boy, including the captain and mate. If the *Concord* was rated at 30 tons, with a water-line length around 60 or 70 feet it was about the tonnage of one of today's medium-sized fishing vessels on the New England coast.

The *Concord* was possibly an old vessel, and certainly one in very bad condition.[2] When well out at sea, it was found that the little ship, as noted in Brereton's report, could not stand the press of full sail. When she heeled under a heavy breeze, there was creaking and groaning of timbers and a dangerous opening of seams, convincing all on board that less speed would assure a more certain arrival on the other side of the Atlantic. The journey across, therefore, was to take seven weeks instead of the five or six which Captain Edward Hayes had reckoned. At that however, as Brereton points out, the passage directly across to their destination was shorter by a thousand leagues than the roundabout course through the tropics, following the fleets sent out by Sir Walter Ralegh.[3]

To those who live on Martha's Vineyard, the first island of Gosnold's discovery off the southern coast of Massachusetts the group of islands called the Azores seems not very far away. This impression is created in part by the presence on the island of thousands whose parents or grandparents crossed over to this region from the Azores in the days of whaling ships, for

owing the course sailed for the first time by Bartholomew
Gosnold two and a half centuries before them. Actually, as seen
on the map, the Azores are a thousand miles nearer to the
southern New England shore than are Portugal and Spain.[4]

The Azores were discovered by the Portuguese sixty or
seventy years before Columbus discovered America. In the
course of the next century, the islands became a port of call
for Spanish and Portuguese voyagers sailing to and from the
New World. They also became well-known to British mariners,
who set their course to the West Indies from them. Inasmuch
as the prevailing wind was from the southwest, these ships sailed
on the starboard tack, which took them far to the south before
they crossed to the Americas in the tropics. Gosnold saw from
his charts that a long reach on the port tack would take him
westerly to the part of the coast in the temperate zone on which
he wished to land. The first leg of his crossing, therefore, led
him to make the familiar run to the Azores.[5]

He nearly missed them, because the sailing-master was
unable to sail close enough to an unusually strong wind. The
island they finally raised was St. Mary's, at the extreme southeastern corner of the group. Beyond this island the helmsman
swung the *Concord* onto its westerly course, and Gosnold was
off for America through uncharted waters. No Englishman had
made that turn at the Azores before him.

Ahead of him on the broad Atlantic there might lurk un-
suspected dangers. On this course they would meet no friendly
sail to give them assistance in case of need. Not even an enemy
ship would be sighted. Some great storm might rage far out at
sea, ready to overwhelm the little ship. There might be more
"western" islands, like the Azores, rimmed with cruel, rocky
reefs. They might unawares run on to a great whale, larger
than the ship itself, whose flailing flukes would spell disaster.
Or the wind might fail, leaving them adrift in a northern equivalent of the equatorial doldrums, caught in a deadly calm until
their water was exhausted and their food rotted. But the *Concord*
sailed on day after day, ever at the center of its own little circle

circumscribed by the horizon. None of the apprehended dangers materialized.

In Archer's narrative, although he was no mariner, there is sufficient information to enable reconstruction of a rough log of this notable voyage. Hundreds of other vessels, on their way to the Newfoundland fishing grounds, had shaped their course from the western tip of Ireland to the vicinity of Iceland, then past the southern tip of Greenland to Labrador, and down the coast to Newfoundland. These fishermen were never more than a few hundred miles from the nearest land.[6] Here, therefore, is a record of the first direct trans-Atlantic crossing to the temperate part of America that is called New England.

Reconstructed Log of the *Concord*

Friday, 26 March, 1602. Sailed from Falmouth.

Wednesday, 14 April. We had sight of St. Mary's.

Friday, 23 April. 200 leagues (600 statute miles) due westward from said Island, in 37° north latitude. The water appeared yellow, the space of 2 leagues north and south, but taken up in a bucket, it altered no either in color or taste from sea water.[7] Brereton commented that "we were loath to press our ships with much sail," so that we made les. than a 3-knot headway during these nine days.

Friday, 7 May. We first saw many birds.

Saturday, 8 May. The color of the water changed to yellowish green. A 70 fathom we had ground.

Sunday, 9 May. We had 22 fathom in fair, sandy ground, having upon our lead many glittering stones, which might promise some mineral matter on the bottom. Near the latitude of 43°.

Monday, 10 May. We sounded in 27, 30, 37, and 43 fathom, and then came to 108. Some thought it to be the sounding of the westernmos end of Saint John's Island.[8] Upon this bank we saw schools of fish in great numbers. Brereton remarked on delays for sounding, on accoun of the fog.

Wednesday, 12 May. Hoisted out half of our shallop, and sounded 8(fathom. William Strete, the Master, observed that there was now no current, although when we were one hundred leagues westward from St. Mary's in the Azores we had encountered seaoare [seaweed] which continually floated past us up to now. These sea-weeds seemed to have their course towards the northeast, a matter to set some subtle mind to work, for comprehending the true cause thereof.[9]

Thursday, 13 May. We sounded in 70 fathom, and observed great beds o weeds, much wood and divers things else floating by, and we could smell the shore.[10]

Friday, 14 May, 1602. About six in the morning we descried land that lay north of us. The northerly part we called the North Land. Twelve leagues west, we saw a great rock, which we called Savage Rock, because the savages first showed themselves there . . .[11]

Bartholomew Gosnold had made his landfall. The site, on the Maine coast, was probably that known as Cape Neddick.[12]

About high noon of May 14th the *Concord* was off Savage Rock. There a shallop came towards them, with sails and oars. From the lines and rig it was recognized as one from the Bay of Biscay, of French or Spanish origin. But as it drew nearer, the voyagers saw to their amazement that it was manned by eight Indians, one of whom was dressed in vest and breeches of black serge, made "sea-fashion", and wore shoes and stockings. Another wore a pair of breeches of blue cloth. Otherwise they were naked, "saving about their shoulders certaine loose Deere-kinnes, and neere their waists Seale-skinnes tyed fast like to Irish Dimmie Troueses [dimity, cotton fabric?]."[13] In the shallop, the voyagers saw the Indians had a copper kettle, an iron graple, and other things of European origin.

As no Biscay fisherman in his senses would willingly give up a shallop — which he needed for fetching water and wood from the shore — these Indians had undoubtedly obtained this one by overwhelming a landing party and robbing their victims even of their clothing. Gosnold and his company, however, apparently entertained no suspicions of this, as the Indians made signs of friendship in their usual fashion and with little urging boarded the English vessel.

The Indians of Savage Rock were described as of tall stature, of broad and grim visage, of a black or swarthy complexion, strong and well-proportioned, their eyebrows painted white, and their hair long, tied up with a knot behind their heads.

In their attempts to make themselves understood, the Indians used several "Christian" words, among them the name "Placentia", by which the bay just west of Avalon Peninsula, Newfoundland, was and is known. Supplied then with a piece of chalk, the non-naked Indians — probably the chief and his

87

entourage — drew a map of the coast thereabouts. It may ever be that they traced the shore-line which Gosnold purposed to follow southwards from the latitude of his landfall, between 42 and 43°, to his destination, the great bay of Verrazzano, opening south at 41° 40′. In that case, the Indians' drawing undoubtedl showed Cape Cod with a great bay beyond it. [14]

It must also be assumed, from subsequent events, that th Indians' map gave Gosnold the impression that the norther. part of Cape Cod was an island. This was presumably the resul of their trying to show two canoe waterways, interrupted b portages, from the head waters of one stream to the waters th travellers wished to reach. Both of these were known from earl Pilgrim sources. One at the southeastern corner of the Bay wa used by Governor Bradford to reach a ship stranded in Chathar harbor. At that time, this harbor not only opened to the se but also had a connection to Nantucket Sound, which migh have appeared on the Indians' chalk map as the bay Gosnol wanted to reach. The other canoe waterway was at the soutl western corner of Cape Cod Bay. This, now a part of the moder Cape Cod Canal, was used by the Pilgrims as their route to landing station on Buzzards Bay for vessels carrying on trad with the Dutch at Manhattan. The Indians could not, of cours make it clear on their map that Gosnold's ship was much to large to use these Indian waterways, even had there been n portages.

Gosnold stayed only three hours at Savage Rock, despit signs made by the Indians which he interpreted to mean tha they wanted him to stay longer. Finding themselves "short their purposed place", as Archer expressed it, and at an expose anchorage with the weather uncertain, Gosnold and his con pany decided to weigh anchor at three o'clock in the afternoo They stood off "southerly into [the] sea the rest of that da and the night following, with a fresh gale of wind."[15]

The next morning, May 15th, those who were on the de early saw ahead of them land which they took to be an island, I reason, Archer remarked, of a large sound that appeared wes ward between it and the mainland. Brereton, who may have appeared on deck somewhat later, reported that they found themselves "embayed with a mighty headland." They sailed on until nine o'clock that morning, coming to anchor a league off shore at the southerly end, or the "bottom", of the body of water known now as Cape Cod Bay. If the identification of Gosnold's "Savage Rock" with Cape Neddick is correct, then they had sailed over 90 statute miles in the course of eighteen hours, averaging better than four knots, a rate of speed to be expected with the fresh gale of wind mentioned by Brereton. The bold course southerly from the coast of Maine, passing the mouth of Massachusetts Bay in the dark, is significant of the courage with which Gosnold undertook the exploration of this strange and uncharted coast.[16]

Now, however, Gosnold was temporarily balked. He had come to the quiet protected waters at the southern end of the great bay that he had entered from the north. His plan of following the coast southerly until he came to the latitude of his destination was thwarted by this hilly and heavily wooded land before him. Was there, as he had understood from the Indians of Savage Rock, a great bay such as he was seeking beyond this land? And if there was, could he find a passageway through the land that blocked his way?

Gosnold was not an explorer with no objective but to plot the shape of the shores of an unknown land; he had a destination, and he had encountered an obstacle in his course to it. Thus, within a matter of hours he was to learn that he had come upon a great cape. Even then, he could not know that this cape, ever thereafter to appear on maps of the New World as he had seen and named it, was to give him everlasting fame.

89

CHAPTER XI

A NEW LANDMARK

Others had seen Cape Cod from a distance, before Bar
tholomew Gosnold stepped ashore in 1602. Cabot had sailed
down the coast from Newfoundland in 1498, perhaps as far a
Cape Hatteras, claiming everything in sight for the King o
England.[1] Following him in ever-increasing numbers, Spanish
Portuguese and French vessels sailed up and down, some ex
ploring, some on voyages to the Newfoundland fisheries. By
1600, Captain Edward Hayes reported, 400 ships yearly were
visiting the fisheries, a large proportion of them undoubtedly
fishermen from Southern Europe who had crossed the tropic
to Florida and then coasted up to Newfoundland. All these
coasting vessels must have passed Cape Cod not far off shore
but only one of them has any semblance of a claim to having
discovered it.

A map made in 1529 by a Spanish cosmographer named
Diego Ribero shows on the American coast a thornlike projec
tion representing a peninsula pointing north and enclosing :
bay. The cape bears the legend C[abo] de Arenas (Cape o
Sands, "Sandy Hook"). This may have been the first European
name given to Cape Cod, although that is highly questionable.

On Ribero's map, C. de Arenas is made a part of the "Tierr
de Ayllón", named for don Lucas Vázquez de Ayllón, an associ
ate of Cortés in Mexico, who set out on some exploring afte
the Conquest (in 1520-1521, and again about 1530), but wh
pretty certainly got no farther than Cape Fear. North of Ayllón
land and its cape is another place, designated "Tierra de Esteva
Gómez". Some scholars believe that evidence points to Gómez a
the discoverer of C. de Arenas. Others protest that not only th
name of C. de Arenas but also the names of places in its vicinit
are those of a more southerly part of the coast, that C. d

Arenas is in fact an exaggerated drawing of Sandy Hook, near New York City.[2]

The uncertainty in fact makes little or no difference so far as Bartholomew Gosnold is concerned. One of the maps which Gosnold undoubtedly used was Dr. Dee's map of 1580. On this, C. de Arenas is plainly placed two or three hundred miles west of Verrazzano's Bay — Narragansett. Bartholomew Gosnold could have had no inkling that in sailing south from his landfall to his destination he would be caught within the great arm of the peninsula which is Cape Cod. No Englishman had known of its existence, and Gosnold's contemporaries, led by Henry Hudson in 1609, ascribe to Gosnold the credit for putting this landmark on the map.[3]

The strange fact that for over a century ships passed by Cape Cod without reporting to the map-makers its peculiar hook-shaped head has a simple explanation. The rocky shoals of its seaward shore, extending south beyond Nantucket, effectually discouraged any attempt to approach close enough to see its configuration. These shoals made the cape region one of the most dangerous spots on the Atlantic coast, and ships evidently passed so far to the eastward that their navigators were unable to see the great bay lying between the outer cape and the mainland. If documentary evidence of this is needed, it is to be found in the terrifying experiences of Captain George Waymouth (1605) and of Captain Henry Hudson (1609), in the bafflement of Captain John Smith (1614), and in the concern of the Captain of the *Mayflower*, the somewhat unsavoury Captain Thomas Jones, for his Pilgrim passengers.[4]

The narrative of Waymouth's voyage at this point tells a story which may be taken as the equivalent of scores of others that might have been told, had navigators in the preceding century attempted to approach Cape Cod.

[Monday, 13 May, 1605; off the coast of Maine.] From ten a clocke at night till three a clock in the morning, our Captain tooke in all Sayles and lay at hull, being desirous to fall with the Land in the day time, because it was an unknown Coast, which it pleased God in his mercy to grant us, otherwise surely we had runne our Shippe upon the hidder Rockes, and perished all: for when we set sayle, we sounded in an hundred fathom: and by eight a clocke, having not made above five or six leagues our Captaine upon a sudden change of water supposing verily he saw the sand, presently sounded, and had but five fathome. Much marvelling because we saw no Land, he sent one to the top, who descried a whitish sandy Cliffe, which bare West North-west about sixe leagues off: but comming neerer within three or foure leagues, we saw many breaches still neerer the Land. At last we espied a great breach ahead us right along the shoare, into which, before we entred, our Captaine thought best to hoist out his Ship-boat and sound it: which if hee had not done, wee had then ended our Voyage, together with our lives: for he bare up the Ship as neere as he could after the Boate, until Master Cam his Mate being in the Boat, weffed [waved] and called to him to winde about and stand off, for in this breach he had very shoald water, two fathome upon Rockes, and sometime they supposed they saw the Rocke within three or foure foot whereon the Sea made a very high strong breach, which we might discern (from the top) to runne along as wee sailed by it, sixe or seven league to the Southward: and we saw no end thereof. Wherefore we were constrained to put backe againe from the Land; and sounding (the weather being faire) wee found our selves embayed with continuall Shoalds and Rocks, in a most uncertaine ground; as by judgement of our Captaine and whole companie, they had never knowne the like; from five and six fathome, at the next cast of the Lead wee should have fifteene and eighteene fathome all hard Rocke over many which (by the unspeakable goodnesse and mercy of God towards us) wee passed. For if we had bar in with it but the day before (which was exceeding tempestuous) or in the night, we could by no meanes have escaped the danger. But God so blessed us, that we had weather and winde as faire as poore men could wish, in this distresse, whereby we both perfectly discerned every breach and with the winde were able to turne, where wee saw most hope of safest passage. Thus we parted from the Land, which wee had not so much before desired: and at the first sight rejoyced: as now wee as joyfully praised God, that it had pleased him so miraculously to deliver us from so imminent danger of death before our eyes.[5]

Three days later, Waymouth, having failed to get sight of any land where his charts placed it, found himself in the vicinity of an island easily identified as Monhegan, off the coast of Maine. This suggests that other navigators in the preceding century having learned the dangers of the shoals off Cape Cod, sailed a course so far to the eastward that they had no sight of the head of the Cape, but made their next landfall somewhere on the coast of Maine or Nova Scotia. Many other seamen, les well-informed or less canny, undoubtedly sailed their ships to destruction in the vicinity of the Cape, as the rough waters surrounding it to this day take heavy toll of unwary fishing vessels and coasters, regardless of navigational aids.

The landsman, who may have ridden in safety through great seas on deep waters, cannot readily comprehend the twisting, rending power of these same seas when they roll in upon the broken bottom of rocky shoals. No one knew that power more than the mariners who sailed cockleshells courageously into the unknown. But once a region pestered with shoals became known, it was avoided. And because the Cape Cod shoals were so fearsomely known, navigators and geographers alike had to wait for Bartholomew Gosnold to tell them the shape and the physical aspects of the Cape itself.

For the last three centuries and a half, everyone who has cast his eye upon a map of New England has carried away an unforgettable impression of the great peninsula at the southeastern corner of Massachusetts, running out for thirty-five miles easterly to a junction with barrier beaches of the outer coast that run another thirty miles northerly and ten miles southerly. The extreme northerly end curves around like the head of a shepherd's crook, forming a harbor of refuge into which the Great Shepherd drew the Pilgrims, far from the shoals that threatened them when first they arrived off these shores. To this whole great cape Bartholomew Gosnold gave the name Cape Cod.

A peculiar situation makes it possible to gauge the appreciation of Gosnold's accomplishment in the minds of his contemporaries. Brereton's *Relation* described the Cape and the codfishing within its great bay, but nowhere mentioned the fact that the name "Cape Cod" was bestowed upon it. The story of the naming of the Cape was told in Archer's parallel account — which did not get into print until 1625. For an interval of twenty-three years, therefore, the written story of the naming of Cape Cod was not available. Nevertheless, within this period we find that the name "Cape Cod" was in common use, the story of Gosnold's exploit having passed like a saga from one mariner to another. The citations that follow suggest how word of the new landmark spread among English seamen. Yet none of these records were printed before Archer's account.

In 1609, two years after Gosnold's death, Henry Hudson sailed down the coast of America on the voyage for the Dutch that led him to the discovery, or rather rediscovery, of Manhattan and the river subsequently named for him. He encountered on his way a great headland, of which his mate Juet recorded, "And this is that Headland which Captaine Bartholomew Gosnold discovered in the yeere 1602. and called Cape Cod; because of the store of Cod-fish that hee found thereabout."[6]

The next year, on June 19, 1610, Sir George Somers and Captain Samuel Argall, each commanding a pinnace, sailed from Jamestown colony bound for Bermuda, in the hope of finding there provisions for the starving Jamestown settlers. They somehow failed to locate Bermuda, and turned north. At this time the name "Cape Cod" was bellowed across the waters of the North Atlantic; Argall's narrative reveals that his ship bore up Somers' lee so that they were within hailing distance and Sir George called out that he could no longer ride out the stormy weather towards Bermuda, "but that hee would presently [right away] steere away North North-west, to see if he could fetch Cape Cod." This occurred on July 16th.[7]

Their next landfall was not, however, Cape Cod, but the coast of Maine, where they spent nearly a month fishing and being tossed about in fog and rain. It was August 19th before Argall could note:

> About two of the clocke in the afternoone I did see an Head-land, which did beare off me Southwest, about foure leagues: so I steered with it, taking it to bee Cape Cod; and by foure of the clocke I was fallen among so many shoales, that it was five of the clocke the next day in the morning before I could get cleere of them. It is a very dangerous place to fall withall: for the shoales lie at the least ten leagues off from the Land; and I had upon one of them but one fathom and a halfe water, and my Barke did draw seven foot.[8] (Somers had meanwhile taken off for Bermuda, without further ado.[9])

94

Another account of this same expedition was written by William Strachey a year or more later:

> Likewise from the North point of our Bay [Chesapeake], which (as aforesaid) the Indians call *Accowmack* and we call Cape Charles hath the Coast all along bene discovered even to the River of Sachadehock; for Capt Argoll in his returne from the search of the Bermudas Anno 1610. after he had lost Sir George Somers the 28. of July in a dangerous Fogge, well beaten to and fro, fell with the Mayne [mainland] (standing for Cape Cod) and made good from 44. degrees what Captayne Bartilmew Gosnoll, and Capt Waymouth wanted in their discoveryes, observing all along the Coast, and drawing the plotts thereof as he stered homewardes unto our Bay . . .[10]

All this leads back to the Velasco map, which was already drawn before Strachey wrote. Not only did Gosnold, Henry Hudson, and Argall supply information, but so also did the so-called Popham colony, which spent the winter of 1607-1608 on the coast of Maine and did considerable exploring. Detailed evidence of just who discovered and mapped just what is lacking, but the map itself is certainly attributable at least as much to Popham's group as to any predecessors or to Argall.[11] The interesting feature of the Velasco map, however, is the fact that the name *Cape Cod* is placed opposite the southeastern corner of the Cape; the northern tip of the Cape bears the legend "Whitson's Head". Although the name is only an ephemeral contribution of Martin Pring (1603), it is noteworthy that for the first time the peculiar convolution of this northern head, which forms the harbor now known as Provincetown Harbor, is more or less correctly drawn.

If Whitson's Head did not survive as a name, there might have been danger that a burst of monarchic loyalty from Captain John Smith might. Smith repeatedly referred to "Cape Cod" in his *Description of New England* (1616), but not once did he mention when or how it got the name. One might think that he must have heard the story from Gosnold himself, since the two were associated for at least two years in the Virginia enterprise. Smith attributed the entire Virginia enterprise to Gosnold, so it cannot be that he omitted the story out of jealousy or disparagement. But he made no mention of who named Cape Cod and nearly ten years after Gosnold's death he felt free to please Prince Charles (who found the New England Indian names "barbarous"), and changed Cape Cod to Cape James, in honor of the King. The misguided effort to flatter royalty proved as short-lived as Pring's "Whitson's Head." Gosnold's homely, practical name has survived all such petty adulation. Yet Gosnold's own name seemed for a few years to be in danger of succumbing to a wave that virtually left little memory of him but the name *Cape Cod*. For as long as the name endures it will be associated with the arrival of the Pilgrims on these shores in 1620.

The Pilgrims are among those who knew about Cape Cod — how is not known — before Gabriel Archer's story of its naming saw the light of day. It is fitting, therefore, to conclude this chapter with the words of Governor William Bradford, telling the story of the arrival of the *Mayflower* at the Cape.

. . . after longe beating at sea they fell with that land which is called Cape Cod; the which being made & certainly knowne to be it, they were not a litle joyfull. After some deliberation had amongst them selves & with ye mr. of ye ship, they tacked aboute and resolved to stande for ye southward (ye wind & weather being faire) to finde some place aboute Hudsons river [location uncertain] for their habitation. But after they had sailed yt course aboute halfe ye day, they fell amongst deangerous shoulds and roring breakers, and they were so farr intangled ther with as they conceived them selves in great danger; & ye wind shrinking upon them withall, they resolved to bear up againe for the Cape, and thought them selves hapy to gett out of those dangers before night overtooke them, as by Gods providence they did. And ye next day they gott into ye Cape-harbor wher they ridd in saftie. A word or too by ye way of this cape; it was thus first named by Capten Gosnole & his company (because yey tooke much of yt fishe ther), Ano: 1602, and after by Capten Smith was caled Cape James; but it retains ye former name amongst seamen . . .

Being thus arived in a good harbor and brought safe to land, they fell upon their knees & blessed ye God of heaven, who had brought them over ye vast & furious ocean, and delivered them from all ye periles & miseries thereof, againe to set their feete on ye firme and stable earth, their proper elemente.[12]

96

CHAPTER XII

CAPE COD

Saturday, May 15th, for Bartholomew Gosnold was a day of disappointment, exhilaration, and decision.

Like a stallion corralled, the *Concord* sailed first to the east and then to the west along the southern shore of Cape Cod Bay, looking for a way of escape through the encircling arm of the Cape to more southerly waters beyond. Having assumed that the Cape's northerly, outer arm was an island, Gosnold sailed easterly until shoaling water forced him to anchor. From the poop and from the masthead keen eyes scanned every yard of the shore, looking for the stream that would separate the northern part of the Cape from the mainland, making the former an island — the stream that the Indians had probably tried to indicate on their chalk map. Nothing of the sort could be descried.

In this vicinity, the white settlers of the next century did in fact cut off the northern part of the Cape by laboriously digging a boat channel to connect the head waters of a creek emptying into the bay with a lagoon on the outer coast called Nauset Harbor. This canal, long since filled in, is well remembered in connection with a famous Massachusetts mariner, Captain Cyprian Southack, who made a chart of New England waters. On this chart he drew this passageway, somewhat exaggerated in width, with the following note appended: "The place where I came through with a whale-boat, being ordered by the government to look after the pirate ship *Whida*, Bellame, commander, cast away the 26th of April, 1717, where I buried 102 men drowned."[1] It was in the vicinity of this first "Cape Cod Canal", where the outer cape begins to narrow, that Gosnold in the previous century had hoped to find a natural waterway, although his search brought only disappointment.

The *Concord* then weighed anchor and sailed slowly to the west a league off shore, looking presumably for the other open-

97

ing which the Indians had seemed to indicate. The voyagers observed, to their discouragement, that the further west they sailed, the higher rose the wooded hills in the background, until, having covered from eight to ten miles — a matter of two hours sailing — they were abreast of those which Brereton said were the "highest hills we saw."[2] But more to the point, in Archer's words, they here "did perceive a large opening."[3] It was the entrance to a shallow harbor known now as Barnstable Harbor. Hope reawakened. From a league off shore, this opening looked as though it might be the outlet of a stream that somehow came from inland around the hills, a navigable passageway to the supposed waters on the other side of the hills. When the *Concord* had anchored, a half-shallop was hoisted in haste out of the hold and launched. Gosnold went ashore, with John Brereton and three others, on a tour of exploration.[4]

When they entered the inlet, they found that it quickly shoaled to a depth scarcely enough to float their landing craft. Archer reported that they called it "Shoal-Hope", a name probably originating with Archer, ever ready with a trenchant expression to record the experiences of the explorers. This particular name was a play on words, for "Hope" at that time still had the meaning, since virtually forgotten, of "inlet, haven". Archer quite possibly meant that this haven had turned out to be a shallow hope indeed.

Gosnold, in no way dismayed by his second disappointment, proceeded to put into effect his alternative plan. He and his four companions made their way southward through the trackless forest, determined to reach the summit of the high hills that they had seen from off-shore. If there was an inland body of water beyond these hills, Gosnold wanted a sight of it. He would know then how to go about a search for a southern entrance to it, such as Verrazzano had described, facing south at 41° 40'.

They marched all that afternoon, Brereton reported, with their muskets "on their necks." Cut off from the prevailing southwest wind by the hills and trees, they found it to be one of those insufferably hot days that frequently occur in this region in the early spring.[5] Nevertheless, they toiled up one slope after another until they reached the highest hilltop.

They marched without fear of the savages of the land, because they saw none. Surely, however, Indians of the Mattakeeset (Barnstable) tribe stealthily followed the noisy Englishmen as they crashed through the woods and shouted to one another about their progress. Indians of this region and period, before their enmity had been aroused by wanton acts of Europeans, seldom attacked mysterious and awesome strangers who came ashore from the *floating islands,* unless they saw booty to be had without danger to themselves.

Indeed, if the Indians had contemplated an attack, it would have been made on the sailors guarding the landing-craft, for that was a prize which might have tempted a bellicose group of savages. These Indians of southeastern Massachusetts, however, were a different breed from those of "Savage Rock", who were found in possession of a Basque shallop, and they were more inclined to deal peaceably with strangers. Furthermore, the Cape Cod Indians had doubtless learned from Maine tribesmen in contact with the French that the long black sticks which the white-men carried could belch forth deadly thunder. Nevertheless, Gosnold and his companions unwittingly — or perhaps we should say courageously — ran great risks in blundering about for five or six hours in the forests of a region well-populated with savages.

The high hill which Gosnold and his party climbed — easily identified on a topographical map as Shootflying Hill, with an elevation of 200 feet — gave them the exhilarating view for which they were looking. Just below them, to the south, began that great expanse of water known as Nantucket Sound, cheering Gosnold for the day with the thought that he had actually found the great bay described by Verrazzano. Although the islands that border the Sound on the south, Nantucket, Tuckernuck and Muskeget, are below the horizon, even from that altitude, the waters had the look of an inland sea — present-day observers agree on this. Far to the east the waters of the great "bay" met the skyline, which seemed to Gosnold to be the end, as Archer later reported, of the inland waters. As Gosnold's eyes followed it from east to west, it seemed to extend in all about thirty miles — a reasonably close estimate, as the actual length of Nantucket Sound is about twenty-five miles.

In the near foreground, on the Cape itself, the men must have seen a beautiful lake studded with islands, although no one mentioned it. Close by the shore of the Cape, a small island stood out which is actually a peninsula now called Point Gammon, or Great Island. Across the Sound they made out a single peak above the horizon, the highland at Cape Poge on the northern end of the island called Chappaquiddick, adjacent to the eastern end of Martha's Vineyard. These indications that there were islands both on the near and on the farther side of this body of water justified Brereton in reporting that there were "sundry islands lying almost round about the Cape." The explorers' interest in these arose from the report of Verrazzano that there were five small islands in the great bay of his discovery.

The view to the west from this hill is an amazing one, quite unlike anything anyone might guess from looking at a map of the region. Brereton's first sentence by way of report when they had reached this vantage point read, "At length we perceived this headland to be parcell of the maine [mainland]." In fact, there was nothing to be seen in the west except a vast verdure-covered land mass, with what seemed to be a river emerging from it and flowing into the bay south of them. The divergence between that which the explorers saw, or thought they saw, and that which is seen on the map, needs clarification.

The East Chop at the northeast corner of Martha's Vineyard lies about six miles from the mainland and marks the division point between Nantucket Sound and Vineyard Sound — the latter lying between Martha's Vineyard and the Elizabeth Islands. This stretch of water between the island and the mainland, for those looking at it from the summit of Shootflying Hill, is at the extreme limit of vision; nothing of the great sound beyond it to the west can be seen. Furthermore, intervening hills of the Cape narrow this stretch of water so that it seems to be a narrow silver thread emerging into Nantucket Sound from between hills. The high, background hills of the Vineyard, visible because of their elevation, seem to be a part of the mainland. Buzzards Bay, the great body of water lying to the west of Cape Cod, is completely cut off by intervening hills, and there is nothing whatever to suggest its presence to the observer. The low-lying Elizabeth Islands are, of course, well below the horizon.

This scenic effect, which may be observed by any who take the trouble to follow Gosnold to the top of Shootflying Hill, leads to the following conclusion. On this day, and for a week thereafter, until he was disillusioned by sailing the length of Vineyard Sound — no river, but an arm of the sea — Gosnold believed that he had seen the outlet of the great River of Norumbega, or the River Dee, as Dr. Dee had called it, flowing into the upper part of the great bay discovered by Verrazzano.

Turning his eyes northward, and gazing out over the protected waters through which he had come to reach this shore of the Cape, Gosnold saw what he must do. Retracing his course, he must round the northern tip of the Cape and follow the outer coast southward until he was beyond the islands enclosing the great bay that he believed to be his destination. Confidently, he expected that somewhere along their southern shores he would then find the entrance which Verrazzano had described.

Returning to their landing-place in such haste as they could, Gosnold's party found that several things had happened during their five or six hours' absence.

The other half-shallop had been launched, rowed ashore, and "set" together with the first half, making a craft capable of transporting twenty-five men — as is learned from a later passage in Archer's account.[6] These divided shallops were an ingenious and practical invention, apparently in common use at that time. They had the advantage of being capable of instant launching. It was otherwise with the one carried by the *Mayflower*, described in this account by Governor Bradford:

Being thus arrived at Cap-Cod ye 11 of November, and necessitie calling them to looke out a place for habitation (as well as the maisters & mariners importunitie) they having brought a large shalop with them out of England, stowed in quarters in ye ship, they now gott her out & sett their carpenters to worke to trime her up; but being much brused & shatered in ye shipe with foule weather, they saw she would be long in mending . . .[7]

It turned out that the *Mayflower's* carpenters had to work on the boat for two weeks or more before it was serviceable.

While Gosnold and his party were off exploring, or perhaps just about the time that they returned, a young Indian appeared on the shore, fearlessly mingling with the visiting strangers. Brereton described him as "a young man, of proper ["good"] stature, and of a pleasing countenance." Archer wrote that he was "armed with his Bow and Arrowes, and had certain plates of Copper hanging at his Eares." Archer further reported that "hee shewed a willingness to helpe us in our occasions [needs]," — no doubt in the gathering of the cypress, birch, witch-hazel and beech, mentioned by Archer as the sorts of wood obtained for firewood.

From the courageous demeanor and copper ornaments of the young Indian, it may safely be assumed that he was some chief's son, one of the "privileged" who were rigorously trained from childhood to meet all the crises of savage life with fortitude.[8] Without disparaging his courage, it may also be assumed that his tribesmen were lurking behind the nearest cover, ready to send a shower of arrows at the strangers if they threatened any harm to the lone lad. As expected of a chief's son, he was at the forefront in an effort to determine the intentions of the ship's company.

This young Indian recalls the chief of these same Barnstable Indians whom the Pilgrims encountered eighteen years later, and found him to be "a very personable, gentle, courteous and fair conditioned savage, indeed not like a savage, save for his attire." The marvel of the incident is that this young man, obviously a brave of "rank", should deign to assist in the gathering of firewood and the bringing of water, tasks ordinarily performed by squaws. Obviously he regarded the strangers as some sort of superior beings whom it was an honor to serve.[9]

On returning to the ship, Gosnold and his companions found that the others "had pestered our ship so with Cod fish, that we threw numbers of them over-boord againe", as Brereton put it. "Surely I am persuaded that in the months of March, April, and May, there is upon this coast, better fishing, and in as great plentie as in *Newfound-land*." He summed up the advantage of the Cape Cod region over Newfoundland in general:

. . . the schools of Mackerell, herrings, Cod, and other fish, that we daily saw as we went and came from the shore, were woonderfull; and besides, the places where we tooke these Cods (and might in a few daies have laden our ship) were but in seven fadome water, and within lesse than a league of the shore; where, in *Newfound-land* they fish in fortie or fiftie fadome water, and farre off.[10]

An interesting commentary on this report by Brereton, is an "Eldridge" chart of Cape Cod Bay, published early in this century, one of an excellent series of practical charts for local coasting vessels and fisherman. On this chart, the precise locality off the shore of Barnstable where the *Concord* did its fishing is marked "Fishing Grounds", and in the soundings for this vicinity seven fathoms predominates — the depth recorded by Brereton.[11]

Why, in Gosnold's generation, Brereton's report did not send a rush of fishing vessels to the bay inside of "the mighty headland" is more or less inexplicable. Possibly there were fishing voyages to this bay which were not recorded. Captain Argall had sailed in 1610 into the shoals seaward of the Cape in search of cod and nearly lost his vessel in doing so. Why did Argall not go into the bay so plainly described by Brereton in 1602 and fish in safe and protected waters?

The only sound reason for this would seem to be the lack of a shore base from which to operate. Newfoundland continued to attract the fishing-fleets because such bases existed. Those really interested in the Cape Cod fishing-grounds held back until bases were established, which took longer than anyone might reasonably have expected.[12]

103

Brereton, it may be noted, did not mention the bestowal of the name *Cape Cod* on this "mighty headland", as he called it. Knowledge of the naming comes from a rather confused sentence in Archer: "The fifteenth day . . . we did perceive a large opening. We called it Shole-hope. Neere this Cape [at the west end thereof] we came to Anchor in fifteene fadome, where wee tooke great store of Cod-fish, for which we altered the name and called it Cape Cod."

Although the text seems to have been pared down somewhat here, it is evident that Archer's name, Shoal Hope, was finally considered too limited in scope and rather meaningless in view of subsequent discoveries, so that he eventually acquiesced in the decision to call the whole cape by the more significant name, "Cape Cod". Who made the decision? Without doubt it was Gosnold. He wanted to tell all England that he had found a new source of wealth from fisheries. That would be a good bargaining point when it came to final plans for a permanent colony.

Another lacuna in Archer's narrative must be filled in, if possible. On May 15, Archer has the *Concord* placed at the west end of the bottom of the sound between the cape and the mainland. On the 16th the scene is abruptly shifted, with the statement that they "trended the Coast Southerly, which was all champaine [open country] and full of grass, but the islands somewhat wooded." This he follows immediately with the story of events that happened twelve leagues, or thirty-six miles, beyond the Cape. When and how did the *Concord* get from the bottom of Cape Cod Bay to the outer coast? How did the *Concord* fare in the shoals?

There is not so much as a single phrase to suggest the answers to these questions, except that Brereton, in his parallel account, reports in typical landsman's fashion:

From this place, we sailed round about this headland, almost all the points of the compasse, the shore very bolde: but as no coast is free from dangers, so I am persuaded, this is as free as any. The land somewhat lowe, full of goodly woods, but in some places plaine.

Others following Gosnold who got into the shoals had breath-taking tales to tell of their hairbreadth escapes from destruction; the list includes the mate of Hudson's *Half Moon,* Waymouth, Argall, Captain John Smith, and the Pilgrims. Why did Archer and Brereton lead their readers to conclude that Gosnold encountered no dangers as he sailed down the outer coast of Cape Cod?

In the first place, literary critics with an eye on the map will agree that Archer's narrative is too disjointed at this point to have been originally written in this form. Someone edited Archer's narrative. That someone was most probably Richard Hakluyt. What, then, was Hakluyt's motive behind his deletions?

At the time Archer gave him his story of what happened, complementing Brereton's, Hakluyt was busy collecting documents, possibly for another edition of his *Voyages.* There is evidence that Hakluyt sometimes edited his material to fit in with promotion ventures which his clients had under way. Archer's narrative turned up at a time when those interested in establishing a colony in the "north part" of Virginia — New England — still logically wanted to keep something of their discoveries under cover. It remained for Captain John Smith, a dozen years later, yet still before the publication of Archer's narrative, to "release" detailed information about the shoals and the general lie of the coast.[13]

> Towards the South and Southwest of this *Cape* [Cod], is found a long and dangerous shoale of sands and rocks. But so farre as I encircled it, I found thirtie fadom water aboard the shore, and a strong current; which makes mee thinke there is a Channell about this shoale: where is the best and greatest fish to be had, Winter and Summer, in all that Countrie. But the Salvages say there is no Channell; but that the shoales beginne from the maine at *Pawmet,* to the Ile of *Nausit;* and so extends beyond their knowledge into the Sea.
> The next to this is *Capawack* [Martha's Vineyard], and those abounding Countries of copper, corne, people, mineralls: which I went to discover [explore] this last yeare [1615]; but because I miscarried by the way, I will leave them, till God please I have better acquaintance with them.[14]

But, to return to the story, not content with Archer's shift of the *Concord* mysteriously from the southernmost part of Cape

Cod Bay to the ocean waters off Nauset outside the Cape, it is to be assumed that on the evening of the 15th, as soon as the halves of the shallop were safely stowed again in the hold, Gosnold weighed anchor and made a night run around the northern tip of the Cape. This assumption is necessary because of the time-element: a greater distance was sailed before the evening of the 16th than could be covered in the hours of daylight. The assumption is furthermore reasonable, since Gosnold had sailed throughout the previous night southward from the coast of Maine, and he knew the waters of Cape Cod Bay to be safe, because he had just traversed them.

It hardly needs to be said that Gosnold passed through or around the shoals safely, else nothing more would have been heard of the *Concord* and Captain Bartholomew Gosnold. Probably, like Waymouth, in the words of Waymouth's Chronicler, James Rosier, Gosnold exclaimed, "God so blessed us, that we had weather and winde as faire as poore men could wish, in this distresse, whereby we both perfectly discerned every breach, and with the winde were able to turne, where we saw most hope of safest passage."[15]

One thing is quite certain. Gosnold did not attempt, as some historians have assumed, to turn into Nantucket Sound past Monomoy Point, the end of the long sandy strip running southwards from the main part of the Cape at its southeastern corner. Nor did he attempt an entrance into this sound by using the channel which Captain John Smith later quite rightly thought that he detected flowing out of it, and which seamen in these days of navigational aids have long regarded as the course to be followed in rounding the Cape into these southerly inland waters. (The cutting through of the Cape Cod Canal between Buzzards Bay and Cape Cod Bay has given coastwise shipping a much safer inland route, obviating the need of passing through any part of the shoals.) Gosnold was much too intent on finding a southern entrance into the great bay that he had seen from the Cape Cod hills even to consider a risky entrance from the east.

Five days later, on Friday, May 21st, Gosnold was again

oasting along a shore of Cape Cod. But this time he was in the quiet waters of Nantucket Sound on his way to his most notable discoveries, searching for a southern entrance to the Sound.

Chapter XIII

AN EXPOSITORY INTERLUDE

This chapter is concerned with certain technical matter of source study and documentary interpretation, of the sor which historians usually leave behind the scenes as not likel to interest the average reader. But perhaps these matters de interest the average reader. If not, let him or her then pass or to the next chapter! They are inserted here, rather than in the notes, because the story of the *Concord's* course among the islands south of Cape Cod — to be told in the next chapter — differs materially from that told in current histories. There may therefore be those among readers of this work who will wan to know immediately the grounds on which the present write ventures to give an entirely new reconstruction of Gosnold' explorations.

The question at issue is whether Bartholomew Gosnol(sailed through the open ocean past a large and beautiful island ignoring it, to explore a small outlying island known to ou early English settlers as Noman's (or No Man's) Land, o whether he sailed through the inland sounds, to explore the large island known as Martha's Vineyard. To which of these islands, the small or the large, did Gosnold give the name o his daughter Martha?

The large island, with an over-all length of twenty-five miles (including the contiguous island of Chappaquiddick a its eastern end), and about nine miles wide from north to south at its broadest point, was known to the Indians as Capawack This was the name used, in various spellings, by Harlow, Hobson Captain John Smith, the Dutch writer de Laet, Thomas Dermer the early Pilgrims, Richard Vines (Agent and Steward-General of Sir Ferdinando Gorges), and by Gorges himself, who became

:nglish proprietor of the island in 1635 by patent from the
Council for New England, confirmed in 1639 by a Royal Charter.[1]

Capawack, of more or less the same geological formation
s New York's Long Island, has along its northern shore a range
f hills rising to elevations between two hundred and three
undred feet.[2] It is the dominant feature of the landscape be-
ween the lower part of Cape Cod and Buzzards Bay, and no
ne sailing from that cape to that bay, as Gosnold undoubtedly
did, could possibly overlook it. Yet the casual reader of the
Relations of Brereton and of Archer, as has already been pointed
ut, is left in ignorance of any such island. This lacuna cries aloud
or explanation. For historians in general have ignored the prob-
em, and therefore one looks in vain for an adequate solution.

Before undertaking a re-examination of the narratives of
his part of Gosnold's voyage, the testimony of two unimpeach-
ble witnesses, unknown in this connection to past historians,
s introduced. Both independently aver that Capawack, not
Noman's Land, was the island named Martha's Vineyard. If
hey are correct — and their knowledge of the matter obviously
:ame from Indians who were living at the time of Gosnold's
landings — then it follows as matter of course that Capawack
was the island explored and named by Bartholomew Gosnold,
despite the apparent evidence of the *Relations* to the contrary.

Edward Winslow, Mayflower Pilgrim and leader of the
colony, published in London a letter written by the young missionary to the Indians, Thomas Mayhew, Jr., dated November
18, 1647. Winslow began this letter with the following words:
"[The] name [of the writer] is Mr. *Mayhew,* who teacheth the
Word both to *English* and *Indians* upon an Island called formerly
Capawack, by us *Mortha's Vineyard* . . ."[3]

It hardly needs to be pointed out that Winslow's information must have come from the Indians with whom he became
intimately acquainted in 1620, eighteen years after Gosnold's
voyage. Among Winslow's friends were Massasoit, the great
chief of the Pokonockets, in whose dominion Capawack was
included, Squanto, the Pilgrims' interpreter, born and raised

at the site of the Plymouth settlement, and Epenow, alias Apannow, who journeyed from Capawack to Plymouth to sign the document acknowledging the Indians' subjection to King James (a document still preserved at Plymouth). Doubtless many other older Indians had stories to tell of the first coming of white men to their lands. It is inconceivable that the Pilgrims used the name bestowed by Bartholomew Gosnold for an island which Gosnold had not visited.

This testimony from Edward Winslow is paralleled by that of Richard Vines, a gentleman in the employ of Sir Ferdinando Gorges, who many years later became Governor in Maine. An agent for Gorges, Vines is reported to have spent the winter of the great plague in an Indian wigwam in Maine, which would place him on this coast as early as 1616-1617, possibly earlier. He ranged up and down New England on behalf of his principal for many years, among other things conducting some sort of business with the Pilgrims in 1631, as the result of which he was one of those to whom the Pilgrims owed over £500.

After Gorges acquired the islands of Capawack and Nantucket in 1635, it was Vines' particular business, of course, to know all about these islands, having available all that the Indian Epenow while a captive in England had reported to Gorges in 1613, eleven years after Gosnold's voyage, all that he had learned from his own conversations with Indians along the coast, and all that his associate in the service of Gorges, Thomas Dermer, had told him as the result of Dermer's visit to Capawack in 1619. He therefore knew precisely what Dermer meant when Dermer reported that Capawack was "an island formerly discovered by the English."[5]

In 1641, Vines, as the Steward-General of Sir Ferdinando, conveyed to Thomas Mayhew of Watertown the "islands of Capawack alias Martha's Vineyard." Again here is a witness who could hardly have been mistaken as to the identification of the island which Gosnold named.[6]

Knowing this evidence furnished by Winslow and Vines, it is somewhat amusing to read the remarks made on the subject the Reverend Jeremy Belknap in 1798. Belknap is entitled respect as the first American historian to use what may be called "modern methods" in the writing of history. Unfortunately, however, Belknap's half-informed study at the scene of Gosnold's voyage has come down in our histories as the final word. Having convinced himself that Gosnold landed only on Noman's Land, and that therefore it was Noman's Land which was named Martha's Vineyard, Belknap betrayed his uneasiness about the matter by adding, "For what reason, and at what time, the name Martha's Vineyard was transferred from the small island so-called by Gosnold to the large island that now bears it, are questions which remain in obscurity."

There are obvious answers to this makeshift theory by which Belknap sought to justify himself. In the first place, there is no evidence whatsoever that any Englishman, at any time after Gosnold, knew Noman's Land by the name of Martha's Vineyard. A name that never came into use could hardly have been transferred. Then, Vines' grant of "Capawack alias Martha's Vineyard" would have lacked validity if any neighboring settlers had thought Martha's Vineyard to be Noman's Land. The island's only neighbors, as a matter of fact, were the Pilgrims at Plymouth and on the Cape, and these, as has been said, had accepted the identification of Martha's Vineyard as Capawack. No one ever disputed the Mayhews' occupation of the "Vineyard" on the ground that the Gorges grant gave them Noman's Land only. Belknap's theory of a "transfer" of the name, therefore, merely covers the fact that he was quite mistaken in his identification of Noman's Land as the island which Gosnold had explored.[7]

If these early seventeenth-century authorities, Winslow and Vines, were convinced by the contemporary evidence of Indians that the present Martha's Vineyard was the island named by Gosnold, why have historians, from the time of Jeremy Belknap down to the present, interpreted the *Relations* of Brereton and Archer otherwise? To answer this question a critical re-reading of the narrative is necessary. The significance of Archer's data

111

may best be established by a running commentary on his cruci
statement, beginning when Gosnold started south on May si
teenth, 1602, as related at the end of the last chapter.

"Twelve leagues from Cape Cod we descried a point . .

In general, interpreters of this sentence have taken th
measure from the northern tip of Cape Cod, with the result th
the point said by Archer to be twelve leagues from Cape C
turns out to be Cape Cod itself.[8] This initial assumption is u
warranted by Archer's use of the name. It did not mean
Archer merely the northern extremity of the Cape.

Archer mentioned Cape Cod elsewhere three times, fir
where the name was given, on a shore that runs "northeast
east", which is obviously the main east-west body of the Cap
as seen from inside the Bay. (Gosnold and his party had ju
observed how the main southern part of the Cape jutted o
from the mainland.) Secondly, he mentioned an opening whic
Gosnold had descried from Cape Cod. It is impossible to se
any opening into Nantucket Sound from the northern part
the Cape: Archer again must have meant the central part of th
Cape where its highest hills were found. As a third instanc
Archer later referred to the cod-fishing at Cape Cod: this fishin
to repeat, was done in the westernmost end, or bottom, of Cap
Cod Bay. To Archer, therefore, Cape Cod meant the main,
southerly, portion of the Cape. A vessel coasting south woul
naturally take a measure from the last point of Cape Cod see
which in this instance was its most southeasterly point, know
now as Monomoy Point. (Incidentally, once again, the nam
Cape Cod is placed on the so-called Velasco map at this soutl
easterly corner.) "Twelve leagues from Cape Cod", taking th
words in their natural meaning of "twelve leagues beyond Cap
Cod", coasting south and then west under Nantucket and i
adjacent islands, there is such a point as Archer describes on th
eastern side of the Muskeget entrance into Nantucket Sound.[9]

The proof that this is a correct interpretation of Archer

words lies in the following observation, which will be borne out by the interpretation to follow. If the measure is taken from the northern tip of Cape Cod, placing the point descried somewhere in the vicinity of Chatham, Archer's whole account is thrown into disorder, and no historian has been able to make anything satisfactory out of it. If, on the other hand, the measure is taken to mean that Gosnold has gone about twelve leagues beyond Cape Cod to a southern entrance into Nantucket Sound, then everything that Archer had to say subsequently falls into reasonable order, and his data become meaningful and correct.

"*We passed over the breach of Gilberts Point in foure or five fadome, and anchored a league or somewhat more beyond it; betweene the last two Points are two leagues, the interim, along shoale water . . .*"
The zeal with which various interpreters have tried to locate these points on Cape Cod, about thirty-six and forty-two miles below an indefinite northern point, and their divergent views, are most amazing — the fact of the matter being that there are no such points six miles apart on Cape Cod anywhere, and any opinion as to their location on the Cape has to be based on a theory that they have disappeared since Gosnold's day.[10] To avoid this confusion, one has only to examine a chart of the coast, from which it will be seen that Archer is correctly describing the points that mark the Muskeget opening into Nantucket Sound, which are just about two leagues — six miles — apart, with the intervening water full of dangerous sandy shoals. It follows therefore that the "passing over the breach of Gilberts Point" was an entrance through the opening, not merely the passing of a point in the open sea. Gosnold had entered Nantucket Sound![11]
This passage well illustrates Archer's peculiar style. He omitted saying definitely that there was an opening, and that the explorers found themselves passing through it into a great sound. Nevertheless, a comparison of Archer's words with a

113

chart of the vicinity shows that he was quite accurate as far as he went. Prolonged study of Archer's narrative as a whole gives the impression that these omissions were intentional, designed to confuse any who would follow, while preserving truthful but fragmentary remarks on much of that which the explorers had seen.

"The Coast from Gilberts Point to the supposed Iles lyeth East and by South. . . [The next day] we went coasting from Gilberts Point to the supposed Iles . . ."

"A little from the supposed Iles appeared unto us an opening . . ."

"From this opening the Mayne lyeth South-west, which coasting along . . ."

These three statements taken together lay out a course first, easterly, then past an opening, then following the coast of the mainland southwest. A chart of Nantucket Sound, shows that Archer is describing a circuit of the sound, first following the northern shore of Nantucket, then turning north, past the Nantucket opening into the sound, and finally turning southwesterly along the south shore of Cape Cod, which runs in that direction.[12] Again, following his usual style of reporting, Archer did not say that the explorers were making a circuit of the Sound; but it is obvious that nowhere else on a chart of the local coast is there a place for this sequence of bearings.

"From this opening the Mayne lyeth South-west, which coasting along we saw a disinhabited Iland which so afterwards appeared unto us: we bore with it, and named it Marthaes Vineyard; from Shole-hope [here, the Nantucket opening] it is eight leagues in circuit, the Iland is five miles . . .

This sentence describes a situation which does not exist anywhere in the region explored by Gosnold. The statement is either wrong in saying that they were coasting along the mainland, or else it is wrong in saying that they arrived at a small island.

114

Historians in general have chosen to assume that the mainland mentioned here is not the mainland, but the southern shore of Martha's Vineyard. This course would have taken Gosnold to the small island already mentioned, known as Noman's Land.

The theory that Gosnold sailed to Noman's Land and made three landings, taking four days to explore its one square-mile area, is supported by only one item in the data furnished by Archer and Brereton, the mention of an island only a square mile in area. All the rest of the information furnished by these reporters becomes a hodge-podge of error, if an effort is made to apply the rest of the items to Noman's Land.

If, on the other hand, it is assumed that Archer is correct in saying that the explorers coasted southwest along a shore of the mainland (i.e., Cape Cod), then it is evident, as may be seen from any chart, that they arrived at the northeastern promontory of the large island Capawack, now known as Martha's Vineyard.

The thought behind this interpretation is that there may have been here some alteration, or alterations, in the manuscripts, by which the large island named Capawack was eliminated from the narratives, as it surely was by some process or other. To make this clear, substitute the word "headland" for "island" in the quotation from Archer: *From this opening the Mayne lyeth South-west, which coasting along we saw a disinhabited* Headland *which so afterwards appeared unto us: we bore with it, and named it Marthaes Vineyard; from Shole-hope it is eight leagues in circuit, the* Headland *is five miles . . .* This revised sentence is correct in every particular, and like a touchstone reveals the accuracy of all the other data furnished by Archer and Brereton.

Approaching the matter from a different angle, one may make this observation parenthetically. Historians have fastened upon the statement that the place named Martha's Vineyard was an island a square mile in area, disregarding all other evidence in the narratives, and leading them inevitably to the conclusion that Noman's Land was the island in question. These historians should have asked themselves, rather, whether the square-mile area mentioned was really a separate island as stated, for no such island as the one described can be reached by sailing southwest along the mainland. But by a curious coincidence, the headland now known as the East Chop of Martha's Vineyard[13], limited in area by injutting salt ponds on either side of its base, is about the same size as Noman's Land, and like that island can be described as four or five miles in compass.

So the question is, are Archer and Brereton reporting on a one-square-mile island standing by itself out at sea, or on an island over one hundred square miles bordering on the Sound south of the mainland? Which was reached when the *Concord* sailed southwest?

The data reviewed in the numbered paragraphs following bear on Archer's statement, italicized above, that an island was named Martha's Vineyard. Which island was it?

> 1. The island named Martha's Vineyard is said to be eight leagues from an opening. Noman's Land is not that distance from any opening, but East Chop is precisely that distance from the eastern opening into Nantucket Sound.[14]
>
> 2. The "island" is said in both narratives to be without inhabitants. This is correct, if the so-called island was the East Chop headland, as there were never any permanent wigwam sites on East Chop. On the other hand, Noman's Land was almost certainly occupied by Indians, for by ancient custom the Indians of Capawack moved over to it for fishing every spring. Later on the narratives state that at the third landing-place, Indians appeared. This could hardly have happened on tiny Noman's Land in the way described, as the whole island can be inspected in half an hour, and any Indians on it would have been seen on the occasion of the first landings. On the other hand, if the island in question is the large island of Capawack, and the explorers had

116

passed from the uninhabited headland to the populous regions further west, then it was to be expected that Indians would suddenly show themselves.

3. On the third day of exploration of this island, the explorers *"weighed, and toward night came to anchor at the Northwest part of this Island."* This report is an utter absurdity, if made of a change of location on Noman's Land: the distance from the north to the northwest shore on that tiny island is hardly over half a mile. On the other hand, if the narratives are telling about the exploration of the twenty-five mile long Capawack, it is quite reasonable to believe that the distance between the locations of the second and third landings was a matter of ten or twelve miles, an afternoon's sail.

4. Brereton says, "At length we were come amongst many faire Islands, which we had partly discerned at our first landing; . . . but coming to anchor under one of them, . . . Captaine Gosnold, my selfe, and some others went ashore. . . ." By no stretch of the imagination can Noman's Land be described as one of the "sundrie Islands lying almost round about" the Cape, which the explorers had seen from the hill of Cape Cod: Noman's Land is far, far below the horizon as one looks out from that hill. The eastern headland of Capawack, on the other hand, can be made out quite distinctly.

5. At the place of the second landing, Brereton describes a spring-fed lake, a mile in circuit. There is no such lake on Noman's Land, but Brereton's words are an excellent description of a fresh-water lake of that size at a place on Martha's Vineyard called Lambert's Cove, seven miles west of East Chop by water.

6. At the scene of the third landing, Brereton reports a "great store" of clay, "both red and white." There are no beds of red and white clay on Noman's Land — at least, none that are visible.

7. According to Brereton, who went ashore at the first landing, the place described as one square mile in area held nothing of particular interest for the explorers, save an old wigwam and the remnants of a fishing weir. The next day, when they land, with no mention in the

117

narratives of a change of location, the explorers fir
themselves in a veritable Garden of Eden, with all sor
of wonders worthy of mention.

Obviously, the place could not have changed ove
night; therefore the only conclusion is that the explore
had changed their location. Such a shift, however,
an entirely different scene could not have taken pla
on the small area of Noman's Land, where everythi
could have been seen in half an hour or so on the occ
sion of their first landing; nor could all the physical fe
tures seen at the three successive landings have be
found together on any one-square-mile area. Hence t
three landings must have been at widely separated plac
on a large island such as Capawack, and not on t
miniature Noman's Land.

8. Brereton places the island named Martha's Vineya
three or four leagues from the mainland. This estima
doubles the distance from East Chop to the neare
point on the mainland, but can be understood as
measure of the distance sailed diagonally from the poi
where the ship began to angle away from the mainlan
to reach the island across the Sound. It is quite in
possible, however, to apply this measure to Noman
Land, which is at least six leagues, eighteen statu
miles, off the mainland shore of Buzzards Bay.[15]

9. Archer reports a distance "from Marthaes Vineya
to Dover Cliffe [Gay Head], halfe a league over t
Sound." This is another measure that is absurdly wror
if one takes Martha's Vineyard to be Noman's Lan
Noman's Land is over five miles from Gay Head at t
nearest point, and there are no parallel shores to form
sound between them. If, however, Martha's Vineya
is understood to be the larger island, the high land
which extends to within a mile and a half of the hi
land of Gay Head, then the statement is correct. T
half-a-league is a chord of Menemsha Bight, and this
as Archer states, a measure "over the Sound."

The sum of the matter in the above paragraphs is that i
ternal evidence from the narratives makes it virtually certa
that the island found by Gosnold on his southwest course w

e present Martha's Vineyard. Both narratives describe places
this island easily recognizable as features of the local scene
anyone who knows this Vineyard well. Other data in the
rratives are true of the Vineyard, too, but not of any other place.

There is no mention or hint in the narratives, however, that
e places described were found on a large island. Readers were
ft to infer that the one-square-mile area was the whole island,
ing misled by the simple device, apparently, of substituting
sland" for "headland" or some such word that originally stood
Archer's narrative. Brereton's account was skilfully worded
give the same impression without directly calling the square-
ile area an island.

There remain a few items to add to the commentary on
rcher's narrative.

*Marthaes Vineyard . . . hath 41. degrees and one quarter of
titude."*

This, to be sure, is the correct latitude for Noman's Land.[16]
evertheless, Archer's use of it for Martha's Vineyard was for-
itous. A correct latitude is one of those things that are just not
und in the annals of exploration in this period. The instruments
use for determining latitudes had not been perfected to the
int where they could give trustworthy observations within
teen to thirty minutes of latitude — corresponding to as many
utical miles. But to the embarrassment of those who trust
Archer's report of this observation as support for their "No-
an's Land theory", it is noted that Archer gives the latitude of
uttyhunk as 40° 10′. Taking Martha's Vineyard at 41° 15′, as
rcher reported, it is clear that Archer placed that island —
gardless of its correct latitude — five nautical miles farther
rth than Cuttyhunk. Noman's Land, however, is ten nautical
iles *south* of that island. At the same time, the northern tip of
artha's Vineyard, as known today, is nearly five nautical miles
r minutes of latitude) north of the southernmost part of Cutty-
ınk. That is about as much as can be made of Archer's reports
latitude.

"The place most pleasant; for the two and twentieth [of May] we went ashore . . ."

The incidence of verbal agreement between the passage from Archer's *Relation* thus introduced, and a similar one in Brereton's *Relation*, makes it certain that they were both reporting on the same landing. The explorers were now in the region of the fresh-water lake at Lambert's Cove, seven miles west of the headland which the explorers first encountered. Therefore here is another typical omission: Archer should have explained this shift of location by stating that the *Concord* had passed from one sound to another. Archer in particular was willing to tell about the great sound called Cape Cod Bay, and that other great sound, Buzzards Bay. But he withheld explicit information about Nantucket and Vineyard Sounds, features of the landscape, or rather seascape, which the ordinary explorer would have described in full. Archer, however, is betrayed by two clauses which evidently escaped the eye of the editor of his manuscript. In one of these, he speaks of Elizabeth's Isle as lying between two sounds. This is quite correct, as may readily be seen by consulting a chart; but Archer failed to describe Vineyard Sound previously, as lying between the Elizabeth Islands and Martha's Vineyard, and therefore the reader is left to wonder what he meant by "two sounds".

"The foure and twentieth, we set saile and doubled the Cape of another Iland next unto it, which we called Dover Cliffe . . ."

The name Dover Cliff suggests that the Gay Head cliffs at the western end of Martha's Vineyard three and a half centuries ago had much more white clay than at present. This is easily accounted for by erosion, and the removal of thousands of tons of white clay for commercial purposes.

The peninsula at the western end of the Vineyard, where Gay Head cliffs are located, was thought to be an island because the explorers had sight of a creek, and of the great pond, called Menemsha by the Indians, which almost separates Gay Head om the rest of the island. On the other hand, if the explorers ad been sailing along the south shore of the island on their ay to Noman's Land, they would have seen the broad sandy each with no break in it which connects Gay Head to the main art of Martha's Vineyard. They would have had no reason ꞁ think of Dover Cliff (Gay Head) as a detached island.[17]

The subject is disputatious. But no matter what interpreta-ꞁon is put upon the data of the two *Relations*, the omission of ꞁny plain account of the large island Capawack, which Gosnold ꞁust have passed either to the north or to the south, presents a ꞁnique and surprising problem. It is much as though a tourist, ꞁailing about New York Harbor on a sight-seeing craft, were to ꞁass by lower Manhattan and its sky-scrapers, thinking them ꞁot worthy of notice or mention.

And now the story of Bartholomew Gosnold amongst the ꞁslands may be told as it ought to be told.

Chapter XIV

MANY FAIR ISLANDS

The Fountain of Youth, legend has it, was first sought that region of the North American coast known as Florida.[1] the centuries that followed, not supernaturally endowed water but the sight of primeval forests to be exploited, vast acreag to be brought under cultivation, and great mountains to searched for mineral wealth, has rejuvenated and stimulate American spirit from generation to generation even down to t present, making our humble and often untutored forebea God-like creators of a new world. Those who are pleasant titillated by travelling about in the well-ordered and high civilized communities of the Old World and this, need a lar amount of historical imagination, in the best sense, to unde stand the emotions of one like Bartholomew Gosnold, as beheld for the first time the temperate zone of America whic he hoped to colonize, building there a new English nation.

Men of vision before him — Sir Humphrey Gilbert, Richar Hakluyt, Captain Edward Hayes — had gathered together fro fragmentary reports a considerable amount of information abo this temperate region and had made plans on paper for its settl ment. The most useful of these reports were made by Englis men who had reached the northern part of Maine from Nev foundland[2], but none had gotten to the Land of Promise foun by Verrazzano. Now Gosnold was to see it with his own eyeand perhaps begin a traffic that would bring to England all th things needed for her prosperity.

After the *Concord* had passed safely through the rock shoals off the eastern shores of Cape Cod and Nantucket, th ship was turned westward, to coast along on the south side the "somewhat wooded" islands — Nantucket ("the Place nea the Rough Water") and Tuckernuck ("the Place like a Roun oaf of Bread") — to the little island of ever-shifting sands, Muskeget ("on the Grassy Place"), a distant Massachusetts cousin of the muskeg of the Arctic.[3] By the dead-reckoning of his navigator, Gosnold knew these to be the islands that enclosed on the south the great sheet of inland water which he had seen from the hill on Cape Cod.[4] These islands had been below the horizon from that elevation, but had betrayed their presence to his trained eye, by affecting the appearance of the sea, as they do to observers of today.

Here, south of the islands, the *Concord* was in deep water, eight to ten fathoms two or three miles off shore, with a smooth, sandy bottom. The in-rolling seas do not break into surf until they strike the sharply-shelving beach. At the southwestern corner of Muskeget Island, however, twelve leagues from Cape Cod, a sand-bar juts out at right angles to the beach, with places where the water is scarcely two fathoms deep.[5]

Seeing this southwestern corner of Muskeget Island as a "point", with the breakers of an opening a good distance beyond it, Gosnold thought that by tacking around it, his sailing-master could take the ship into the enclosed waters north of the islands. Before this could be accomplished, however, the seamen discerned the hidden sand-bar beneath them, with only a few feet of water between their keel and the treacherous sands. Speedy and skilful action got the ship about and withdrawn again into deep water; they had "well quitted themselves" of the place. Archer, here telling the story with unusual detail, thought that the point ought to be remembered as Point Care, a reminder that caution was needed in these unknown waters. At the same time, one Tucker (who may have been a "gentleman" rather than a member of the crew) evinced such excited fright that Archer named the *breach* through which they passed "Tucker's Terror." (The *breach*, of course, was the break in the boiling surf that stretches across a good part of the six-mile-wide opening into Nantucket Sound from the south.) Beyond the breach, they "bore up again with the land."

This land on the further, or western, side of the Muskeget

Channel is the island called Chappaquiddick. It lies at the easter
end of Martha's Vineyard, separated by a bay with an openin
in the north to the sound, and at its southern end opening t
the ocean through a channel that cuts through the connectin
tongue of land at one location or another, according to the whi
of the shifting sands. The anchorage off this Chappaquiddic
shore was made after nightfall, the *Concord* having sailed we
over a hundred miles since departing from the bottom of Cap
Cod Bay the previous evening. The anchor was dropped "in eigh
fadome, the ground good."

On the following day, the mariners found themselves su
rounded by a lively but not dangerous surf. In these presen
days fishermen with an eye to the sport stand on this shore an
make a long cast with their lines out in the breakers, on th
chance of hooking a fighting bass or a bluefish, and some ventur
out in sturdy motor-boats to do their casting farther off shore
Except in a southeast gale, the waters here are ordinarily no
dangerous. Gosnold and his crew, unaware of these facts, "con
tinued that day without remoove." Possibly there was a south
easter.

The next day, "being faire", it was possible to launch th
ship's boat for soundings. These, according to Archer, were mad
in or over a breach that in their course "lay off another Point
by us called Gilberts Point." This was the point opposite Poin
Care, at the western end of the Muskeget Channel into Nantucke
Sound. The soundings showed a depth of from four to seve
fathoms, making the passage reasonably safe for a ship the siz
of the *Concord*.

This entrance into Nantucket Sound is now very little use
except by fishing vessels. In 1776, however, when the Britis
Admiralty made very precise charts of this part of the America
coast, a course through Muskeget channel was plotted on th
chart for this area. The advantage of an entrance into the Soun
through this narrow channel, with dangerous sand shoals to th
east, was that the approach — through the open sea — hel
no dangers whatsoever, in contrast with the perils of entering

the Sound from the east, where many miles of outlying rocky shoals and uncertain waters guarded the entrance.[6]

There must have been wild excitement and rejoicing on board the *Concord* when it was announced that the latitude of "Gilberts Point" was 41° 40′ — exactly the latitude of Giovanni da Verrazzano's haven that "lieth open to the South." It happens, as a matter of fact, that the observation giving this latitude erred above the average.[7] By this reckoning with a faulty instrument, he was given good reason to believe that he had actually found the opening to a great bay, facing south, at the "right" latitude. It seemed to be the dramatic climax of the long months of preparation and the many weeks of sailing through strange waters, to find himself finally at his chosen destination. To be sure, the entrance was four times as wide as Verrazzano had reported, and there was no "rocke of free stone" ready for fortification in the center of the opening, but these were unessential details that Verrazzano might not have remembered accurately. Gosnold had seen the great bay, and here was a southern entrance to it in the latitude where Verrazzano had said it was to be found.

A few days later, Gosnold was to be disillusioned. When he had sailed the circuit of Nantucket Sound and continued westward through Vineyard Sound, he knew that he had not entered the estuary of a river, and although he had passed many islands, there were not five small islands within the bay, to be counted as Verrazzano had counted them. Nevertheless, he believed to the end that he had reached the vicinity of Verrazzano's discovery, since in a letter to his father, written after the return of the expedition, he wrote of the Indians whom he had encountered that a description of them would be found in Verrazzano's *Letter*.[8]

Archer gave no reason for the use of the name of Gosnold's co-captain in the naming of Gilbert's Point; Archer did not like Gilbert, it seems, and probably with good reason. Possibly Captain Gilbert assumed a personal responsibility for the soundings off the point that bore his name. Earlier it was noted that a reasonable explanation of Captain Gilbert's presence on the ship may be that he was a representative of the owner of the *Concord;* if that is so, he would have been particularly concerned for the safety of the ship in passing this dangerous place.

While the long-boat was out making these soundings, Indians paddled up in their dug-out canoes.[9] A canoe of this sort was fashioned out of the bole of a great tree, frequently an oak, three or four feet in diameter. Such trees are known to have grown in the swamps of the Vineyard, as stumps of that size have been found. The canoe was made by a process of alternately burning and scraping with a chipped-stone scraper or chisel, until it was hollowed out, leaving sides of the desired thickness. Both ends were shaped to make a handsome, elevated prow. These canoes varied of course in size and carrying capacity. While Gosnold and his company were ashore at Cuttyhunk they were visited by a party of fifty Indians, who arrived in nine canoes, indicating that the average dug-out could carry five or six natives comfortably.

The use of dug-out canoes, around the island, rather than those covered with bark, is mentioned in the story of two Quakers who visited the Vineyard in 1657. They complained that a constable thrust them out of the meeting where they had tried to speak and turned them over to an Indian, "in order to be carried in a small canoo, or hollowed piece of timber, to the mainland over a sea nine miles broad (dangerous enough for any to pass over), having first took their money from them to pay the Indian." (The Indian had to wait three days for a calm day to do the ferrying, anyway.)[10]

The savages who boarded the *Concord,* according to Archer, were apparelled much as those previously seen at Savage Rock. They were more timid about coming aboard, but once there, were more active in petty thieving. They were adorned with copper pendants hanging from their ears, and one had a plate of rich copper about twelve inches by six that he wore as a breastplate. They offered for barter tobacco, pipes "steeled with Copper" (with copper stems), skins of animals, artistically strung beads, and other trifles. One, probably a pawwaw (powwow) or medicine-man, had his face painted, and feathers stuck in his hair.[11]

The next day, waiting no doubt for a favorable tide, the ship worked its way three or four miles up the channel into the Sound, and anchored in the quiet waters between the eastern shore of Chappaquiddick and Muskeget Island. The men had noted, in passing the land on their left, water streaming from two outlets, and thought these might possibly be streams from the interior carrying freshwater to the ocean. They could not see, even from the masthead, that these were merely channels for salt-water flowing into and out of a great bay and a pond — the former between Chappaquiddick and Martha's Vineyard, and the latter a pond enclosed by beaches on the northern side of Chappaquiddick. The second of these channels, an outlet from the southern part of the pond known as Cape Poge Pond, was closed by shifting sands in a hurricane in 1723, and has since remained closed. It is therefore not to be found on any present-day chart.

As the ship lay at anchor the rest of this day and all of the next in the quiet waters of the Sound, great auks (then known as penguins) swam about the ship, exhibiting their speed in swimming and their skill in diving for fish. Some of the ship's company shot them for pleasure. These birds, long since extinct, could not fly, and were awkward and slow on the land; they were edible, if one could stand the fishy taste, and failed to survive on the North American coast because they could be taken so easily.[12]

The *Concord* passed the whole of the next day, May 20th, at anchor in this spot. It is easy to guess that they awaited a clear day with a good breeze for the circumnavigation of Nantucket Sound. The Sound, like Muskeget Channel, is full of shallow, sandy places, amongst which a ship can be conned with a man at the masthead accustomed to gauging the depth of the water by its changing colors. This sort of navigation must wait, of course, on a day of clear atmosphere and brilliant sunshine.

On May 21st, Gosnold started out easterly, looking, Archer reports, for the "supposed islands." As there is nothing in the way of small islets at the eastern end of Nantucket Sound, no doubt the explorers, when they "trended" the outer coast southerly a league or two off-shore in the open sea, had observed on the meeting line of water and sky high dunes or "hummocks", which appeared from that distance to be islands. These were located on the Great Point of Nantucket and on Monomoy Island, which extends southward from the eastern part of Cape Cod. The explorers were looking, of course, for the islands described by Verrazzano as being within the bay.

At the eastern end of Nantucket the shore facing the Sound turns northward, and the *Concord* had to alter its course accordingly. Presently the explorers came to the beginning of an opening — the eastern opening into Nantucket Sound ten miles wide from north to south, possibly a bit more in Gosnold's day. Archer avers that Gosnold had descried this opening from the hill on Cape Cod and taken it to be the end of the Sound. Of this the most that can be said is that Gosnold probably saw a merging of water into sky here on the horizon which he took to be an opening. Actually, the opening is a bit beyond the limit of vision from the hill which it is assumed that Gosnold climbed.

The *Concord* sailed the length of this opening, on the inside — that is, remaining in the Sound. About a league off-shore — Archer did not report which shore — the ship was hove to, to take a sounding. They found the depth to be three and a half fathoms, not enough to assure a safe passage through. As a name for the place, Archer again used "Shoal Hope", the name rejected at Barnstable Harbor. It seemed good that Gosnold had not tried to enter the Sound from the east.

Sailing on north beyond the opening, the explorers found themselves again in proximity to the mainland of the Cape, but now in the Sound south of it. This shore ran southwesterly, or rather west by south to west-southwest, and taking their course from it, the explorers sailed in that direction. After four hours or so they raised ahead of them, well-separated from the mainland, the high sandy bluffs of the so-called East Chop of Martha's Vineyard. (This designation for the "chops" or "jaws" of a harbor or channel was given to Vineyard Haven by very early settlers — and was one of the earliest recorded uses of the word in that sense.[13])

The explorers "bore with" this promontory — that is, they sailed directly for it and anchored off its shore in eight fathom of water. Archer immediately announces that they named it *Martha's Vineyard.* He is a bit premature with his information, as he furnishes a name before the explorers had seen the vines at the second place of landing, vines which suggested the name. Yet it is probably a mistake to blame Archer for this inadvertence. As shown earlier, there is internal evidence that Archer's narrative has been subjected to editing, and in the course of deletions and dislocations the naming was awkwardly inserted where there is nothing in the context to explain it.

Gosnold, Brereton, and the others who landed on this promontory apparently found nothing interesting about it. It is a high, sandy plateau with no springs, and therefore not adapted either to Indian or white-man's habitation, except that in these latter years there have been built upon it summer cottages provided with "town water" piped from nearly three miles away. While there are stands of old oak trees near the broad base of the peninsula, it is doubtful whether the greater part of the upland was ever forested. Gosnold probably got a clear view of the place by walking ten or fifteen minutes to its highest points.[14]

By following the east shore of the Chop, Gosnold would have come to a creek flowing out of a salt-water pond, which in turn was fed by a fresh-water pond — the drainage basin of a swampy area to the south of the pond. There he would have seen the southernmost of these ponds disappearing in the southwest behind a screen of huge trees. Likewise, if Gosnold followed the western shore south, he would have come first to ponds at the north end of a large lagoon and then to the lagoon itself. These ponds on the east and west sides of the base of the peninsula come within three-quarters of a mile of meeting and there-

129

fore give a well-defined boundary on the south. Brereton, who
walked about the Chop, estimated the circuit to be four miles
Archer, who stayed on board ship, reported it as five miles.

The ponds on the east side of the Chop, before contamina
tion by civilization's drainage, were herring-ponds, ponds with
fresh-water source to which herring ascended for their spawning
It is not surprising, therefore, that the explorers found the re
mains of a fish-weir, presumably at the outlet of one of thes
ponds. Near the fish-weir they saw at close hand their firs
Indian wigwam — "a little old house", Brereton wrote, "made o
boughes, covered with barke." This construction marked it a
a summer construction, since wigwams for winter occupatio
were covered with two thicknesses of woven-straw mats. The
also saw "one or two places, where they [the Indians] ha
made fires."

This was obviously an isolated place to which Indians cam
to catch fish when the herring were running. Why the weir ha
been allowed to fall into disrepair is hard to say; possibly
great storm had closed up the outlet from the lower pond t
the Sound, as happened from time to time two centuries later.

The shore here, incidentally, as well as the sandy cliffs a bi
to the north, is subject to rapid erosion; the shoreline in Gosnold'
day may have been as much as three or four hundred fee
farther to the east than it is now, but the configuration and th
general aspect of the place has merely moved inland, and nc
changed in characteristics or appearance. The writer has know
this shore intimately for fifty years and more, and is aware b
surveyor's measurements that the shoreline has receded at leas
fifty feet during his lifetime but to a casual eye it looks jus
about as it did half a century ago.

The explorers next landed, on the following day, in a plac
with very different physical features. There is no statement, as ha
already been pointed out, explaining how they got there, but ther
is no mistaking the locale. The explorers must have weighe
anchor early in the morning of the twenty-second, sailed pas
East Chop and the entrance to Vineyard Haven Harbor, an

:irted an island on the north side of Vineyard Sound which is
ientioned in Brereton's narrative as a place where they saw
iany Indians on the shore.[15] Gosnold, who seems to have been
dverse to landing on a shore where he might be thronged or
ven overwhelmed by Indians, then crossed the Sound back to
s Vineyard shore. Here, about seven miles from East Chop,
iere is an inviting place for anchorage now called Lambert's
'ove. The depth of the water where the *Concord* halted was
ight fathoms.

While this cove, as seen on the maps, is only a slight inden-
ition in the shoreline, it is interesting to mention in passing
iat for two or three generations it served the early settlers of
ie Island as the only harbor, or port, on the north shore. This
: difficult to understand, as Vineyard Haven, which Gosnold
nd his company had passed by, became in the course of the
ears one of the best known harbors on the coast, and a refuge
ir all sorts of coastal shipping. The explanation lies in the fact
iat there was early established in the center of the island, about
venty-five years after the settlement at Edgartown on the
land's eastern shore, an agricultural community. This farming
illage grew rapidly, before there was any sort of community at
ie head of Vineyard Haven. The consequence was that this
iland community, in the place now called West Tisbury, found
 more convenient to keep their boats and small vessels at Lam-
ert's Cove than to drive five or six miles farther along through
ie sand to the harbor now called Vineyard Haven. Conse-
uently two or three wharves were built at Lambert's Cove
efore there were any in Vineyard Haven harbor. The settle-
ient that flourished at Lambert's Cove in colonial days sur-
endered not long ago to the incursion of a "summer colony", and
ractically all the land around Gosnold's landing-place is now
ccupied by the owners of vacation estates. Fortunately, this has
ept it a region of woods and open spaces, almost as it was in
iosnold's day.

The two reporters of the scene at Lambert's Cove were
nthusiastic in their descriptions. They spoke of great trees —

131

beeches and cedars — and of the fruit-bearing bushes in "the outward parts", three or four feet in height, bearing raspberries, huckleberries, gooseberries, with strawberries on the ground better, says Brereton, than those in England. (In the heyday of commerce at Lambert's Cove, an enterprising resident loaded up his small vessel every summer with these assorted berries and transported them to Nantucket, where they found ready sale.)

The most impressive feature of this place to this company of Englishmen looking for profitable products were the wild grape vines running up the trees and along the ground in such confusion that, as Brereton remarked, they "could not goe for treading upon them."[16] In the list of commodities appended to Brereton's *Relation* appears the phrase, "Vines in more plenty than in France." These wild grape vines, even to this day fairly plentiful on the west side of the pond at Lambert's Cove, held the promise that in these new lands there might be developed cultivated vineyards which would supply England with wines to replace those imported from France and Spain. It was an idle day-dream, but had its propaganda value when incorporated in the name of Martha's Vineyard. For some reason, the settlers of this island with English antecedents apparently never even tried to cultivate grapes here, either through lack of skill or will Present-day residents whose forebears came from the Azores make a wine of these wild grapes.

The Vineyard became, as a matter of fatherly sentiment, the namesake of Gosnold's little daughter Martha, perpetuating in the name of this beautiful and enduring island the given name of the child's grandmother, Martha Golding, of whom much has been said in earlier chapters.

Brereton was particularly interested in "a great standing lake of fresh water, neere the sea side, an English mile in compasse which is mainteined with the springs running exceeding pleas antly thorow [through] the wooddie grounds which are very rockie [boulder-strewn]." This lake is now known as Great James Pond, or simply James Pond — "Great", according to Massa chusetts custom and law, indicates a pond of such size that it is not subject to individual ownership.[17]

The northern end of the lake is only about three or four hundred feet from the salt water of the Sound. A sluggish creek wends its way through the sands to form its outlet. The surrounding terrain is just as Brereton described it. Most of the springs — six or seven of them — bubble out of the hill on the western side of the pond and send little rivulets down to replenish its fresh-water. Brereton correctly called it a "standing" lake, as it shows no perceptible flow of water — in fact, in mid-summer it is apt to develop the scum of a semi-stagnant pool. The explorers saw it in the springtime, when it was overfilled with fresh-water. The tracks of many animals both large and small were seen all about the pond. Both narrators reported that here they saw deer.

Archer was interested in the game-birds he saw nesting on the sandy, boulder-filled cliffs just west of Lambert's Cove. Brereton gave a somewhat more extended list of them than Archer, and between them the lists include cranes, heron, shovelers [spoon-bill ducks], bitterns, mallards and teals.

Archer waxed enthusiastic about the great "store" of cod which they caught from the ship in the Cove. He declared them even better than those caught at Cape Cod. This was perhaps because the cod here had been feeding longer on the oily herring which came to swim up the outlet to spawn.

For the better part of two days — May 22nd and 23rd — the whole ship's company ambled and gambolled, after the manner of sailors ashore, about this garden spot of the Vineyard. Some probably climbed the adjacent hill, which affords a magnificent view out over the waters, leaving no possible doubt that the voyagers had come into a great sound, lying between the island on which they stood and the Elizabeth Islands to the north. It is passing strange that no Indians arrived to interrupt this sylvan idyll. There was an Indian village located, at this time, probably not more than two or three miles away. The

133

savages here, like those who boarded the ship four days before, may have been somewhat timorous. Or else the place where these landings were made might have been under some sort of religious taboo, making the region a sort of game-preserve with the abundant fauna under the protection of the great god, Manittou. This is suggested by the fact that the great hill overshadowing the place bore a name in the Indian language which means Manittou's Hill. A level place on one of the shoulders of this hill has always been known to the Island's white settlers as the Indians' "dancing floor", although nothing is known of the ancient rites that were presumably conducted there.[18]

In mid-afternoon of the second day at this place, the *Concord* weighed anchor and sailed on to the west, coasting along the northern shore of the Vineyard. Towards night, reported Archer, they "came to anchor at the Northwest part of this Iland." From the mention of fresh-water fish, and of red and white clay, in Brereton's account of this landing, it may be safely assumed that it was near the outlet of an innocuous, gurgling little stream, now known by the impressive name of "Roaring Brook."

When Gosnold and his party went ashore the next morning thirteen savages came running to them, armed with bows and arrows and all naked, "saving", Brereton wrote, "they cover their privy parts with a black tewed [dressed] skin, much like a Black-smiths apron, tied about their middle and between their legs behinde." These Indians offered the white-men a wicker basket filled with boiled fresh-water fish, probably served with sorell, which the Indians used as a salad.[19] Among their other gifts, the Indians of this place presented their visitors with deerskins, a mark of honor, as the wearing of these was a privilege reserved for the nobility in these tribes.[20]

Archer stressed the fact that this group of natives came "fast running". From this manner of approach, it is probably to be inferred that they constituted a welcoming committee stationed on the summit of Prospect Hill, which lies about half a mile from Roaring Brook and is the highest hill on the Vineyard (308 feet). They would have been placed there to observe what the strange visitors might do at dawn. When they made out just where the landing boat was to be beached, they rushed to the spot ready for battle or peace, according to the mind of the invaders. It is probably significant, although not mentioned in the narratives, that at both of Gosnold's landing-places on the main part of the Vineyard there were high hills, higher than any on Cape Cod, within easy climbing distance from the shore. These two widely separated hills give views that between them cover most of the island, although inland there is little to be discerned but an unbroken sea of green treetops. Gosnold may have been attracted to the shores where he saw the possibility of climbing hills that would enable him to look out over the interior of the island.

Brereton, who seems to have been a confirmed smoker, took particular interest in the Indians' tobacco. This was made of green leaves, he observed, "dried into powder." He found it very strong and pleasant and much better than any he had tasted in England. The "necks" of their pipes were made of clay, hard dried; "the other part" was a piece of hollow copper, "very finely closed and cemented together." The clay of these pipes led Brereton to comment on the abundant "store" of red and white clay on "that Island" — not on the island beyond, Gay Head, which Gosnold called Dover Cliff.

Along Roaring Brook is a bed of clay which, for several generations in the last century, served as a source of supply for a brickyard. This, with the aid of a great water-wheel placed in the brook to supply power, and a kiln with a towering chimney, produced locally-made red brick for the chimneys of the island. A half mile to the west of this brickyard is a great outcropping of white clay at the foot of a high sandy cliff. Here, in the last century, a China Clay works was started also, but its career was brief. Nevertheless, Brereton was quite justified in remarking that the "store" of clay, both red and white, was great.

Brereton was interested, too, in the shaly beach, where he found many huge bones and ribs of whales, and saw all sorts of stones fit for building, many of them glistering and shin-

135

ing like mineral stones. He noted that this beach was "verie rockie". By this he meant that it was covered by small, round boulders, as it is today.

Gosnold and his men gave their new Indian friends "certeine trifles, as knives, points [laces, much used instead of buttons], and such like, which they much esteemed", and rowed off to their ship to sail on westward. They passed the creek leading out from the large Menemsha Pond, which seemed to make an island of the land beyond, on which were located the many-hued Gay Head cliffs, unique deposits made by a river in the tertiary geological age. They doubled the point of this promontory, getting a full view of the pure white cliffs at the extreme western end of the island, which caused them to call the place Dover Cliff and established the fact that they had come to the end of the island — or rather, from their point of view, the islands — on the south side of Vineyard Sound. Possibly they sailed the few miles southward necessary to get a good look at the outlying Noman's Land, which they could see had no harbor, and little else to invite closer inspection.

The next anchorage mentioned by Archer, where they rode all night, was unmistakably on the Vineyard Sound side of the island known now as Cuttyhunk. This island was reached by sailing northwest across the wide opening at the western end of Vineyard Sound. Brereton made no mention of Dover Cliff (Gay Head), and therefore shed no light on its doubling, or encircling. He merely remarked, "From hence [i.e., from the place where the Indians had presented them with boiled fish] we went to another Island, to the Northwest of this, and within a league or two of the maine." Archer, however, having placed the *Concord* in the open sea beyond Dover Cliff, reported in a curiously misleading phrase that they "then came into a faire Sound" — obviously withholding the information that they had just left this same "faire Sound", having sailed the full length of it. He evidently felt it necessary at this point to acknowledge the existence of this magnificent stretch of water. (It had dropped out from the earlier part of his narrative, along with a passage which had described the length of the Vineyard, and of its Sound as well.)

Little did Archer or his editor reckon that ten thousand times ten thousand words would be written to replace his parsimonious, single-word description of Vineyard Sound! The logs of innumerable ships, from the humble packets of the seventeenth century to the swift steam passenger vessels of the twentieth, the tales of shipwrecks and battles in these waters, the annals of yachting, and latterly the honeyed words of travel and vacation agencies, not to mention the studied, official aids to navigation, have made known to the world every deep fathom and mile of this celebrated inland waterway. But for reasons that seemed good at the time, Gosnold and his companions, after their return to England, decided that they wanted none to know the full story of his Martha's Vineyard and its encompassing waters.

CHAPTER XV

ELIZABETH'S ISLE

Cuttyhunk is the outermost of a sixteen-mile string of islands jutting out in a straight line from the southwestern corner, or heel, of Cape Cod. They average about two miles in width, and separate the waters of Buzzards Bay on the northwest from those of Vineyard Sound on the southeast. On the map they look as though they might have been, in some remote geological age, a long narrow peninsula, now intersected by several channels. Through these, the higher tides of Buzzards Bay flow furiously into Vineyard Sound, only to flow out again later, equally furiously. The three largest of these gaps, which make islands of the peninsula, are called by the homely, descriptive name "Hole" — there is Woods Hole, separating the first island from the mainland, then Robinsons Hole, and Quicks Hole. The islands all still bear their Indian names.

Between Cuttyhunk and the island next to it to the east, Nashawena, there is no designated "Hole" — obviously because until recent times the two islands were connected by a sandy beach on the Vineyard Sound side. The small body of water between these two islands has been called a harbor ever since the islands were first occupied by white settlers. Archer called it an "increek, or sandy cove", to which the Indians resorted for crab-fishing. In Gosnold's day, although not now, the beach certainly connected the two islands to make one, as Brereton reported that Elizabeth's Isle was "16. English miles at the least in compasse" — a reasonably accurate measure of the two islands joined, Cuttyhunk alone being somewhat less than two miles long.[1] But when it came to counting the islands, Brereton was at a loss. He went on to say of "Elizabeth's isle" that it contained "many pieces or necks of land, which differ nothing from severall islands, saving that certeine banks of small bredth do, like bridges, joine them to this Island."

The difficulty of correct description persisted down to the days of Thomas Mayhew, the first English owner of the islands. In 1666, desiring to sell a tract of land on the largest of them, Mayhew referred to "the greater island of Elizabeth Island" — a neat turn of phrase. The islands are now called the Elizabeth Islands, the name Gosnold gave to the outermost having been extended to cover the whole group.

When Gosnold late in the afternoon of May 24th sailed across the western opening of Vineyard Sound, six miles wide, he saw extending out from the seaward end of Cuttyhunk a reef of rocks running out a mile into the ocean. He wanted to get around this point into the waters on the other side of the islands, which could be seen from the masthead, but he had no way of knowing how far this rocky reef might run out under water. Earlier in the day, off Dover Cliff shore, he had gotten safely around a submerged reef, not mentioned in the narratives, known today as "the Devil's Bridge", where he must have escaped disaster only by the grace of God and a good masthead lookout.[2] He was taking no chances with hidden rocks of this sort off the point of Cuttyhunk. Bartholomew Gosnold anchored for the night in the exposed, but for the moment safe, waters on the southeast side of the island.

In the morning the ship's boat was sent out for soundings, and Gosnold found that deep water began just beyond the last of the visible rocks. He then sailed around the point, entering waters that Archer was pleased to call "one of the stateliest Sounds that ever I was in", and anchored in eight fathoms a quarter of a mile from shore. This "Sound", known as Buzzards Bay, the explorers named *Gosnold's Hope*, evidently because in this great "hope", or inlet of the sea, Gosnold hoped to find his dreams fulfilled.[3]

From the Buzzards Bay side it was seen that this seagirt island had a lake only a short distance from the shore. Like the one found on Martha's Vineyard this turned out to be "a stand-

139

ing Lake of fresh water", but it was somewhat larger, being almost three miles in compass. In the midst of it was a small island, an acre or so in extent and well wooded. It seemed to be a good place to establish headquarters. Here a substantial building, well screened by tall trees from the rest of the island, could be erected, to serve as their abode, storage place, and "fort". The lake would form a natural moat around it.

Gosnold doubtless had in mind words almost prophetic, written in 1584-1585 by the elder Richard Hakluyt:

> And for the more quiet exercise of our manurance [occupation, tenure] of the soiles where we shall seat, and of our manual occupations, it is to be wished that some ancient captaines of milde disposition and great judgement be sent thither with men most skilfull in the arte of fortification; and that direction be taken that the mouthes of great rivers, and the Islands in the same (as things of great moment) be taken, manned, and fortified; and that havens be cut out for the safetie of the Navie, that we may be lords of the gates and entries, to goe out and come in at pleasure, and to lie in safetie . . .[4]

Bartholomew Gosnold was able to carry out this precept. The island called Cuttyhunk today commands the entrance to both Buzzards Bay and Vineyard Sound.

But there were other advantages to a location on this outer island, as Gosnold saw later. It could be reached easily by Indians wishing to trade, who could come to it in safety under the shelter of the string of islands from the mainland. At the same time, and this is perhaps significantly not mentioned in the narratives, there was a single isolated hill less than a mile from the place where they proposed to erect a building, rising to an elevation of a hundred feet, and giving an unobstructed view of all approaches.[5]

The decision to build their "abode" on the wooded islet in the middle of the lake was not made until three days later, the intervening time having been used, apparently, to explore the island and its surroundings more thoroughly. The *Concord* had anchored off Cuttyhunk on May 25th. On the 26th, Archer reported, the company "trimmed and fitted up" their shallop. Brere-

n gave the details, calling their means of conveyance a "light-
orseman [light boat]", which was presumably the same "gig"
s the shallop. In any case, the company voyaged along the shore
: the islands to the mainland, and then turned north, examining
he eastern shore of Buzzards Bay for some distance above mod-
n Woods Hole. They stopped, however, when they first reached
he mainland, to go ashore — probably between the localities
ow known as Quisset and Sippowisset.

Here Brereton grew rhapsodic over the beauty of the scene.
We stood a while", he wrote, "like men ravished at the beautie
nd delicacie of this sweet soile[6]; for besides divers cleere Lakes
f fresh water (whereof we saw no end) Medowes very large
nd full of greene grasse; even the most woody places (I speake
nely of such as I saw) doe grow so distinct and apart, one tree
om another, upon greene grassie ground, somewhat higher
han the Plaines, as if Nature would shew her selfe above her
ower, artificial." By the last word Brereton meant that Nature
ad here exceeded herself, creating a scene of beauty hardly
atural.[7]

Near this place the explorers espied seven Indians. On
pproaching them, the white-men saw that the Indians were at
rst inclined to hide or retreat, but were reassured by the
iendly demeanor of the strangers and the offering of small
ifts. These Indians in their canoes followed the explorers' swift
raft up the coast to a place thought at first to be an island,
ut on closer view found to be connected with the mainland by
narrow neck. This was probably the peninsula now known as
happaquoit Point, four and a half miles north-northwest of
almouth. Here the explorers entered a harbor or broad river-
nouth, apparently the outlet of a stream flowing from the interior
f the land.

This seems to have been the shallow harbor at West Fal-
nouth, although the changes in the shoreline which have un-
oubtedly taken place since 1602 make it impossible to be cer-
in. In any case, whatever point was reached on the shore of
uzzards Bay by the party in the "light-horseman", they did

141

not find a location more suitable for their purposes than th island at the outer end of the Elizabeth Islands. "The eight an twentieth", wrote Archer, "we entred counsell about our abo and plantation, which was concluded to be in the west pa of Elizabeth Iland."[8]

There is a startling contrast between the Cuttyhunk tha Bartholomew Gosnold knew and named Elizabeth Isle and th island as it appears today. The whole of the western part the island is now a treeless plain, recently given over to th grazing of sheep, bred in experiments to obtain finer grades wool. Before that this plain was under cultivation, even inclu ing the little islet in the lake, where there now stands a tall tow to mark the location of Gosnold's trading station. The ston placed by Gosnold's men for a foundation, discovered and e amined by a party of historians in 1797, were scattered or r moved by farmers tilling the soil, and could not be found aga when the memorial tower was built in 1903. Strong, salt-lade winds sweep over the place now and keep it barren except f grass. Brereton's description no longer holds:

> This Island is full of high timbred Oakes, their leaves thrise so bro as ours; Ceders, straight and tall; Beech, Elme, hollie, Walnut trees aboundance, the fruit as bigge as ours, as appeared by those we four under the trees, which had lien all the yeere ungathered; Haslenut tree Cherry trees . . .; Sassafras trees great plentie all the Island over, a tr of high price and profit; also divers other fruit trees, some of them wi strange barkes, of an Orange colour, in feeling soft and smoothe li Velvet . . .[9]

Archer mentioned many of these same trees, giving mo particular attention to the shrubs, among which he listed wi peas, [grape-]vines, eglantine, gooseberry bushes, hawthorn and honeysuckle. They found also many edible herbs and root among which were ground-nuts (a tuber with an odd taste, eate by Indians when other foods failed).[10] Brereton called the so "fat and lustie, the upper crust of gray colour; but a foot lesse in depth." He and some others cleared a few places an planted them ("for a triall") with wheat, barley, oats and pea

142

hich in fourteene dayes were sprung up nine inches and
re." No animals were mentioned in the descriptions of the
and, but there were many small turtles in the pond, and
und the outer shores edible shell-fish such as scallops, mus-
s, cockles, lobsters, crabs, oysters and whelks, "exceeding
od and very great."

Ten men were put to work building the house that was to
ve as a fort, and completed it in nineteen working days. This
is the first structure put up by Englishmen in the region that
came known as New England. Nothing is told about the
inner of construction except that it was thatched with sedge,
lich grew plentifully around the lake. The building was made
ge enough to house twenty men and their stores.

After Gosnold had decided upon this island as the place
his first abode in America, he named it *Elizabeth's Isle*. The
izabeth thus honored was presumably his sister, named in
e records as the oldest of the daughters of Anthony Gosnold.
ere is nothing in either of the *Relations* to support the com-
on modern assumption that Queen Elizabeth was meant.
ereton merely placed the name *"Elizabeths Island"* in the
argin toward the bottom of page 6, and later, toward the top
page 12, mentioned in an off-hand way in a parenthesis that
snold called the island *Elizabeths Island*. This, coupled with
e naming of Martha's Vineyard for Gosnold's daughter, seems
point to Elizabeth Gosnold (by then married to Thomas
lney) rather than Elizabeth Tudor, Queen of England, France,
d Ireland, as the lady honored by an island in New England.[11]

In residence, as it were, at Cuttyhunk, with the *Concord*
chored close by and most of the ship's company busied on
e island, Gosnold and his gentlemen companions became hosts
a number of visiting Indians. The first of these appeared on
ay 27th, while the group in the "light-horseman" were explor-
g the coast of the mainland. The visitors were a single Indian
ave accompanied by two squaws, whom the Englishmen took
be his wife and daughter — they might well have been his
st and second wives. This was a bit unusual, to say the least,

143

judging by the accounts of the earliest contacts between white-men and Indians. Ordinarily the braves of a tribe travelled in a group and left the squaws at home. Possibly this Indian was a local inhabitant, living in a wigwam concealed in the woods at the eastern end of Cuttyhunk, that is, the part that is known to-day as the island Nashawena, or perhaps on the next island. Indians of "noble" rank frequently had a single-family domain, such as a neck of land or a small island. This one may have been the resident owner of all of Cuttyhunk, who came driven by naive curiosity to find out what was going on in his front yard, so to speak.[12] The squaws, as Archer told the story, were both "cleane and straite bodied, with countenance sweet and pleasant." The Indian with them "gave heedfull attendance" to them, because of their "much familiaritie" with Gosnold's men; but these dusky ladies were circumspect in that "they would not admit of any immodest touch."

The Indians of the islands, as well as those of Cape Cod, were under the dominion of the Great Chief of Pokonocket, the grand-sachemdom which extended from the eastern shores of Narragansett Bay to the Atlantic, where the Pilgrims later estab-lished themselves at Plymouth. The small sachemdoms beyond this area on the cape and on the islands, were ruled by petty chiefs or, as Matthew Mayhew called them, "princes." In the Pilgrims' treaty with the Great Chief, Massasoit, these "princes" were designated as his "neighbors confederate." They paid nominal tribute to their Great Chief, and were leagued with him in a mutual defense pact, bound to render assistance to him if he needed warriors in his never-ending warfare with the Nar-ragansetts to the west. These Indians of southern New England had no tribal names other than those, like Pokonocket, derived from the place of residence of their chief.[13]

It is to be remembered that the Indians with whom Bar-tholomew Gosnold came into contact were still living in what may be called a "golden age". They were a forest-people, well provided with the necessities of life, and in good health.[14] But about ten years after Gosnold's visit the picture began to change.

First, there were devastating tribal wars, beginning about 1612. Then came the Europeans, some of whom were guilty of ruthless atrocities, such as that which (according to Thomas Dermer, who could not discover whether the men were English, Dutch or French) cleared the ship's decks of Indians with a "murderer", a small cannon which fired brass and iron pieces, anticipating by two centuries the invention of shrapnel.[15] Then there was Captain John Smith's disloyal man Hunt, who descended upon the Indian villages at the site of Plymouth and on Cape Cod, taking by foul treachery captives whom he sold as slaves in Spain.

Semi-starvation as always followed the internecine warfare, but this was nothing compared with what came next. Some European ship, quite likely a French vessel, was wrecked on Cape Cod in 1616. In its sequence followed a pestilential disease, not small-pox but possibly syphilis, which raged for several years, reducing the Pokonocket and Massachusetts Indians quite literally to one-tenth of their former strength. The entire Indian settlement at the site where the Pilgrims landed was wiped out, and the Pilgrims who travelled inland during their first year in New England found unburied corpses everywhere. Proud, happy Indians had become a weakened, dispirited remnant.[16]

It was far different in Gosnold's day. He was welcomed by savages who were friendly, inquisitive, annoyingly thievish in a childish way, and delighted with the Englishmen's gifts of trinkets and small steel cutting implements, the like of which they had never seen. One of the first names used by these Indians for white-men meant "the Knife-Men" — *Cháuqua-quock*.[17]

Saturday, May 29th, found Gosnold's company busied about the little islet in the pond, or working elsewhere. Some were clearing away the undergrowth in preparation for building. Some were making "a Punt or Flat bottome Boate to passe to and fro our Fort over the fresh water." Others were in the woods gathering sassafras roots. Still another group was engaged in putting a new keel on the shallop, presumably working on the shore of the small harbor. While they were scattered about engaged in these pursuits, most of them well hidden in the woods, an alarm was sounded.

Indians in eleven canoes had been seen approaching the island — a party reckoned to be fifty in number, coming from the mainland where Brereton and the others in the "light-horse man" had landed two days before. Gosnold, Brereton, and presumably a few others, unwilling that the Indians should see what they were doing in the matter of fortifications, rushed out to the seaward or southeastern side of the island, where the Indians came into the little harbor and disembarked. The two parties approached each other. Then the Indians seated themselves on stones, calling and motioning to the white-men to do likewise at a little distance from them. And there they sat, gazing at one another.

The situation puzzled Gosnold, for he did not understand, of course, the etiquette of the occasion. Matthew Mayhew, the historian, explains this in an amusing story of a visit to his grandfather on the Vineyard by the Great Chief of the Pokonockets (probably King Philip) in a much later period. The two in Mayhew's house, the Great Chief and the Governor of the white settlers, sat staring at each other for a long period because Indian custom required that the one of lesser rank speak first; and neither was willing to assume that role. Gosnold not knowing what was expected of him, broke the ice by sending Brereton over to greet the party.

On approaching them, Brereton recognized an Indian to whom he had given a knife two days before on the mainland. This Indian smiled and said something to his Chief. The latter "presently [immediately] rose up and tooke a large Beaver skin from one that stood about him", and gave it to Brereton, a gift which Brereton acknowledged as best he could by giving a few trifles in return. Then, pointing toward Captain Gosnold, he made signs to the Chief that Gosnold was the Captain, who desired to be a friend of the Indians and in league with this Chief. This sign-language seems to have been understood, beause Brereton reports that the Great Chief made signs of joy. In the meantime the rest of the English company, being twenty in all, came up to them, and there was pleasant intercourse by signs. Gosnold himself made further gifts to the Indians and sent to the shallop for food, giving them such dishes as were ready.

The casual reader of the two narratives at this point may find himself confused, as each narrator has a different story to tell of a visit by fifty Indians. Brereton, contrary to his usual custom, dated his account, placing the visit which he describes two days after the exploration of the nearby mainland, that is, on May 29th. This party of Indians promised to return — "pointing five or six times to the Sun, and once to the maine, which we understood, that within five or six dayes they would come from the maine to us againe." It is not surprising, therefore, that Archer's narrative, but not Brereton's, told of a party of fifty which arrived on June 5th. Brereton evidently combined into one continuous account, with some loss of clarity in chronological sequence, the incidents of two separate visits by a large party of Indians. He implied that the visitors of May 29th stayed around for three days, departing on the fourth day; but a comparison with Archer's calendar of events indicates that the extended visit was the second one, not that of May 29th. Brereton probably had in mind the second visit also, when he remarked that six or seven of the Indians remained at Elizabeth's Isle, bearing the Englishmen company every day into the woods, where they helped cut and carry sassafras. Some of them slept aboard the ship.

It is somewhat surprising not to find in Archer's dated day-by-day narrative any mention of the first visit, placed by Brereton on the second day after his visit to the mainland. One inference is that Archer was taken violently ill, and lost all interest in the happenings that day, beyond those indicated. He broke off his account of activities on May 29th to write: "the powder of Sassafrage [sassafras] in twelve houres cured one of our Company that had taken a great Surfet by [gotten very sick from] eating the bellies of Dog-fish, a very delicious meate."[18]

147

He might well have been reluctant to admit that it was he himself who committed this gastronomic indiscretion, and even more reluctant to confess that he was too sick on that day to bother about Indian visitors.

On May 30th, probably in the afternoon after the first visiting delegation of Indians had departed, Captain Gosnold with a few of his company sailed over in the shallop to the little speck of an island which Archer named *Hills Hap*, obviously that known today by its Indian name, Penikese. It lies about a mile and half north of the harbor of Elizabeth's Isle, with an area of about 40 acres. Archer called it half a mile in compass — somewhat less than it measures today — and reported that it had a stand of cedar trees.

An Indian canoe was found hidden in the brush on this islet, "that foure Indians had there left, being fled away for feare of our English." The canoe was taken aboard ship and later transported to England. Connected with this incident is another story, told by Archer among the events of June 11th, twelve days later. Archer had been left at the fort on Elizabeth's Isle with nine men, while Gosnold went off to explore Buzzards Bay, remaining away much longer than he had anticipated. The party left behind began to run out of food and Archer sent out four men to get what they could in the way of shellfish, warning them to stay together. They separated, however, two by two, and one of the couples was assaulted by four Indians, "who with Arrowes did shoot and hurt one of the two in his side." The wounded man's companion, "a lusty and nimble fellow", jumped in and cut their bowstrings, whereupon the Indians fled.[19] Their surprise at this totally unexpected form of attack is readily imaginable, as they were not accustomed to sharp knives that could slice through raw-hide in a trice. These four Indians were undoubtedly the same four who had abandoned the canoe, bent on reprisal. As for the white-men, they had to spend the night in the woods, since darkness came upon them and they were unable to find their way back to the fort through the underbrush

On May 31st, Captain Gosnold, wanting to see the mainland

148

iled for the head of Buzzards Bay. He visited two inlets at the
ead of the Bay, one at its northwestern corner where the city
' New Bedford now stands, and the other at the northeastern
rner, where the town of Wareham is now located. The latter
cation bore the Indian name of Agawam, and is probably the
ace where Captain Harlow, in 1612, met with a friendly recep-
on by the Indians. It is impossible to make out from Archer's
arrative which of these places Gosnold visited first. Whichever
was, he anchored and went ashore with certain members of
s company. Immediately "there presented [themselves] unto
m men women and children, who with all curteous kindnesse
ntertayned him, giving him certaine skinnes of wilde beasts,
hich may be rich Furres, Tobacco, Turtles, Hempe, artificial
kilfully made] Strings coloured, Chaines, and such like things
; at the instant they had about them."

Gosnold was much impressed with the mainland in this
cinity. "This Maine[-land]", Archer wrote, "is the goodliest
ontinent that ever we saw, promising more by farre than we
ay way did expect: for it is replenished with faire fields, and
them fragrant Flowers, also Medowes, and hedged in with
ately Groves, being furnished also with pleasant Brookes, and
eautified with two maine Rivers. . . ."

The distance between these two rivers, Archer reckoned to
e about five leagues, fifteen modern "statute" miles, adding
and the Coast betweene bendeth like a Bow, and lyeth East
nd by North." By this he meant that the *Concord*, to get from
ne of these rivers to the other, had to sail an arc-like course,
ulging to the south, to get around the long points that run out
'om the shore between the two rivers. It may be remarked here
arenthetically that if Captain John Smith, in the brief months
f his friendliness with Archer at Jamestown, Virginia, in 1607
'as privileged to read this journal, the conclusion is justified
aat it was this particular region that Smith in 1619 recommended
) the Pilgrims, when he applied for the job of leading them to
ae New World.[20]

The most remarkable thing about Archer's report is that

after mentioning the two main rivers he added this clause "that (as wee judge) may haply become good Harbors, an conduct us to the hopes men so greedily doe thirst after." Th seems to be rather exaggerated language to use of two litt streams, which are comparatively short and too shallow fe navigation. Evidently Gosnold did not have opportunity to in vestigate them.

So the great hope remained, awaiting further exploration that one or the other of these rivers might be the great wate way which the adventurers of that day hoped to find, leadin into the interior of the continent and perhaps through it to th "South Sea", the Pacific Ocean. "With this taste of Discovery Archer concluded his remarks about the excursion, "we now con tented our selves, and the same day made return unto ou Fort, time not permitting more sparing delay."

The discovery of the Great River of Norumbega was Gos nold's hope. If instead of entering Buzzards Bay, he had saile on westward around the next point of the coast, less than twent miles beyond Elizabeth's Isle he would have found the grea bay which Verrazzano entered, with a river flowing into it northeastern corner, navigable for his ship over thirty miles int the interior. But Elizabeth's Isle was well suited to his immediat purpose, and he saw no reason for exploring further.[21]

On June 4th, after several hard days had been put in gathe ing sassafras and working on the Fort, there came to the ship side in a canoe the Chief of the Indians who had visited the on May 29th. This Chief did not stay long, but pointed to th sun, holding up one finger, as a sign that he would come agai on the next day. He came on June 5th with his full retinue, a he had signified, but this time "amongst them there seemed t be one of authoritie, because the rest made an inclining respec unto him."

The prior arrival of a herald reminds one of the way i which Massasoit, the Great Chief of the Pokonockets, announce his first visit to the Pilgrims, years later, by sending ahead th English-speaking Indians Samoset and Squanto, together wit everal others. Judging by this, it seems likely that the first isit to Gosnold and his company on Elizabeth's Isle was made y a local Chief, probably seated at Succonesset (at the site of ne present town of Falmouth), four miles east of Woods Hole, nd that "high dignitary" who accompanied the group on the econd visit was none other than the Great Chief of the Poko-ockets himself, Massasoit's father. The time interval of five or ix days indicated by the Indians on their first visit as the date f their return is just about what would be required to summon ne Great Chief from his home on the shore of Narragansett Bay. o extraordinary an event as the coming of the white-men on a great ship" sailing up from over the seas made imperative the ersonal attention of the Chief of the Chiefs of the Pokonocket onfederacy.[22]

Gabriel Archer was the master of ceremonies, as it were, n the occasion of this second visit, Gosnold and Gilbert both eing on shipboard a league offshore, leaving only eight men vith Archer. The arrival of the fifty Savages at that moment produced a tense situation. In Archer's words, "These Indians n hastie manner came towards us, so as we thought fit to make . stand at an angle between the Sea and a fresh water [lake or ond]", that is, in a corner where the Englishmen could not be asily surrounded. Archer then stepped out in front of his com-anions and went through an elaborate pantomime designed to ind out whether they wanted peace or war — a rather needless question, as the Indians were obviously on pleasure bent. The Chief was probably amused at these antics, but he returned the ompliment with Archer's "owne signes of Peace", whereupon he latter "stept forth and imbraced him", as was proper on the pattlefields of Europe when an honorable peace had been achieved. The Indians hunkered down "like Grey-hounds upon heir heeles", there evidently being no stones to sit on as at the previous visit.

The eight men with Archer began to barter. If the bartering was for furs, as seems likely, these could have been the furs listed by Brereton: "Beavers, Luzernes [lynx], Martens, Otters,

151

Wild-cat skins, very large and deepe Furre, blacke Foxes, Conie Skinnes, of the colour of our Hares, but somewhat lesse [smaller], Deere skinnes, very large, Seale skinnes, and other beasts skinnes, to us unknowen." In that case, since it was well past the hunting season for fur-bearing animals, it would seem that the Indians had had previous experience in trading for furs, either directly (with the French?) farther north, or through the Maine Indians with Europeans still more distant from Narragansett. In any case, furs were then the Indian commodity most prized by the white traders.[23]

Presently Gosnold arrived from the ship with twelve men who had been aboard the *Concord* with him, bringing the English company on shore up to its full strength of twenty men (Gilbert, Archer comments, "almost never went ashoare.") Archer then staged a bit of military ceremony, to impress upon the visiting Chief that Gosnold was the captain of the white men. A guard of honor was formed, and Gosnold passed between the rows, thus advancing with dignity into the presence of the Chief, whom he greeted "with ceremonies of our salutations." The Chief evidently did not know what to make of all this, as Archer remarked that "he nothing mooved or altered himselfe." Gosnold then presented the Chief with a straw hat and a pair of knives. The Chief wore the hat for a while, but "the Knives he beheld with great marvelling, being very bright and sharpe this our courtesie made them all in love with us."

That night the Indians retired to the furthermost part of the island, two or three miles from the fort, according to Brereton. This means that they passed over the connecting sandbar to the island known as Nashawena, Cuttyhunk itself being too small to permit a withdrawal of that distance. The next day it rained and the Englishmen spent the day "idlely aboard." The Indians likewise seem to have remained under cover, whereve exactly they were.

On the third day of their visit, June 7th, the Great Chief and his fifty retainers again appeared. As they were hanging

round at noon, the voyagers invited them to dinner. They ate
ɔdfish, English style, with mustard, Archer says, and drank
ɔme beer, "but the Mustard nipping them in their noses they
ɔuld not indure: it was a sport to behold their faces made
eing bitten therewith."

While the meal was in progress, in the midst of the great
ᴇerriment over their efforts to understand one another, some of
ᴂe "lesser" Indians sneaked down to their canoe, carrying off
"target", or round arm shield, part of the martial equipment of
ᴂe of the gentlemen. No notice was taken of this at first, but
ᴂally by pantomine Gosnold made known to the Chief what
ad happened, to test the Chief's authority over his men (and,
resumably, to get the target back). The Chief ordered it re-
ᴢored, which the Indians did "with feare and great trembling,
ᴂinking perhaps we would have beene revenged for it." But
ᴌeasant relations continued, and the Indians prolonged the
ᴇast by roasting crabs, red herring, ground-nuts and so on, as
•efore. After the meal, the Great Chief took his leave and de-
ᴨarted.

Somewhat later (or, as Brereton reported it, early on the
ᴚorning of the fourth day) the rest of the delegates returned
ɔ the mainland. A day or so after this, another Indian turned
ᴑp, who stayed all night on board the ship. He seemed to be
ᴚore "sober" — quiet, sedate — than the rest, and the voyagers
ᴛhought that he had probably been sent as a spy. Nevertheless,
ᴛhey treated him kindly. The next forenoon he "filched away"
ᴛheir pot-hooks, "thinking he had not done any ill therein."
ᴛhey caught him, but instead of punishing him they asked him
ᴑo show them how he made fire. This he did, taking from a little
ᴘouch a flat emery stone ("such as the Glasiers use, to cut
ᴸlasse"), a "mynerall stone" (presumably containing iron) and
ᴧ piece of touchwood, or tinder. Striking the mineral stone with
ᴛhe emery (or flint), he produced sparks which fell on the
ᴑouchwood which "forth with kindled with making of flame."
ᴃrereton added the detail that the Indian tied the emery stone

153

to the end of a little stick, before digressing into the subject o flax which the Indians had given them, "wherewith they mak many strings and cords."

Another interesting and instructive incident had taken place on one of these visits by the fifty mainland Indian: Brereton, sitting alongside of an Indian, was prompted by th Indian's actions to say to him, smiling, "How now (sirrah) ar you so saucie with my Tabacco?" To Brereton's amazemen without any further repetition, the Indian suddenly spoke th same words as plainly and distinctly as if he knew the language which of course he did not. The point is that the Indian wa well practiced in what students of linguistics call "echolalia" the repetition of words or phrases without understanding thei meaning, which characterizes a child's first attempts to speak.

The Indian languages in fact require an unusual develop ment of this "skill" because of their structure. Imagine, fo instance, an Indian infant learning that the old gentleman in th wigwam is *wuttootchikkineasin*, "grandfather", or learning t ask his mother whether he may go out and pick some *wuttoh kohkoominneonash*, "blackberries." The child either learned t echo back these syllables, or else he remained inarticulate. Th odd moments of several years dedicated by the author to a attempt to gain an insight into this language has produce in him a profound respect for the intelligence of these native of America. Only a highly intelligent race could have mad long, grammatically correct speeches in a language more com plicated than classical Latin or Greek.[24] John Eliot of Roxbury John Cotton, Jr., of Plymouth, and Experience Mayhew of th Vineyard became masters of Indian rhetoric, using it in transla tions of the Bible and in other works.

Brereton concluded his account of Gosnold's guests by writing: "These people, as they are exceeding courteous, gentl of disposition, and well conditioned, excelling all others that w have seene; so for shape of bodie and lovely favour, I think they excell all the people of *America*." They were taller tha the Englishmen, dark olive in complexion, and their hair black

154

ed up in a knot behind, into which feathers were stuck. Some
ad thin black beards, others wore artificial beards of the hair
f animals. One of the Indians offered a black beard to a sailor
hose beard was red, because he thought it was artificial and
ould be changed. And, to conclude the description of their
ppearance, Brereton added, "They are quicke eyed, and sted-
ist in their looks, fearelesse of others harmes, as intending
one themselves. . . ."

The second and last withdrawal of the nine canoes with
heir fifty Indians brought forth mutual salutations. The depart-
ig guests "made huge cries & shouts of joy unto us", said
rereton, "and we with our trumpet and cornet, and casting up
ur cappes into the aire, made them the best farewell we could."

155

CHAPTER XVI

COMMODITIES

After the resounding farewell to the last of the visiting
Indians, Gosnold's company set about dividing the food-supply
into two lots, under the direction of Captain Bartholomew Gil
bert, commissary of the expedition.[1] The twenty prospective
settlers took stock of their allotment with dismay, for it appeared
that they would have only enough to last them for about six
weeks. The ship's crew, likewise, had a supply only for the same
number of weeks, but they were bound for England and could
make it do. There immediately "fell out a controversie" — a
wrangling discussion as to how the twenty settlers could hold
out until the return of the ship with a further supply of provi
sions. There were some, Archer reported, and he was possibly
one of them, who voiced the conviction that Captain Gilbert
had no intention at all of returning as planned, with additional
settlers and with an adequate food-supply for all — purchased
— optimistically — with the proceeds of the cargo they were
going to ship back to England with Gilbert. They maintained
that he secretly intended to sell the cedar and sassafras with
which they were loading or about to load the ship, and pocket
the money himself, leaving Gosnold and those remaining with
him in the settlement to starve, like Sir Walter Ralegh's colonists
in the southern part of Virginia (modern North Carolina).
Others of the company, more fair-minded, probably disputed
these allegations as slanderous, expressing at the same time
optimism as to their ability to cope with the food situation.

To those who have read tales of our later American pioneers
able to live from nature's bounty in the forests, it seems strange
that these first English voyagers to America should have felt
themselves, in the midst of a land of plenty, so dependent upon
the maggoty flour and other spoiling foods transported from

England. Had they been capable of a quicker adjustment to a new environment at Jamestown and at Plymouth, instead of dying of scurvy and malnutrition, they would have begun immediately to live as the Indians lived.[3]

Present residents of Gosnold's *Martha's Vineyard* replenish their larders continually, gathering the foods free for the taking that the Indians enjoyed centuries ago, in fine independence of cultivated and transported provisions. In season, there are all sorts of fish, including five to ten pound bluefish, and twenty to forty pound bass, to be had by casting from the shore; later, there are great schools of pollock easily caught; in the spring the herring run so plentifully that many eat only the roe, discarding the bony body which is sometimes used as fertilizer.[4] In the summer several sorts of berries grow wild in the woods in great profusion. In the hunting season, there are deer for a few lucky hunters, and rabbits for the stew-pot in unlimited supply, duck, geese, and occasionally a pheasant. Clams, both soft and hard-shell, the latter being locally known as quahaugs, may be dug along the beaches throughout the year. In the winter season there are "bay" scallops, although few of the island-born like them. Until quite recently, lobsters swarmed around the island. To these, which are still the Vineyard's natural foods in the middle of the twentieth century, the Indians added nuts, including acorns, green herbs and edible roots such as ground-nuts, which our civilized generation does not bother to gather from the woods.

Gosnold's party would have needed, of course, the Indians' staple cultivated food, corn (maize), to carry them through the lean months of early spring, when even the Indians of the Pilgrims' day suffered food shortages. Supplies of this commodity would have been plentiful in the untroubled period of Gosnold's visit, as it was the custom of Indians to store away a superabundance of dried corn against contingencies. In 1634, for instance, Governor Winthrop of the Bay Colony sent to Narragansett for corn and obtained five hundred bushels. He was disappointed, as "the Indians had promised him one thousand bushels, but their store fell out less than expected."[5] Gosnold's Indian neighbors could easily have supplied the white-men with enough corn to see them through the winter, if the settlers had enough in trade goods to give in exchange for it; but Gosnold, because of his inability to converse with the Indians, did not learn of this food. One of the pleasures of life that he missed was clam chowder, thickened Indian fashion with corn-meal.[6]

Gosnold's immediate task was to fill up the hold of the *Concord* with such commodities as would bring a profit in England. The first of these in importance was sassafras root, which Captain Edward Hayes had suggested as a commodity easily obtained, and sold to offset the expense of fitting out for the voyage. Gosnold's men and the Indians loaded on board a ton of it, the value of which in London, as reported by Brereton, was three shillings a pound, or three hundred and thirty-six pounds sterling for the long ton. Sir Walter Ralegh said that sassafras was worth ten, twelve and twenty shillings a pound before the *Concord's* cargo was brought in. But he undoubtedly exaggerated its value for the sake of his argument that the dumping of the *Concord's* cargo on the market in London would depreciate the value of sassafras root to the point where it would no longer be profitable to import. His fears were groundless, as the merchants of Bristol, knowing the price to be three shillings the pound, the next year sent out a voyage under Captain Pring, organized by Robert Salterne (who was with Gosnold in 1602) and aided by Richard Hakluyt, which returned to Bristol with both the fifty ton and the twenty-six ton vessels of the expedition loaded with sassafras root.

The medicine made by infusing the powder ground from the root's "bark", or cortex, was in great demand as a specific for the cure of the disease then commonly known as "French pox" a disease named syphilis by Fracastoro in 1530, but not so known in England until long after Bartholomew Gosnold's day. The use of this medicine, however, was not limited to that deplorable pox, but was regarded as a general curative of great value. It is in fact a diaphoretic, and would have helped in any illness where an induced profuse sweating hastens recovery. It was certainly a great advance over blood-letting as a general cure.

One of the documents used in planning Gosnold's voyage, printed in the second edition of Brereton's *Relation,* has a note on the subject reading as follows:

> Sassafras, called by the inhabitants *Wynauk*: of whose soveraigne and manifold vertues, reade *Monardes* the Phisician of *Sivile* [Seville], in his booke entituled in English: *The joyful newes from the West Indies.*[7]

This English translation of Monardes' work made by a John Frampton, had been published in 1577.

As the sassafras tree, indigenous to America, ranked high for a while in importance, along with potatoes and tobacco, among America's first gifts to the old world, Hakluyt's more extended remarks on the subject in his *Discourse of Western Planting* are noteworthy.

> Moreover, Doctor Monardas that excellent physician of Civill [Seville] writing of the trees of the West Indies, maketh mention of a tree called sassafras which the Frenchmen found in Florida. Folio 46 of his book has the following; From the Florida they bring a root and wood of a tree that groweth in those parts of great virtues and excellencies, healing therewith grievous and variable diseases; it may be three years past that I had knowledge of this tree, and a Frenchman that had been in those parts showed me a piece of it and told me marvels of the virtues thereof, and how many and variable diseases were healed with the water which was made of it; and I judged that which now I do find to be true and have seen by experience. He told me that the Frenchmen which had been in the Florida at the time when they came into those parts had been sick the most of them from grievous and variable diseases, and that the Indians did show them this tree and the manner how they should use it, and so they did and were healed of many evils, which surely bringeth admiration that one only remedy should work so variable and marvelous effects. The name of this tree, — it is called 'Parrane' [*Pauame* in Frampton's *Monardes*], and the Frenchmen call it 'sassafras'; to be brief, the Doctor Monardus bestoweth eleven leaves in describing the sovereignties and excellent properties thereof.[8]

For Gosnold, sassafras roots had to be accepted as a poor substitute for the gold that he had hoped to find in the land discovered by Verrazzano in 1524. Archer appended to his May

28th description of Elizabeth's Isle — obviously not a place where gold might be found — this rather despairing note: "These Indians call Gold Wassador, which argueth there is thereof in the Countrey." Archer's logic was good, but his premise quite wrong. New England Indians had no word for gold. When Experience Mayhew translated the Psalms into "Massachusetts" Indian a hundred years after Gosnold had come and gone, he retained the English word "gold" in his Indian text, as was his custom with words for which the Massachusetts Indians had no equivalent. Archer did not get the word *Wassador* from his contact with the local Indians, but from the description of southern Virginia written by Master Ralph Lane.[9] This description is cited in another of the documents used in preparing for the voyage, printed at the end of Brereton's *Relation*. The reference to gold reads in part:

> The constant report of many of the Salvages to the worshipfull Master Ralfe Lane then governour of the English colonie in *Virginia* of the rich mine of *Wassador* or Gold at a place by them named *Chaunis Temoatam*, twentie dayes journey overland from the *Mangoaks* [dwelling to the westward], . . . is much to be regarded and considered by those that intend to prosecute this new enterprise of planting nere unto those parts.[10]

Needless to add, the foothills of the Alleghenies, to which Lane referred, were far, far from Cuttyhunk.

There was disappointment also in the hope confidently expressed by Captain Edward Hayes and the Reverend Mr. Hakluyt, that a copper mine might be found on this voyage. The Indians of the islands and the adjacent mainland, to be sure, were well provided with ornaments made of copper, but the explorers found that it had come from some distant region. While Gosnold's men were entertaining one of the visiting parties of fifty Indians, Brereton had made signs to one of them asking the source of the copper. The Indian, taking a piece of it in his hand, made a hole with his finger in the ground and pointed to the mainland from whence they came. He was undoubtedly pointing beyond the nearby mainland to the present state of

Maine, where in the early years of white settlement a good deal of free copper was to be found lying about.

Indians, it should be pointed out, could not or at least did not produce sufficient heat to smelt copper ores, and therefore could use only the fragments found loose in the soil. These could be beaten with stone hammers into very thin plates. The ornaments of the Indians, while showy, were made of this thin sheet-copper, and did not require much metal. Their chains were made of small pieces rolled into a tube, the joined edges somehow cemented. These tubes, some the length of a finger and some only about an inch long, were strung on strings to form chains, or held together by a knotted network in rectangular designs, making of the shorter pieces a bandolier, or collar, worn about the body and a "hand-full broad" — four inches. Brereton reported that four hundred of the short tubes were necessary to make such a collar. He also mentioned earrings, plain plates of this copper worn as a breast-plate, and drinking cups made of the same material. Copper arrow-heads were also observed, but these were probably for show rather than use in actual hunting, where arrow-heads were lost by the score and by the hundred. Uncounted thousands of arrow-heads have been picked up on the surface of Martha's Vineyard by farmers and amateur searchers, apparently with never a copper one among them. Archaeologists have found a few elsewhere.

Some have assumed that copper for these ornaments was brought by trading Indians from as far away as Lake Superior. But this seems hardly necessary as a supposition, because the free bits of copper referred to above were to be found not only in Maine, but also in the nearby enemy territory of the Narragansetts, in the country around the present inland city of Bristol and farther north, in the state of Connecticut. The copper found in Indian graves in these parts by archaeologists is said to be of European origin, but when these archaeologists assume a French Trade in these parts before Gosnold's day they would seem to be quite mistaken. There is no evidence whatsoever that the Indians visited by Gosnold, Champlain, and others in

161

the first decade of the seventeenth century were in possession of any sort of European trade goods, although it is possible that the Indians got some copper from the wrecks of Spanish and French vessels headed for Newfoundland and stranded in storm or fog on the southern shores of the islands or on Cape Cod. However this may be, the fact pertinent here is that Gosnold returned to England without any store of copper.

On June 10th, Gosnold sailed the *Concord* over to the little islet called Hill's Hap (Penikese) to fill the hold with great cedar logs — according to Ralegh's letter about the cargo brought back, there were in all twenty-six of them. This was a valuable addition to their freight. Captain Edward Hayes had included cedars among the trees that would "make masts for the greatest shippes of the world: Excellent timbers of Cedar, and boords for curious [beautifully wrought] building." The elder Hakluyt had written: "Sawed boords of Sassafras and Cedar, to be turned into small boxes for ladies and gentlewomen, would become a present [immediate] trade." While the selling price of the twenty-six cedar logs in the *Concord's* hold is unknown, it is possible that they brought the value of the whole cargo up to five hundred pounds sterling or more, topping the costs of fitting out the voyage.[11]

Archer's narrative reports that the *Concord* on this excursion "was gone cleane out of sight." This is somewhat puzzling, as Hill's Hap is only about a mile and a half from Cuttyhunk. However, the *Concord* may have sailed around to the north side of it, or, more likely, the usual June mists of this vicinity may have set in, making visibility poor. Then, too, Gosnold may have gone farther afield for his logs than he at first intended — perhaps to the little hilly island which Archer called Hap's Hill, at the mouth of one of the rivers flowing into the north part of Buzzards Bay. This more distant islet seems also, as Archer described it, to have been covered with cedar trees. In any case, Gosnold's trip to fell and load cedar logs, intended to take one day only, lasted three days.

Archer and nine men had been left in the fort with provi-

ions for three meals only, Gosnold having promised to return
he next day. Archer seems to have yielded to panic when Gos-
old "came not, neither sent." He and his companions were left
o sustain themselves as best they could with the edibles that
ould be gathered. Archer sent four of the company to "seek
ut for Crabbes, Lobsters, Turtles, &c.", but this project went
wry, and they were forced to eat "Alexander [horse-parsley,
aten like celery] and Sorrell pottage", and ground-nuts. This,
vith the smoking of tobacco, "gave nature a reasonable content."
But nothing could ease the strain of being marooned with no
roper food available, a thousand leagues from their homes in
England, and means of transport thither visibly lacking. "The
vant of our Captaine", Archer wrote, "that promised to returne,
s aforesaid, strooke us in a dumpish [melancholy] terrour, for
hat hee performed not the same in the space of almost three
days." At last they heard Captain Gosnold "to lewre", or call
oudly to them, probably out of the mists, "which made musike
s sweeter never came unto poore men."

On June 13th, a Sunday, the day after Gosnold's return
and five days after the shortage of provisions had been revealed,
"beganne some of our companie that before vowed to stay",
Archer bluntly put it, "to make revolt." In other words, although
hey had gone into the adventure intending to become settlers,
having promised Gosnold to remain with him in America, they
enounced that role and demanded the privilege of returning to
England with Captain Gilbert.[12] Brereton said of them that they
vere gentlemen who had "nothing but a saving voyage [neither
winning nor losing] in their minds." The game, in short, was
not worth the candle — the prospects for profit were outweighed
by the risks involved.

Eight men in all seem to have abandoned the project, out
of twenty, "so as captaine Gosnold", Brereton continued, "seeing
his whole strength to consist but of twelve men, and they but
meanly provided, determined to returne for England." This is
substantially what Archer wrote.

Three more days were "spent in getting Sasafrage and fire-

wood of Cedar", Archer remarks plaintively, "leaving House
and little Fort by ten men in nineteen dayes sufficient made to
harbour twenty persons at least with their necessary provision.'
Obviously, Archer had had a hand in building the fort.

On June 17th, the fourth day after the "revolt", they set
sail. Doubling the rocky point of Elizabeth's Isle, they passed
the brilliant Dover Cliff again on their way back to the place
on Martha's Vineyard, five leagues from the fort on Cuttyhunk,
where they had seen the nesting fowl in the sandy cliffs. There
they laid in a supply of young cranes, heron, and geese, "which
now were growne to pretie bigness", to eke out their provisions
for the homeward voyage.

The next day, they made their way out safely into the open
sea again, "cutting off" their shallop — setting it adrift as no
longer needed for landing parties. Then with what Brereton
calls "indifferent faire winde and weather", they sailed back
across the Atlantic, coming to anchor five weeks later, on July
23rd, before Exmouth. Why they passed Falmouth and Plymouth
to run up to Exmouth is not explained. But a few days later
they went on to Portsmouth, near Southampton.

Both Brereton and Gosnold — Gosnold in a letter written
to his father some weeks after their return — expressed devout
thanks for the good health enjoyed by the voyagers. Brereton
wrote in his *Relation:*

> For the agreeing of this Climat with us (I speake of my selfe, & so
> I may justly do for the rest of our company) that we found our health
> & strength all the while we remained there, so to renew and increase, a
> notwithstanding our diet and lodging was none of the best, yet not one
> of our company (God be thanked) felt the least grudging [symptom] or
> inclination to any disease or sicknesse, but were much fatter and in bette.
> health than when we went out of *England.*[13]

Gosnold, in the letter to his father, spoke of the good health
of the natives he had seen, and then continued:

> . . . for our selves (thankes be to God) we had not a man sicke two
> dayes together in all our Voyage; whereas others that went out with us

or about that time on other Voyages (especially such as went upon re-prisall) were most of them infected with sicknesse, whereof they lost some of their men, and brought home a many sicke, returning notwithstanding long before us.[14]

Scurvy, of course, was the scourge of voyagers of that day, but Gosnold's company did not fall prey of it. This perhaps may be attributed in part to fresh foods sent to the *Concord* at the outset of the voyage from the broad acres of the Gosnolds in the valley of the Finn River, easily shipped down the Deben to Gosnold's point of embarkation, and also in part to the eating of green, leafy salads, and berries while the company of voyagers were on the islands.[15]

Gosnold's letter to his father was dated September, 1602. It adds but little to knowledge of the voyage and is strangely barren of intimate personal references. Bartholomew apologized for his failure to get home to see his father in person. The reasons for this delay were not given in the letter, but he probably was overwhelmed by the troubled situation to be discussed else-where. He referred with some feeling to the shortage of food and the haste in returning made necessary by that shortage. A ton of sassafras, he explained, had been obtained rather easily — enough to cloy the market in England. Then he again referred to their haste:

. . . further, for that we had resolved upon our returne, and taken view of our victuall, we judged it then needefull to use expedition; which after-ward we had more certaine proofe of; for when we came to an anker before *Portsmouth*, which was some foure dayes after we made the land, we had not one Cake of Bread, nor any drinke, but a little Vinegar, left: for these and other reasons we returned no otherwise laden than you have heard.[16]

In other words, no gold, no silver, not even copper to make his family wealthy!

Gosnold's failure to effect a settlement on this voyage of 1602 is not entirely to be regretted. It is abundantly clear that cir-cumstances beyond his control changed this expedition, planned to start a plantation, into a trading voyage. This, however, in the grand scheme of things, was a fortunate mischance. The truth of the matter is that the time was not ripe for an English settlement on the coast of "northern Virginia." If Gosnold had succeeded in starting a trading colony of small dimensions, it surely would have been wiped out in the troubled second decade of the century.

Gosnold's actual accomplishment was that he had shown the way to the part of the American coast that was to become New England. He had shown the feasibility of a short, direct crossing that ordinarily could be sailed in about six weeks. He had demonstrated the healthfulness of the climate and the fertility of the soil to be cultivated here. He had shown that the land had products available at any time, which could readily be sold in England.

These things became known to the English public, and more especially to the great merchants of England, through the publication of Brereton's *Relation*. This report brought about the expedition of Captain Pring in the year following and set up a goal and destination for other voyagers. This new knowledge, enlarged, became the stock in trade of Captain John Smith, who made a desperate effort, with support from Sir Ferdinando Gorges, to reach the "abounding country" of Gosnold's discovery. But Smith likewise was balked by fate.

A few years later, Smith did his utmost to persuade the Pilgrims to settle in this region under his leadership. They declined his services, but thought that his books and his maps would lead them to this land of wealth. In short, it may truthfully be said that, although Bartholomew Gosnold failed to begin the English colonization of New England in 1602, nevertheless his work did not die with him, but brought his desire into being long after his death in "southern Virginia."

CHAPTER XVII

SIR WALTER RALEGH

Captain Bartholomew Gosnold, standing on the docks at Southampton, felt himself aggrieved. He had been reviled by the whole ship's company for the hungry days at the end of the voyage. He had finally gotten rid of his passengers. The gentlemen adventurers with their shares of sassafras had been transported to Southampton and were on their way to London. Then the blow fell. An agent of the Lord Admiral, from Southampton, intervened — on information that a cargo of sassafras had been landed. He believed it to be a prize cargo taken from the French or other foreigners and therefore liable to the ten per cent levy due to the Lord Admiral on all prize goods landed. After some discussion, Gosnold got off with losing only part of his share of the sassafras — keeping the logs intact.

As for Captain Bartholomew Gilbert, his final responsibility was to sail the *Concord* back to its home port of Dartmouth, which he did. There he turned the twenty-six cedar logs over to one Staplyne of that place, presumably a dealer in fine woods for cabinet work. Gilbert then went in search of his patron, Lord Cobham, who probably had previously known nothing of Gilbert's latest employment: the transportation of Gosnold and his company. Lord Cobham — Henry Brooke, brother-in-law of Sir Robert Cecil — was at the time an intimate friend of Sir Walter Ralegh, at least on the surface. One would have thought that if Cobham had known of Gosnold's intention to "settle" in northern Virginia he would have talked the matter over with Ralegh before Gosnold started, in which case much misunderstanding would have been averted. (A year later Cobham was accused of conspiring with Ralegh against King James, tried, and condemned with Ralegh to death, but with sentence for both remitted to life imprisonment in the Tower of London.[1])

167

Cobham took Gilbert to Weymouth, where he knew that Ralegh would presently appear. Sir Walter had to attend to the cargo of sassafras, china root and other commodities from "southern Virginia" brought back by Captain Samuel Mace of Weymouth. Ralegh had employed Mace to look for his lost colony, without necessarily sacrificing any profitable trade that might be forthcoming.

When the three met in Weymouth, Gilbert, doubtless with Cobham's help, apparently obtained from Ralegh the promise of employment in another voyage to be sent to Virginia, the voyage which he commanded the following year in the *Elizabeth* of London and which cost him his life. And for the more immediate present he got employment as bearer of an important letter which Ralegh wrote in haste to Sir Robert Cecil, Secretary of State.[2]

This letter is one of those annoying documents which raise more questions than they answer. As it is of primary importance in the study of Gosnold's expedition of 1602, it is here printed in full.

SIR,

Whereas as I wrate unto yow in my last that I was gonn to Weymouth, to speake with a pinnace of myne arived from Virginia, I found this bearer, Captayne Gilbert, ther also, who went on the same voyage. Butt myne fell 40 leaugs to the west of it [Roanoke], and this bearer as much to the east; so as neather of them spake with the peopell [of the colony]. Butt I do sende both the barks away agayne, having saved the charg in sassafras woode; butt this bearer bringing some 2200 waight [2200 lb.] to [Sout] Hampton, his Adventurers have taken away their parts, and brought it [all] to London.

I do therfore humblie pray yow to deale withe my Lord Admirall for a letter to make seasure of all that which is come to London, either by his Lordships authority or by the Judge: because I have a patent that all shipps and goods are confiscate that shall trade ther, without my leave. And whereas sassafras was worth 10*s.*, 12*s.*, and 20*s.* a pound before Gilbert returned, his cloying of the market will overthrow all myne, and his owne also. Hee is contented to have all stayde; not only for this present: butt, being to go agayne, others will also go and distroy the trade, which, otherwize would yeild 8 or 10 for one, in certenty, and a returne in xx [20] weekes.

I desire butt right herein; and my Lord Admirall, I hope, will not be a hinderance to a matter of trade graunted by the Great Seale of Inglande; his Lordship havinge also freedome and an interest in the countrye. A man of my Lord's, of Hampton, arested part of Gilbert's, for the tenths. I hope my Lord will not take it; [it] belonging not unto hyme; having also hyme self power to trade ther [in Virginia] by his interest. And it were pitty to overthrow the enterprize; for I shall yet live to see it an Inglishe nation.

Ther was also brought 26 cedar trees by Gilbert, which one Staplyne of Dartmouth hath. If my Lord will vouchsafe to write to C[hristopher] Harris to seize them, we will part them in three parts — to ceil [line] cabinets, and make boards [e.g., chessboards, for book-covers, etc.] and many other delicate things. I beseech yow vouchsafe to speak to my Lord [Admiral]. I know his Lordship will do mee right herein. I, for haste, have not written. For, if a stay be not made, it will be spent, and sold into many hands.

This bearer, Captayne Gilbert — who is my Lord Cobhame's man — will find out wher it is. Hee came to mee with your post letter. It is he, — by a good token [sign], — that had the great diamonde.

I beseech yow, favor our right; and yow shall see what a prety, honorabell, and safe trade wee will make.

Your's ever to serve yow,
W. Ralegh.

[Postscript.] I hope yow will excuse my cumbersome letters and suits. It is your destiny to be trobled with your friends, and so must all men bee. Butt what yow thinck unfitt to be dun for mee shall never be a quarrell, either internall or externall. I thanck yow evermore for the good, and what cannot be effected, farewell [to] it! If wee cannot have what we would, methincks it is a great bonde to finde a friende that will strayne hyme self in his friend's cause in whatsoever, — as this world fareth.

Weymouth, this 21 of August [1602].

[Second postscript.] Gilbert went without my leave, and therefore *all* is confiscate; and he shall have his part agayne.

This letter stands alone — that is, there are no letters on the same subject preceding it or following it — from either Ralegh or Cecil. Its interpretation, apart from certain statements that can be accepted as objective fact, is largely a matter of conjecture. Deductive reasoning sheds some light, but the letter itself raises questions. It is strangely silent on some matters, and seems to betray remarkable ignorance on others. Why was Bartholomew Gosnold's connection with the voyage not mentioned? Why did Ralegh not say that it was a voyage intending to make a settlement, which only by chance turned out to be a trading voyage? Why was there no mention by name of those who were to suffer financial loss through the confiscation of the cargo. Did Ralegh not know that the Earl of Southampton had invested in the voyage, or that the adventurers, Brereton and Salterne, were friends of Hakluyt?

Merely asking these questions brings a choice of three possibilities, all containing their portion of the truth. The first deduction is that Gilbert had given Ralegh only a partial and naturally one-sided account of the circumstances surrounding the voyage. The second is that Ralegh suspected that Cecil knew more about the voyage than he had chosen to reveal. And the third is that Ralegh was not entirely frank with Cecil, which seems "unthinkable", yet, in an age of fine deception, is not to to be ruled out. In short, Ralegh's letter, based on the not entirely veracious Gilbert's tale of the why's and wherefore's of the voyage, was probably a mixture of sincere ignorance, perhaps intentionally beclouded by Gilbert, and hesitant or "tactful" probing into what Cecil knew about the matter.

Turning to the more positive side of the letter, it appears that Ralegh was primarily concerned with not suffering a financial loss because of the unauthorized voyage — unauthorized by *him*, and he held the patent. Ralegh was apparently not on too close terms with the Lord Admiral and therefore asked Cecil, whom he did know intimately, to intervene, so that the argument about the sassafras could be settled quickly and informally as a civil action in the Admiralty Court. It is not a question of "politics" in this aspect of Ralegh's letter at all.[3]

Another point that is fairly clear in the letter is that Ralegh did not want the Lord Admiral to seize any part of the cargo, because it was not his to seize. The cargo was not "prize goods", but trade goods. Furthermore, the Lord Admiral himself had an interest in such overseas trade matters — he was an adventurer in Ralegh's earlier Virginia venture.[4] In other words, without knowing all about the details of Gosnold's voyage as yet, Ralegh seemed to be trying to clarify the picture, and to keep the Lord Admiral as much out of it as possible — with the tactful insinuation that the latter himself was interested in just such projects as Gilbert was now returning from.

The matter seems, in fact, to have been more serious to Ralegh from the point of view of the Lord Admiral's possible moves than from the point of view of what Gilbert (and Gosnold) had done, in violation of his patent. For that aspect of the story was cleared up in less than two months after the letter was written. Sir Walter was pleased to accept the following dedication of Brereton's *Relation:*

> Honourable sir, being earnestly requested by a deere friend, to put downe in writing, some true relation of our late performed voyage to the North parts of *Virginia;* at length I resolved to satisfie his request, who also emboldened me to direct the same to your honourable consideration; to whom indeed of duetie it perteineth. [The narrative proper follows immediately.][5]

Furthermore, on the title page of the little volume there also appeared the information that the voyage of *"Captaine Bartholomew Gosnold, Captaine Bartholowmew Gilbert,* and divers other gentlemen their associats" was made "by the permission of the honourable knight, Sir WATER RALEIGH, &c."

The story of the voyage, the Lord Admiral, and Ralegh's letter becomes twice confounded when, of necessity, another element is introduced. This was a plot that would involve Ralegh, and in bringing about his downfall by association, contribute a tragedy of errors to England's dramatic "Elizabethan" history.

Precisely in the month when Bartholomew Gosnold sailed for America (March, 1602), an unpleasant gentleman named Lord Henry Howard (the second son of Henry Howard, Earl of Surrey, the Lord Admiral's first cousin), for a multiplicity of reasons was drafting a letter to James VI, King of Scots, outlining the steps of a plot for ruining Sir Walter Ralegh and Henry Brooke, Baron Cobham. Howard, "in whom the truth did not dwell"[6], had in mind to involve Ralegh and Cobham in treasonable association with Spain, and so to bring about Ralegh's dismissal from high office by Queen Elizabeth. The plot was not set in motion, however, while Elizabeth lay dying, but was ready to be used as soon as James came to the throne of England. Howard's poison worked. James I succeeded Elizabeth on March 24th, 1603, and on May 7th he arrived in London. On May 8th, the new King dismissed Ralegh as Captain of the Guard; on June 7th he sent a peremptory note to Ralegh to vacate Durham House granted to Ralegh by Queen Elizabeth in 1584. By mid-July Ralegh had been arrested, along with Cobham, and sent to the Tower, accused of high treason. Lord Henry Howard's star was rising rapidly at James's Court, and the trial and conviction of Ralegh and Cobham followed inevitably.

Gosnold's voyage of 1602 was not a mere incident of maritime history — a voyage by a man of no significance or importance in English politics — but was somehow connected, at a critical time, with the vital question of Ralegh's prestige in the minds of the Queen and the public. Unfortunately, it would seem impossible to tie together the ravelled threads of this situation, but the general picture is reasonably clear. Ralegh was in no position, when he learned the names of the important personages back of Gosnold, to antagonize them by persecuting this potential rival in colonization. In the end he was obviously glad to take to himself such credit as he could for furthering Gosnold's voyage.[7]

The question must be asked, therefore, as to whether Ralegh did or did not give permission in advance for the voyage. Ever since Edward Edwards published Ralegh's letter on "Gilbert's" voyage, nearly a hundred years ago, historians have accepted Ralegh's words in the letter as final evidence that he did not give this permission, and that in consequence the information printed on the title page of Brereton's *Relation* was a fabrication.

There is something to be said, however, on the other side. It is quite possible that Gilbert's misrepresentation of the voyage as a trading venture under his own command failed to call to Ralegh's memory his permission, given some years previously for a colonization effort by a person or persons not mentioned by

172

Gilbert in his plea for a return of his sassafras. The changed attitude on Ralegh's part, therefore, as it appears in Brereton's *Relation,* may have been merely a correction of the record to Ralegh's advantage.

There are two sound reasons for thinking that Ralegh had given his permission for the voyage, in spite of his hasty denial. To begin with, it is to say the least extremely doubtful that the Rev. John Brereton would have lent himself to a bare-faced misrepresentation in the publication of his *Relation.* This becomes stronger if it is admitted that Richard Hakluyt, Brereton's friend and neighbor among the Suffolk clergy, was the "dear friend" who urged Brereton to write the book, who persuaded Brereton to dedicate it to Sir Walter, and who became the un-named "editor" responsible for seeing the narrative with its added documents through the press. Hakluyt would have been the last man in all England who would deliberately lend him-self to a falsification of a vital fact in the record of a significant overseas voyage.

A second and weightier consideration is the difficulty in believing that Bartholomew Gosnold would have started out on a voyage to America without Ralegh's permission. Gosnold was a well-educated and well-informed young man, in contact with important people and fully aware of the privileges conferred by a royal patent. He must certainly have known the repercussions that would follow upon the discovery that he had made an unauthorized voyage to a region included in Ralegh's exclusive right to colonization and trade.

Such a proceeding on Gosnold's part would have been more than a mere trespassing on Ralegh's trade preserves. Ralegh was under severe censure for having lost English lives in his coloniza-tion ventures. If Gosnold had succeeded in planting a small colony for a year or more without loss of life, Ralegh would have been made to seem in public opinion a blunderer in his chosen field of activity. The success of a young man without Ralegh's resources would have stood out in painful contrast to Ralegh's failure. While it might be hypothesized that someone

173

put Gosnold up to accomplish this result as a first step in the plot against Ralegh, on the whole the hypothesis would seem ill-founded. It seems therefore untenable that Gosnold would have defied the thunder-bolt of justice by making an unauthorized voyage, in defiance of Sir Walter.

Under what circumstances, then, might Ralegh have given a forgotten permission for a voyage, taken by Gosnold to be an authorization of his expedition to northern Virginia? Before suggesting an answer, it may be well to point out, using the only available analogy, that Gosnold himself would have had little or nothing to do with obtaining this permission — his part being merely to accept appointment under the permission as Captain of the expedition. The analogy is in the record of Martin Pring' voyage from Bristol the following year. The record of that voyage reveals that young Robert Salterne, with a companion named John Angell, and accompanied by the Rev. Richard Hakluyt — all three representing the merchants of the city of Bristol — waited upon Sir Walter and obtained his permission to send out an expedition. Martin Pring did not enter into the picture except as the experienced Captain, selected to lead the venture. No doubt any other equally capable mariner would have done as well.

This voyage has come down in the records with the short title of "Pring's Voyage", but if the opening paragraph of the narrative he wrote had been omitted in the printing the question would be when and how Ralegh's permission had been obtained. So in Gosnold's case, while one may be justified in assuming on the evidence furnished in Brereton's *Relation*, that Gosnold did sail under a permission granted by Ralegh, it does not necessarily follow that Gosnold himself had anything to do with obtaining that permission.

After long consideration and the rejection of several alternative hypotheses, it is suggested, without too much elaboration, that the permission under which Gosnold's company sailed was one granted to Captain Edward Hayes, some time previously. Hayes had been a loyal subordinate of Ralegh's half-brother ir Humphrey Gilbert, and had been rewarded by Gilbert's xpressed desire that Hayes lead an expedition to search for the ay and Indian kingdom described by Verrazzano — a project bandoned in 1584.[9] Hayes therefore is by all odds the most kely one to have secured Ralegh's permission for a revival of he project. The appearance of Hayes' *Treatise* in the little olume called Brereton's *Relation*, together with the convincing vidence that Gosnold used the *Treatise* as his prospectus, bears vitness to a kind of follow-up character in Gosnold's voyage and ies it to Gilbert's. On that slim basis, then, the assumption is hat Ralegh had recognized his half-brother's wishes, had granted Iayes permission for a voyage, had never revoked it, and had uite forgotten about it until it was recalled to him sometime etween the date of his letter to Cecil and the date of the publica- ion of Brereton's book. This pure surmise at least is plausible, nd it has certain bases in known facts.

There is little more to be said about Sir Walter Ralegh's amous letter, except to call attention to its most famous phrase: I shall yet live to see it [Virginia] an Inglishe nation." Unwit- ingly, however, with the same pen and on the same sheet of aper, Ralegh nevertheless demanded financial ruin of the very nan who was to be so vital a factor in the realization of Ralegh's rophecy.

In Gosnold's letter to his father, dated September 7th, artholomew intimated that he was too busy in London to take ime to visit him. Ralegh had made a good point in his note to Cecil, when he protested that the unrestrained sale of the *Con- ord's* sassafras would cloy the market. It may therefore be that vhen the matter of "permission" and customs duties was settled o everybody's satisfaction, Gosnold and Sir Walter joined forces n restraint of trade to keep up the price of the rare panacea.)therwise how explain that sassafras continued to be a profitable ommodity for import?

Ralegh's first postscript expressed a touching but vain eliance on Cecil's friendship: "methinks it is a great bonde to inde a friend that will strayne hyme self in his friend's cause

175

in whatsoever . . . " A year or so later Ralegh was in the Tower c
London, under sentence of death. Cecil had not strained himse
in his friend's cause — perhaps quite the opposite. Was it tha
like Brutus, he loved his country more?

Within the year following Ralegh's incarceration, Barthol
mew Gosnold had begun the talks with nobles, merchants an
gentry which won him the distinction of being called "the Firs
Mover" of the plantation of southern Virginia — the settlemer
of Jamestown.

CHAPTER XVIII

A NARRATIVE AND MORE

Twenty years after Sir Humphrey Gilbert, with Hakluyt as his publicity man, aroused interest in Norumbega but failed to effect its settlement, two young men from the neighborhood of Wetheringsett, Suffolk, and one or two from Bristol, made successful voyages to that part of the American coast. This of course did not come about by chance, for Wetheringsett and Bristol were places where Master Richard Hakluyt held offices which gave him opportunity to be in personal touch with the young men who took the lead in these voyages — Bartholomew Gosnold, John Brereton, Robert Salterne, and probably John Angell. Therefore, a study of Brereton's book, called on the title page *A Briefe and true Relation of the Discoverie of the North part of* VIRGINIA; *being a most pleasant, fruitfull and commodious soile,* begins with the confident expectation that Richard Hakluyt will be found guiding through the press this latest addition to the narratives of American voyages.

In 1600, Hakluyt had completed and published *The Third and Last Volume of the Voyages, Navigations, Traffiques, and Discoveries of the English Nation . . . Collected by* RICHARD HAKLUYT *Preacher.* His interest in the publication of geographical works did not then abate, however, as he immediately gave his attention to the printing of two translations, one from the Italian and another from the Portuguese. Then, in 1602, came Bartholomew Gosnold's notable contribution to the series of English voyages. Obviously Hakluyt would have felt his life's labors on the principal voyages of the English nation unfinished and incomplete, if he had not been able to persuade his favorite printer at the time, George Bishop of London, to bring out a small volume on Gosnold's success in finding a place suitable for English settlement in the northern part of Virginia.

177

This work appeared in the book-stalls late in October, 1602 about three months after Gosnold's return to England. It did not bear in any part of it the signature, the imprimatur so to speak, of Richard Hakluyt. Yet, as has already been noted by George Bruner Parks in his life of Hakluyt[1], it seems likely if not certain, that Hakluyt was responsible for the editing and publishing of Brereton's book.

The first of the appended documents printed immediately after Brereton's narrative — a note on the voyage of Samuel Mace — furnishes an excellent illustration of the method to be used in reaching such a conclusion. The reader should first compare attentively the following two passages.

A. [Title: *A briefe Note of the sending another barke this present yeere 1602, by the honorable knight, Sir Walter Ralegh, for the searching out of his Colonie in Virginia.*]

Samuel Mace of Weymouth, a very sufficient Mariner, an honest sober man, who had beene at Virginia twise before, was imployed thither by Sir Walter Ralegh, to finde those people which were left there in the yeere 1587. To whose succour he hath sent five severall times at his owne charges. The parties by him set forth, performed nothing; some of them following their owne profit elsewhere; others returning with frivolous allegations. At this last time, to avoid all excuse, he bought a barke, and hired all the company for wages by the moneth: who departing from Weymouth in March last 1602, fell fortie leagues to the Southwestward of Hatarask, in thirtie-foure degrees or thereabout; and having there spent a moneth; when they came along the coast to seeke the people, they did it not, pretending that the extremitie of weather and losse of some principall ground-tackle [anchor and mooring tackle], forced and feared them from searching the port of Hatarask, to which they were sent . . .[2]

B. [Title: *The third voyage made by a ship sent in the yeere 1586, to the reliefe of the Colony planted in Virginia, at the sole charges of Sir Walter Ralegh.*]

In the yeere of our Lord 1586 Sir Walter Ralegh at his owne charge prepared a ship of an hundred tunne, fraighted with all maner of things in most plentifull maner, for the supply and reliefe of his Colony then remaining in Virginia . . .

Immediately after the departing of our English Colony out of this paradise of the world, the ship abovementioned sent and set forth at the charges of Sir Walter Ralegh and his direction, arrived at Hatorask; who after some time spent in seeking our Colony up in the countrey, and not finding them, returned with all the aforesayd provision into England.[3]

Most readers will agree that the selections read as though they were taken from a single account, by the same hand, of Ralegh's attempts to find his lost colony. As a matter of fact, the second is a sample of Hakluyt's style, chosen for comparison with the first, written by an unknown hand and appended to Brereton's *Relation*. Here, therefore, is the first clear indication that Hakluyt was the editor of the appended documents, since the earlier paragraph may reasonably be taken as a note written by Hakluyt in his editorial capacity.

The next step is to review briefly by title the other appended documents. This is the more necessary because Brereton's work is generally so difficult of access in its complete, second-edition state that few historians have studied it.

The first edition, which is somewhat easier of access, comprised Brereton's narrative and list of commodities (pages 3 to 13, inclusive), the note on Mace's voyage (just discussed), and (pages 15 to 24) the *Treatise* by Captain Edward Hayes (analyzed in Chapter VII).

The second edition, which reprinted all that was in the first, contained twenty-four additional pages.

Pages 25 to 36 contain a document entitled *Inducements to the liking of the voyage intended towards Virginia in 40. and 42. degrees of latitude, written 1585. by M. Richard Hakluyt the elder, sometime student of the Middle Temple*. This document, ostensibly written by the Rev. Richard Hakluyt's older cousin, a lawyer, who started him on his geographical career, is not to be confused with the one printed among the writings of the Hakluyts with the same title, except that the latitudes for the intended voyage are given in the latter as between 34° and 36°, instead of between 40° and 42°. The relationship between the two versions of the *Inducements* is obscure, but it would seem that someone — who else could it have been except the Reverend Richard Hakluyt — revamped the elder Hakluyt's article to make it applicable to Bartholomew Gosnold's voyage, and appropriate for inclusion with Brereton's *Relation*.[4]

179

Pages 37 and 38 have *A briefe note of the corne fowles, fruits and beasts of the Inland of Florida on the backeside of Virginia.* According to the sub-title this wa taken from the 44th chapter of the discovery of the saic country, begun by Fernando de Soto, Governor of Cuba in the year of our Lord 1539.[5]

Pages 39 and 40 have *A Note of such commoditie as are found in Florida next adjoining unto the South part of Virginia.* The words *next adjoining unto the South part of* are underlined (italicized), and the title add that this was "taken out of the description of the saic countrey, written by Mounsieur Rene Laudonniere, whe inhabited there two Sommers and one winter."[6]

Pages 41 to 45 have *A briefe extract of the mer chantable commodities found in the South part of Vir ginia, ann. 1585 and 1586,* with explanation: "Gatherec out of the learned works of master Thomas Herriot which was there remaining the space of eleven monenths." This is an epitome of material that Richard Hakluyt had printed in his *Principal Navigations.*[7]

Pages 46 to 48 contain the last of the appended documents. The title, as long as the text is brief, reads as follows: *Certaine briefe testimonies touching sundry rich mines of Gold, Silver, and Copper, in part found and in part constantly heard of, in North Florida, and the Inland of the Maine of Virginia, and other countreys there unto on the North part neere adjoining, gathered out of the works, all (one excepted) extant in print, of such as were personall travellers in those countries.* This document is full of citations from the *English Voyages* (the three-volume *Principal Navigations . . .* of 1598-1600), giving in each case the page from which the remarks are taken. It is noteworthy that these para- graphs were written in the first person singular. They bear the characteristic book and page references which set Hakluyt apart from most of the writers of his day.[8]

It would be difficult to find a group of citations and notes which give better expression to Hakluyt's mind in these matters than the seven assembled for inclusion with Brereton's *Relation.*

ndeed, it may be stated unequivocally that the group, including,
s it does, information about Florida, was motivated by Hakluyt's
nterests rather than by a desire specifically to illuminate a
voyage "to the North Part of Virginia."

The evidence of Hakluyt's hand in the preparation of
Brereton's *Relation* as it appeared in its expanded second edition
may be summed up as follows:

> The first and last of the notes appended show
> characteristics that may be taken as evidence that
> Hakluyt himself wrote them. (These are the note on
> Mace's voyage and the "briefe testimonies" at the end
> of the volume.)

> The *Treatise* by Captain Edward Hayes, apart from
> other considerations set forth in earlier chapters of
> this study, was written by the man from whom Hakluyt
> obtained an account of Sir Humphrey Gilbert's expe-
> dition for inclusion in his *Principal Navigations*.

> The document called *Inducements*, by the elder
> Hakluyt, in one version or the other, was almost cer-
> tainly inherited by Hakluyt after his cousin's death in
> 1591.

> The extracts from the account of de Soto's "Inland
> of Florida" explorations (extending to the Mississippi),
> were to be found only in a Portuguese work, of which
> Hakluyt had a copy, perhaps the only one in England;
> it is mentioned in parentheses in the second paragraph
> of the last item appended (the *briefe testimonies*) in a
> phrase reading "to be seene in print in the hands of
> Master Richard Hakluyt." The editor, if he be Hakluyt,
> is saying: "the only place where you can consult it is in
> my home." Hakluyt in any case finally translated this
> Portuguese work on de Soto, publishing it in 1609.[9]

> The Laudonnière work cited was Hakluyt's own
> special discovery. He had found the manuscript in
> France, and it was published there in 1586 at his ex-
> pense. The next year Hakluyt made a translation of it
> into English, which was first published in London in
> 1587, and then incorporated into his *Principall Naviga-
> tions* (1589).

181

The work on Virginia by "Herriot" (Hariot Ralegh's observer sent over to report on the land, ha been published in 1588. Hakluyt reprinted it, too, in h *Voyages* (both *Principall* and *Principal Navigation* of 1589 and 1598-1600 respectively).

In addition, the editorial touches, here and there throughou the appended documents, particularly the glosses or parenthet asides obviously added by the editor to the documents befo: him, also shed light on the personality of the man who prepare this work for the press. These may be listed as follows:

In Brereton's list of commodities the editor ha added in the second edition, "Iris Florentina, where(apothecaries make sweet balles." To Brereton's mentio of "clay, red & white", has been added the clause, "whic may prove good Terra Sigillata" — an astringent cla then esteemed as a medicine.[10]

After Laudonnière's mention of "the tree calle Esquine" there is a parenthesis, "which I take to be th Sassafras." Here a voice of authority such as Hakluyt is speaking. A few paragraphs later the same extrac says "there are mines of Copper", to which is addec "which I think to be Gold."

Among the extracts supposedly from Hariot occur this remark about a certain kind of root: "Monarde calleth them *Beades*, or *Pater nostri of Sancta Helen*(and master Brereton Ground Nuts." The last five word are obviously not in Hariot ((the latest edition of whic: was Hakluyt's, in 1600), and so were added by an edite familiar with Brereton's narrative.[11]

In the last of the added documents, the "brief testimonies", there are several striking personal remarks "This place in mine opinion cannot be farre from th great river that falleth into the Southwest part of th Bay of Chesepioc [Chesapeake]." — "The large descrip tion and chart of which voyage . . . being intercepte(afterward by the English at sea, we have in London t be shewed to such as shall have occasion to make us of the same." — "I could give large information of th(

182

rich copper mine . . . whereof I my selfe have seene above an hundred pieces of the copper, and have shewed some part thereof to divers knightes of qualitie, . . . But I reserve a furthere relation heereof to a more convenient time and place."

The sum of the matter is that if the unnamed editor of rereton's *Relation* was not Richard Hakluyt, then Richard [akluyt must have found or developed an alter ego indistinuishable from himself in learning, interests, or authoritative tterance. Hakluyt might have educated his disciple, Bartholo-1ew Gosnold, to the point where Bartholomew could think, 1uote and write like his master — in other words, Gosnold might imself have edited Brereton's *Relation*. But there is no hint lsewhere that Gosnold ever functioned as a profound student f the *Voyages*. There remains only the conviction, therefore, 1at Hakluyt himself edited and published the little book that ; known as Brereton's *Relation*.

"A deere friend", says the opening paragraph of the *Relation*, equested Brereton to write out his narrative, and "emboldened" im to dedicate it to Sir Walter Ralegh. Again, circumstantial ut significant evidence points to Richard Hakluyt as the man /ho did this persuading. It was quite in character for Hakluyt) secure a voyager's narrative for publication. His long-range 1otive would be the justification of his belief, expressed to)ueen Elizabeth in his *Discourse on the Western Planting* of 584, that Norumbega was a suitable place for English settle-1ent. The immediate occasion of the publication, however, was ndoubtedly furnished by Ralegh's hasty attempt to confiscate he cargo brought back, together with the need of having a mooth and persuasive propaganda document for the benefit f the merchants of Bristol, who, as Pring's narrative reported, /ere being urged to finance and send out another voyage to the egion visited by Gosnold.

If there were any suggestion that the book was limited 1 intent to the enlightenment and encouragement of Bristol 1erchants, the name of young Robert Salterne occurs as the "deere friend" who brought about the writing of the *Relation*. The many weeks at sea undoubtedly brought together in close companionship the ordained clergyma . Brereton and the young man who was later to enter the ministry. But the broad scope of the book as a whole, with its seven appended documents assembled to support and to illuminate the central narrative leaves little doubt that Richard Hakluyt himself was the "deer friend" in question.

Whatever part Bartholomew Gosnold may have had in the publication of Brereton's *Relation* must remain as a matter of conjecture. However, Brereton's silence in regard to the geographical aspects of Gosnold's approach to Martha's Vineyard probably betray Gosnold's hand in censorship. A summary of these silences is repeated for emphasis and to serve as a clue to the circumstances surrounding the publication of the book. They are silences which can be detected only by those familiar with the physical features of the Cape Cod region. The original readers of Brereton's narrative were not and for that matter many modern students of the voyage are not, in possession of the information which would enable them to realize that Brereton was misleading them by a clear case of *suppressio veri* — suggesting what is false by keeping hidden what is true. Here are three examples:

1. Nantucket Sound was seen by Brereton, together with Gosnold and others, from a hill on Cape Cod. This is a geographical fact that cannot be gainsaid. Brereton mentioned islands "lying almost round about" the Cape but he did not anywhere say that these islands enclose a great sound, approximately the size of the great bay described by Verrazzano.

2. Brereton reported: "From this place [i.e., the southern part of Cape Cod Bay], we sailed round about this headland, almost all the points of the compass, the shore very bolde; but as no coast is free from dangers so I am persuaded, this is as free as any." No one not familiar with these waters could possibly guess from this sentence that Gosnold passed over or around the

most dangerous shoals on the coast of New England. Every other voyager of the period who sailed down this coast, and lived to leave a record of his experiences, gave a lurid description of the shoals. Why did Brereton (and Archer) omit mention of them?

3. South of Cape Cod, Gosnold and his companions must have observed at close quarters the imposing island which he named Martha's Vineyard — an island containing about 100 square miles, and prominent because of its high hills. Why did Brereton (and Archer as well) give the impression that this island was only four miles in compass, about one square mile in area? Why did he fail to tell about the great sound, now called Vineyard Sound, lying between the north shore of this island and the Elizabeth Islands?

The only logical conclusion to be drawn from the fact of his and other omissions (which in Archer's narrative have left indications that they were deletions) is that the narrators purposely withheld information from the public that would be useful to others who might want to find again Gosnold's Martha's Vineyard. Other and graver reasons quite possibly existed, involving other nations. It is idle today to attempt to specify the reasons. A number of significant omissions of detail still confuse the reader: that they were intentional there can be little doubt.

In that connection, it is interesting to observe that Brereton's narrative was written in conformity with the revised day-by-day account of Gabriel Archer. This can be taken as rather certain evidence that Archer's narrative had been prepared for publication in 1602, suffering deletions in the process, but had finally been rejected in favor of the rhetorically superior propaganda produced by the Rev. Mr. Brereton.

Another astonishing bit of silence lies in the absence of any satisfactory information either in Brereton's narrative or in Archer's about the purposes of the voyage and its destination, except that Archer in passing mentioned a "purposed place" and later on reported that the *Concord* passed a point (at one side of the opening) whose latitude was 41° 40′, which is, of

course, the precise latitude given by Verrazzano for the entrance
to his great bay.

Brereton's silence on the objectives of the voyage may be
compared with the opening paragraph of Pring's narrative of his
voyage of 1603, as printed by Samuel Purchas:

> Upon many probable and reasonable inducements, used unto sundry
> of the chiefest Merchants of Bristoll, by Master Richard Hakluyt Prebendary
> of Saint Augustines the Cathedrall Church of the said Citie, after divers
> meetings and due consultation they resolved to set forth a Voyage for the
> farther Discoverie of the North part of Virginia.[12]

Neither Brereton nor Archer chose to give any such information about the inception of Gosnold's voyage of 1602. Instead
a *Treatise* by Sir Humphrey Gilbert's man, Captain Edward
Hayes, is offered in explanation of the voyage.

In conclusion, the present author would spin a gossamer tale
as a literary "introduction" to Brereton's *Relation*, trusting his
readers will understand how unsubstantial are some of the
threads used in the weaving.

> He assumes that when Sir Robert Cecil received
> Sir Walter Ralegh's letter demanding the confiscation
> of the cargo supposed to be Gilbert's, Cecil communi-
> cated with the Lord Admiral about settling the
> dispute in the Admiralty Court, or otherwise amicably.
> Then, in view of the importance of the voyage geo-
> graphically, he called in his geographical adviser, Rich-
> ard Hakluyt.
> The author assumes then that Hakluyt sought a
> conference with his friend Sir Walter and explained to
> him tactfully that the noble knight's permission had in
> fact been obtained, not by Gilbert or even by Bartholo-
> mew Gosnold, who had led the expedition, but by the
> old mariner, Captain Edward Hayes, who had dele-
> gated the leadership of the expedition to Gosnold. And
> at this first conference, or at a subsequent one, Hakluyt
> proposed that an account of the voyage be published
> which would redound to Sir Walter's credit. Hakluyt
> would make bold to write for it a note on Ralegh's

186

earnest efforts to find and succour his lost Colonies. Captain Edward Hayes' *Treatise*, to be published with a story of the voyage, would make reference — as indeed it did — to Virginia "lately planted in part by the Colonies sent thither by the honourable knight, Sir Walter Ralegh."[13] Furthermore, and this was the most important of all, the Rev. John Brereton, a gentleman of the voyage, would be asked to write a *Relation* of it, which with the noble Knight's kind approval would be dedicated to him, with the fact plainly stated on the title-page of the projected work that Sir Walter Ralegh had given his permission for the voyage. Thus, the Queen, and all of England, would know that the holder of the Queen's Patent to Virginia was continuing his efforts to bring about the plantation of America, that it might someday become an English nation.

These proposals were welcomed by Ralegh, as he sorely needed something of the sort to restore confidence in his colonizing plans. Perhaps, and this is not essential, Bartholomew Gosnold was brought in to complete the arrangements about the sassafras — amicable arrangements, so that there would be no cloying of the market, as it was put.

In return for all this, Sir Walter Ralegh was asked graciously to give his permission to the merchants of Bristol to send out another voyage to the northern part of Virginia (the part visited by Gosnold) to obtain a further and larger supply of sassafras. To this end, Richard Hakluyt brought to Sir Walter his young friends, Robert Salterne and John Angell of Bristol, as representatives of the Bristol merchants.

In consequence of this, and it was a great deal, Brereton's *Relation* was duly published. One may be certain that a goodly number of copies of it went to the merchants of Bristol, to assure them that a profit was to be made by sending two more vessels to the northern part of Virginia.

187

PART III

Bartholomew Gosnold
Prime Mover of the Jamestown Colony
by *Philip L. Barbour*

PRIME MOVER OF JAMESTOWN

Newtown, Connecticut.
January, 1962.

i.

Bartholomew Gosnold arrived at Exmouth on Friday, July 23, 1602. He had been gone from England seventeen weeks to the day. He had visited unknown lands beyond the seas, and had brought his ship and all his crew — gentlemen and others alike — safely home. Contrarieties he had had, but his voyage was notable for its morale, its expedition, and its maintenance of health. It was also notable for its secrecy.

What had Gosnold achieved in those four months?

He had blazed a new trail, so to speak, across the trackless wastes of the Atlantic that was little longer than the shortest possible route. He had found and explored part of the coast of New England, the first to do so systematically in eighty years. He had found a place suitable for a trading-post, and set up a building — that it was abandoned was beside the point. He had made friendly contact with the Indians there. He had, in short, carried out his mission as well as time and circumstances permitted. And he had brought back raw materials of sufficient value to defray, or nearly defray, the cost of the expedition: the balance, if any, could be charged off to exploratory expenses. This much, apart from the exact balance sheet, is known.

Among the things not known are such particulars as whether or not he was sent by the Earl of Southampton, as William Strachey later stated, whether or not he was aware of the violation of Ralegh's patent implicit in his unauthorized trip, and

191

whether or not he actually expected to winter on an island off the American coast with what little he had by way of men and supplies. These unknowns are relatively unimportant. The important side of his story, about which fact must be combined with possibility and probability, involves the backing he had (regardless of the Earl of Southampton), why he went (regardless of whether he stayed or not), and what he did when he got back to England.

As for the backing, it is reasonable to assume that Gosnold had the support of his wife's cousin, Sir Thomas Smythe — how much is uncertain. It is reasonable to assume that through Sir Thomas he met Captain Hayes, a man over twenty years his senior but whose urge to colonize "Virginia" (including New England) never flagged. It is reasonable to assume, finally, that he knew Richard Hakluyt, through the combination of his father, Lady Stafford, and the living Hakluyt received at Wetheringsett, as country parson. Hakluyt and Hayes were already known to one another, at least since the Gilbert North American venture of 1583. These assumptions, based on fact and on sound inference, sum up the important fundamentals of Gosnold's career: connection with successful and wealthy merchants, connection with the mariners who made colonizing possible, and connection with the leading geographer and propagandist of English expansion of his day, if not of all time. Other connections of course grew out of these, but are subsidiary.[1]

Why Gosnold went on his voyage in 1602 cannot be answered categorically. It may be that residence near such a port as Ipswich stimulated his imagination, and that tales of Ralegh's ill-fated colony reached his ears through Suffolk families which had lost a son or husband there. These would almost without doubt have made more vivid a fancy born of life near a busy port.[2] By comparison, legal studies were dull. And so, between the time when Hakluyt received the living at Wetheringsett, near Bartholomew's home, and the last mention of Bartholomew as law student, everything points to his having abandoned a sedentary

192

career in favor of a restless one. This would have been, on these grounds, between 1590 and 1592, when Gosnold was eighteen or twenty.[3]

Despite the historical blank that broadly covers the years from 1592 to 1602, one isolated bit of fact testifies to some knowledge of the sea on Gosnold's part. In 1599, Bartholomew returned to England from a privateering voyage with booty valued at £1,625 17s 6d, piously hijacked from a Spanish ship at sea. This gave him funds, and possibly contributed to his determination to follow in the footsteps — in the wake, would be more nautical — of Giovanni da Verrazzano (1524) and Sir Humphrey Gilbert (1583). This also perhaps explains how and why, as the year 1602 rolls around, he seems to have planned from the outset to establish some sort of colony in what Verrazzano called "Norumbega."[4]

Yet the size of the planned colony, twenty men at the outside, raises some doubt. He may have intended only to see what location for a colony he might find and, having found a moderately satisfactory one, have determined to hold the site pending the arrival of reinforcements of men and supplies, to be sent quickly by his associate, Bartholomew Gilbert. This again is relatively unimportant. That he planned eventually to found a colony there can be no doubt. Consequently, whether the first one, the short-lived "fort" on Elizabeth's Isle, was to remain the permanent colony is immaterial.

Thus it is apparent that Gosnold deeply intended to found a colony, that he had connections, and that he found a suitable site. What, then, did he do on his return to England?

Again, the breaks in the historical records prevent a clear-cut answer. Clio, the muse of epic poetry and history, seems to have been busier keeping her first interest ship-shape than her second. Indeed, granted the gift of song, it would be much easier to write a poem about Gosnold or most of his known contemporaries than it is to put down just what happened — to record their history. To do that, we must once more weigh possibilities and probabilities, steadying the scales with such facts as we have, and then reconstruct the story according to our best lights.

Gosnold, to repeat, got to Exmouth on Friday, July 23, 1602. The next thing known about him is that he wrote at least a *second letter* (from there, or from London?) to his father by September 7th. This letter intimates that he had written immediately upon his return, and that he had already received an answer in which his father wanted to know more about him and his trip. Then, for at least three years, no record of Bartholomew Gosnold has survived, beyond the notations in a parish register that a daughter and two sons of his were baptized: Susan, apparently in his absence, on August 2, 1602; Bartholomew, on December 16, 1603; and Paul, on December 11, 1605. Let us attempt to fill in the gaps by logic.

In the first place, the documents and narratives preserved by Samuel Purchas (*Purchas His Pilgrimes*) show that two exploratory voyages were sent from England to Virginia in 1603: one, with two ships, under Captain Martin Pring and Master Robert Salterne, the latter of Gosnold's 1602 voyage; the other, with Bartholomew Gilbert as Captain, Gosnold's co-captain in 1602. The former of these voyages had thirty men and boys on one ship, and thirteen men plus one boy on the other. The latter had some sixteen men all told. The former was sent by the merchants of Bristol, under the aegis of Richard Hakluyt, had for its objective the gathering of the panacea *sassafras*, and incidentally (although not without some purposefulness) skirted parts of the Massachusetts coast "which Captaine Gosnold overshot the yeere before."[5] The latter was sent by Sir Walter Ralegh and had for its objective trade in the "southern part of Virginia," the search for the lost Roanoke colony, and the exploration of Chesapeake Bay — still known mostly if not entirely by hearsay. Why was Bartholomew Gosnold not put in charge of either of these expeditions?

In the case of Pring, his was purely a trading voyage, with some exploring. Gosnold's interest seems by that time to have

194

become concentrated on colonizing. In addition, Pring was sent out of Bristol, and all of Gosnold's mercantile contacts surely hinged on Sir Thomas Smythe, of London. Bristol did not like "East Country" interlopers. It was not *logical* for Gosnold to have any part in this at all.

In the case of Gilbert, the absence of Gosnold from the roll is perhaps even more inevitable. Sir Walter Ralegh chose Gilbert to head the voyage as an outcome of his dealings with Gilbert on the latter's return from the 1602 expedition. He had apparently originally thought of sending Samuel Mace out again, despite that Captain's failure to obey orders implicitly in 1602, but in the end sent Gilbert instead. Gilbert's record argues that he was a "good talker", and his association with the successful Gosnold expedition would have been a selling-point. Furthermore, Gilbert obviously had a more important part in that expedition than has commonly been indicated. This appears in the obscure detail that the first geographical feature discovered in 1602 was named *Gilbert's* Point, and only the second *Gosnold's* Hope — in those days, discoveries were generally named with a great eye to relative importance. Other details were that Gilbert, a neighbor of Gosnold and very likely in a sense a friend, was also "Lord Cobham's man", and Lord Cobham was still, though in even less of a sense, a friend of Sir Walter. The result was that Ralegh seems never even to have heard of Gosnold, and therefore, quite logically, could not have employed him to go to Virginia.[6]

This need not mean, however, that Gosnold was, or felt, left out of the colonization plans. The fact is that the death of Queen Elizabeth, just after Pring had started and just before Gilbert left, brought a halt to all such plans for a number of months. Royal influence on all sorts of human affairs being then immeasurably greater than a modern mentality can easily conceive, no merchant, no rich nobleman even, would have dreamed of spending money on colonial projects until the character and attitude of the new monarch from Scotland could be tested. The populace welcomed James Stuart with signs of great joy, the ministers of state sighed with relief that the difficult matter of the succession to the throne was solved without any complication. But the merchants and nobles with money to lose watched King James for a while before indulging in any extravagant gestures.

There were two basic reasons for this, from the point of view of Gosnold's career, the more important of which was probably Spain. Elizabeth had been in an undeclared but unmitigated war with Spain since 1584. James was suspected, or known, to want Peace. Peace might involve English expansionistic behavior overseas — for nearly twenty years without exception designed to harass, thwart, or rob Spain. Colonial plans must wait until James declared himself on that score.

Then there was the matter of patents. Sir Walter Ralegh held a patent on all Virginia, which in theory kept out of America south of Newfoundland all colonial entrepreneurs not authorized by him. But Sir Walter was in disfavor in certain influential circles and was most cordially disliked by one of the truly dangerous and unprincipled men in all England, Lord Henry Howard, soon to be created Earl of Northampton by King James. Howard had poisoned the ear of the new King before he ever laid eyes on Ralegh, and Ralegh was in the Tower, on pretty well trumped-up charges, even before Bartholomew Gilbert's expedition of 1603 returned to London — Gilbert himself had been killed by the Indians somewhere along the central Atlantic coast of what is now the United States.

All in all, then, it behove Gosnold to wait patiently with other colonialists until James's attitude could be known. What specifically Gosnold did, is not known. But it is likely that he profited by this inactivity to lay plans for the future on a broader and sounder base.

Then came a bit of a surprise. Ralegh being held in the Tower "for life", his un-friend (which better represents the state than "enemy"), the Earl of Southampton — highly popular with King James — entered into close association with his Roman Catholic brother-in-law, Thomas Arundell, soon to be known as Baron Arundell of Wardour. They gathered funds and a group

196

of twenty-nine mariners and adventurers and sent the now famous Waymouth voyage fleeting to the shores of New England. It was another voyage of exploration, but this time it may be that a site was being sought for a Roman Catholic colony, where English law would be less severely administered in religious matters. Whatever their real purpose, the entire group returned, filled with praise of the scenery and fertility of "north Virginia." They returned also with five Indians.

This matter may seem trivial, but Waymouth's arrival at Dartmouth with his kidnapped Indians attracted the attention of the Governor of Plymouth Fort, Sir Ferdinando Gorges, under whose jurisdiction the port of Dartmouth lay. Sir Ferdinando, though himself apathetic to the overseas will-o'-the-wisp, was the son of a first cousin of Tristram Gorges of Budockshed, who was related on his mother's side to Sir Humphrey Gilbert and Sir Walter Ralegh and was "imbued with the spirit of American discovery."[7] For that, or some even more obscure, reason, Sir Ferdinando promptly seized three of the abducted Indians for himself, and shipped the other two off to Sir John Popham, Lord Chief Justice of England. This Indian impoundment occurred shortly after Waymouth's landing, July 18, 1605.

Bartholomew Gosnold meanwhile had presumably returned to his home in Bury St. Edmunds, perhaps then twenty-five miles from Wetheringsett by country road and horse-path. Hakluyt had married for the second time in the spring of 1604 and was undoubtedly easily accessible there. (It is known that he had no curate to help him at Wetheringsett in 1603 and possibly he still had to care for his two hundred communicants in person in 1605.) Gosnold more likely than not saw something of him. Sir Thomas Smythe, fresh back from a special embassy to Boris Godunov, "Emperour, and great duke of all Russia", certainly saw him — and not only on Russian affairs. Virginia plantations were very much in the air.

But sometime before this, perhaps very early in 1605, Gosnold must have made the acquaintance of a young farmer's son from Lincolnshire named John Smith, seven or eight years

197

his junior, who had just returned from rare adventures in such unknown places as Hungary, Transylvania, Muscovy, and Morocco. Smith bore the military grade of Captain, bestowed on him by Hanns Jacob Khissl, Lieutenant Colonel of the Arsenal under Archduke Ferdinand of Styria, first-cousin of the Emperor Rudolph II.[8] Captain Smith was casting about for something to do, had some savings and some ill-gotten gains, like all adventurers of the times. He had shown his stamina by escaping from a Tatar prison-camp on the Don and returning to civilization through the unknown and virtually untrodden steppes of southern Muscovy. Captain Gosnold, of no known military experience, apparently saw in Captain Smith a potentially useful associate and began to elaborate verbally: he had plans to establish a colony among the Indians of the New World.

Smith had already given fleeting consideration to joining a relief expedition to an infant colony in Guiana, which for undisclosed reasons he failed to do. But, caught by the fire of Gosnold's enthusiasm, he reacted more than warmly to the substitute plan. He became the first "stranger" to join Gosnold's local group of friends — that is, he was unrelated and he came from "distant" Lincolnshire. (His meeting with Gosnold seems to have stemmed from Smith's landlord, Lord Willoughby, whose uncle, Sir John Wingfield, was a first cousin of Gosnold's aunt, Ursula Naunton.[9])

In later years, Smith wrote that "Captaine *Bartholomew Gosnold,* the first mover of this plantation [of Virginia], having many years solicited many of his friends, but found small assistance, at last prevailed with some Gentlemen, as Maister *Edward Maria Wingfield,* Captaine *John Smith,* and divers others, who depended a yeare upon his projects [before anything happened]...."[10] This means that by early 1605 Gosnold had already approached, and interested, his distant cousin, Edward Maria Wingfield, in his plan. (Edward was a second cousin of Richard Wingfield and Elizabeth Naunton nee Wingfield, father and mother respectively of Sir John on the one side and Ursula Naunton on the other.) But with his wife's cousin, Sir Thomas

198

Smythe, away in Muscovy, with Smythe's associates perhaps dragging their feet on account of the new King, and with Southampton suddenly setting off an expedition like a fire-cracker, neither Gosnold nor Wingfield got much beyond what would be called today "the planning stage"; nor did John Smith's appearance on the scene help materially.

At this juncture, everything happened all at once, as the saying goes. Lord Chief Justice Popham, "a huge, heavie, ugly man",[11] received his two naked Indians from America via Ply-mouth Fort, properly robed, no doubt, in his judicial scarlet. And he marvelled. Time and again, for some years past, he had bethought himself of America — of Virginia — as a place to which undesirable subjects of his Britannic Majesty might be sent, to relieve some of the current ills of the realm which he had continued to observe from the loftiness of his Bench.[12] Now that the dirty-brown, paint-bedaubed bodies of the two denizens of the Unknown Continent grovelled before him, his interest suddenly awakened. Despite his unwieldy bulk, there was nothing slow about the mind of Sir John Popham.

First Secretary Sir Robert Cecil, now created — and to be remembered as — the Earl of Salisbury, was asked to call to-gether all the many individuals who would be interested in schemes to "plant" America — with colonists, not with parsnip seed. Salisbury of course knew of the Earl of Southampton's ex-pedition of that same summer, and undoubtedly remembered the return of Gosnold and Gilbert three years before. (Ralegh's letter made sure of that.) In a word, he was not uninformed on the whole American question. Nevertheless, there had been reasons for not moving too quickly. By the time he received Popham's communication, one important aspect of colonization had cleared up notably.

King James, as everyone had almost feared (fear mixed with contrary hope), had arrived in England clothed in Peace. Scarcely had he arrived at Whitehall than he recalled the "letters-of-marque" that permitted — indeed, authorized — English priva-teers to plunder Spanish ships; and within a year and a few months of his accession to the throne had negotiated and signed a Peace Treaty with Spain. Spain had maintained the decorum of pretending to be in less of hurry to sign, but by June 15, 1605, Philip III had ratified it. Salisbury's conscience was at least clear in regard to colonies: they could legally be established under the terms of the Treaty — more accurately, there was deliberately and carefully not a single word about them there. Oddly, it had so happened that the Lord Admiral brought the Treaty, with Philip's signature, to King James only one week before Waymouth brought the Indians to Plymouth.

Sir Ferdinando Gorges, mystically stimulated by his three Indians, for the first time began to propagandize colonial ventures in America himself. More trivially, playwright Ben Jonson, aided by a couple of collaborators, produced a satire just then, on the gold-seekers who were exciting the metropolis with tales of wealth in Virginia to rival the gold of Ophir.[13] All in all, between Gorges and the Indians and Ben Jonson such an effervescence was frothed up that Gosnold almost disappeared from the scene.

But when the sober Lord Chief Justice, and the sober merchants of London and elsewhere, met with the shrewd and sober First Secretary, Salisbury, solid plans began to emerge. Sir Thomas Smythe, restored in grace and knighted by the King before he went to Muscovy, was by then one of England's leading merchant-princes. Governor of the East India Company and entrepreneur in many merchandising fields, Sir Thomas settled gradually and almost inevitably into place as the pivot on which the American plans would turn. This meant the return of Bartholomew Gosnold to a key position.

Then came catastrophe, in the form of the Gunpowder Plot. (The outbursts of plots attest the disturbed character of the age: Essex' plot in 1601, the Bye plot — involving Ralegh — in 1603, the Gunpowder plot of Guy Fawkes' fame in 1605.) It is unnecessary here to go into what or why that was, but it caused the incarceration of more than one innocent subject — among them, Henry Percy, Earl of Northumberland —

and distracted the attention of the Lord Chief Justice for some weeks. It also brought clearly before the public the cleavage between Catholics and Protestants and exacerbated the tensions and rivalries that had flourished over the religious issue since the days of Henry VIII and his first divorce. The Gunpowder Plot consequently was not merely an incident that slightly delayed Gosnold's realization of his hopes and plans to found a colony. It affected the essence of that colony, and reflected (and perhaps aggravated) the canker that almost destroyed it.

But by the time the Christmas festivities ended with Ben Jonson's masque for the marriage of the new Earl of Essex and Frances Howard, daughter of the Earl of Suffolk — mere children — and the Twelfth Night entertainment, also by Jonson, on January 6, 1606, normality had returned to England. By the end of the month the trial and execution of the plotters had passed into history. The Lord Chief Justice could return to his colonial planning. (The only possible serious obstacle — a Catholic contract of private nature arranged between Sir John Zouche and Captain Waymouth — had been washed away by the flood of anxiety loosed on November 5, "Guy Fawkes' Day.")

ii.

The charter which finally authorized Bartholomew Gosnold's long delayed "English pale" on the shores of aboriginal America was, of course, a compromise. The English have been conspicuous throughout their long history for realizing that nature abhors black and white almost as much as she abhors, proverbially speaking, a vacuum. The pastel shades are better suited to nature's works — men, for instance, are never all black or all white. So must human relations, plans, and aspirations be; some black of imperfection in the purity of white, some white of innocence in the black of depravity.

The black and white in this case were, without specifying which was which, the tradition which provided individual,

201

private monopolies to plant feudal domains across the seas, and the "socialistic" aim of the Lord Chief Justice to form royal colonies under the administration of the Crown. The end result was, to risk oversimplification, investment by private enterprise, by individuals, with the administration, or government, reserved to the Crown. It proved to be a makeshift arrangement, soon changed, but it was good enough to start the movement. English colonies so founded would be backed by men of enough wealth and political power to make the Spaniards think twice (perhaps) before moving to annihilate the colonies planned, *and* to make King James think twice (perhaps) before he backslid under Spanish pressure. Then, and it was equally important, the private investment, necessarily shored up if not quasi-guaranteed by the Crown, could supply the vast capital needed over the first few years. For the investment might well produce no returns for a long time. This private capital took the form of a joint-stock company, but it was strictly private in the sense that subscription was not, in the modern sense, open to the public.[14]

It seems on the surface ridiculous to attribute to the 1602 explorer who, "seeing his whole strength to consist but of twelve men, and they but meanly provided, determined to returne for England [from Elizabeth's Isle]" the elephantine solemnity of the final plan for colonization. Yet there is no real reason to doubt Captain John Smith's word that Bartholomew Gosnold was the "prime mover". Bartholomew moved where he could and, where he could not, other forces moved for him — even Providence, in the form of five naked Indians. Gosnold was in all probability the one Englishman of the time (discounting Ralegh, in the Tower) who combined the vision, the practicality, and the persistence, to make colonization possible. It was a fortunate accident that allied him through his marriage with a business-man of equal vision and even greater capacity for persistence.

The moving picture, then, that like the Moving Finger of Omar Khayyám writes and having writ moves on, is of a young, adventurous soul that found its goal in what was called Virginia, and never stayed nor stopped until that goal was realized. Bartholomew Gosnold, obscure would-be lawyer from a Suffolk village, became the *Deus ex machina* of that consummate planner and idealist, Richard Hakluyt, as neither Gilbert nor Ralegh, knighted for their deeds, could. He, with an even more obscure farmer's boy, planted — for all eternity — an English birthright in Virginia's virgin soil.

The historical details from here on are simple to relate. So far as Gosnold's life and activities are concerned, and to all practical purposes, the Lord Chief Justice drew up a document for the King's signature which satisfied the merchants (including Sir Thomas Smythe) and "the Crown" (including Sir Robert Cecil, Earl of Salisbury). Sir Thomas may well have had a hand in drafting it; so may Sir Francis Bacon, then soaring into fame on the rocket of his *Advancement of Learning;* so may Sir Edwin Sandys, already a great leader in the House of Commons; so may Sir Ferdinando Gorges, he of the five kidnapped Indians; so may others. The crucial matter was the final writing and the securing of the King's approval. Popham and Smythe put it through the mill. Then action once more devolved on those whose idea it really was: Gosnold and the other adventurers who would risk their lives to carry out what the charter permitted them to do.

It is unnecessary to confuse the issue here with minutiae, such as the authorizing of two separate, but overlapping, colonies — one in Gosnold's "Norumbega" (the land that waited for John Smith to name it "New England"), the other in Ralegh's "Virginia" (the North Carolina of the unsuccessful colony). West Country rivalries with London over who should get there first, and what was wrong with the plans, have no bearing on Gosnold's life. Gosnold had "found" the northern part of Virginia, but he was ready to "find" the southern part, and plant his colony there. How the mighty divided the virtually undiscovered land mattered little. The thing was to discover it, plant it, and keep it planted: no one had done that yet for England.

There is no question but it may be argued that the big merchants, nobles, and so on were more likely to have hired mariner Gosnold than that Gosnold went looking for nobles. Yet, it was so common in those days — and still is — for the Columbuses, Cabots, Verrazzanos, and Cartiers to seek support from the magnificent for their magnificent ideas that although the story *may* have been the other way around, the probabilities are against it. It is much more likely that Gosnold, having somehow obtained the backing of the Earl of Southampton and, most probably, Sir Thomas Smythe for a voyage in 1602, put a sort of pressure on Sir Thomas for another voyage — a pressure that was only delayed in its results by Sir Thomas' absence in Muscovy and by the unexpected Waymouth expedition. Delayed by the latter, but helped, for Waymouth's entirely unprincipled kidnapping of five Indians seems to have turned the trick.

Whether, for instance, Edward Maria Wingfield, Gosnold's first associate in the Virginia Venture of 1606, would himself have moved toward the promotion of an English colony in Virginia may well be doubted. Edward Maria was by a dozen years the senior of his cousin of briefer recorded genealogy. Edward Maria, judging by surviving records, had never succeeded in obtaining long-sought acres in Ireland or recompense for services in the Low Countries which resulted in his imprisonment by the Spaniards (in 1588 or so) and despite his illustrious blood he was without land or glory. However, Edward Maria had a tie with the Earl of Southampton — he was the grandson of a lady named Bridget Wiltshire by her first husband, while his first cousin Sir William (later Lord) Hervey, her grandson by her second husband, married the Earl of Southampton's widowed mother. And Southampton was interested in Virginia, and had sent young cousin Gosnold there (to the northern part). Thus Edward Maria and Bartholomew got together — like enough at the asking of the younger man. For him, an illustrious and literate figure-head would lend dignity to his expedition, if he would go along. John Smith, his old companion Archer, and others, would do the work, and gladly.

So it was that when Lord Chief Justice Popham was ready with the basic material — the Charter — Sir Thomas Smythe, with Gosnold at his elbow, was ready with the men: Richard Hakluyt as chief sponsor, and with him Edward Maria Wingfield, Sir Thomas Gates, and Sir George Somers — all "old soldiers" who were far from dying. Edward Maria Wingfield agreed to go along, perhaps with an eye to being Governor. Hakluyt, who had been offered the Chaplaincy, almost went, but sensibly gave up the idea and relinquished the job to a protégé of Wingfield's, a Robert Hunt, of more suitable age for hardships.[15] Gates and Somers remained in the wings until it was their turn to step on stage. So far as Gosnold's story is concerned, they are mere names.

On April 10, 1606, at least a year after Gosnold had really begun to work on his plans, James, by the Grace of God, King, etc., "greatly commending and graciously accepting" so noble a proposal, granted to Gates and Somers, Hakluyt and Wingfield, and divers others not named, his "license to make habitation, plantacion, and to deduce a colonie of sondrie" of his people in that part of America which was commonly called Virginia — that is to say, between the indeterminate line where Spanish influence was supposed to stop and the lands where French influence was supposed to begin. Of Gosnold, Smythe, or Smith never a word.

As has just been said in passing, King James authorized two groups of colonial entrepreneurs, one for the "north part of Virginia", the other for the "south part", the Virginia of today. Hakluyt was with the *southern* group, Popham (in the persons of members of his family) and Gorges took over the "northerners." Their story, like the eventual history of Gates and Somers, is beside the point. Gosnold, ephemeral planter in the north, joined Hakluyt's group, as was to be expected. The merchants financing the expedition gathered together — under Sir Thomas Smythe, judging by subsequent events — to provide proper government as well as the necessary funds, and the active participants set about procuring supplies and enlisting prospective colonists. In John Smith's words, "his Majestie by his letters patent, gave commission for establishing Councels, to direct

205

here, and to govern and to execute there. To effect this, was spent another yeare."[16] Well, not quite. In eight months the expedition was ready to sail.

King James was not so speedy about appointing a governing Council as Smith wrote, for the official list of members was not published until 20 November. Since someone must have been in charge in the meantime, it may be taken for granted that Sir Thomas Smythe dedicated a good bit of time to general direction. Perhaps he was aided by his associate in the East India Company, Sir William Romney, who had already shown interest in the exploration of a "Northwest Passage" to China, across the top of North America. They, or whoever was then in charge, selected ships and ship-captains; Gosnold, Wingfield and Smith busied themselves with "gentlemen" and others (laborers) to go along.

On the basis, presumably, of Ralegh's Roanoke Colony of 1587, it was determined to send three ships (a "fleet", with an Admiral in charge) and a body of roughly one hundred colonists (Ralegh had sent three ships, with about a hundred men and boys — disregarding the women. The 1606 expedition included no women at all.) To command the fleet, Captain Christopher Newport was chosen, an old hand at privateering in West Indian waters, who had left an arm there in defense of his ship.[17] Newport's Vice-Admiral was, need we say, Bartholomew Gosnold. These two were the only appointed officers of the expedition during the voyage. Upon arrival in Virginia, a permanent governing body would take over.

The third ship, which may have been the same pinnace which was Pring's second ship in 1603, was placed under the command of Captain John Sicklemore, alias Ratcliffe, who is still the most obscure figure among the leading colonists.[18]

Newport, Gosnold, and Ratcliffe, as he is more commonly known, were eventually entrusted with three copies of secret and sealed *Instructions* for the foundation and government of the Colony, not to be opened until arrival in Virginia. These *Instructions* contained the names of those appointed by the London Council to the Council of and in Virginia, which proved

cause of considerable dissent despite the fact that secrecy was
chosen just to avoid that very thing. How far Newport and
Ratcliffe influenced the choice or enlistment of other colonists
is not clear. But there is evidence that Gosnold and Smith had
a large hand in this aspect of the plans.

Here brief mention may be accorded to some of those lesser
lights in the colonial experiment, some who are known or surmised to have been relatives or friends of Bartholomew Gosnold.
In addition to his friend Gabriel Archer, Gosnold took with him
his younger brother, Anthony, and the son of his first-cousin
Robert, another Anthony, aged not over eighteen. George Gould-
ing, a laborer who went along, was also most probably a relative
— a close one, perhaps, of Bartholomew's wife, or a distant one
of Bartholomew himself.

Then there was John Asbie or Ashby — Bartholomew's
uncle Robert of Otley married a Naunton whose brother married
an Ashby. Roger Cooke, another colonist, may have been another
connection, also through the Nauntons. Robert Ford may have
belonged to the Fords of Essex into whose family Bartholomew's
cousin Robert of Langham married. Nicholas Skot or Scot may
have been connected through Bartholomew's distant cousin Sara
Carter, who married an Edward Scot, or through Sir Thomas
Smythe's sister who married Sir John Scott, a member of the
London Council in 1607. And Thomas Webbe, "Gentleman", may
have been a cousin through Bartholomew's great-aunt Alice, who
married a Thomas Webbe who had died more than half a century before.

Some or all of these may be but coincidences of surname.
No one has determined as yet who these colonists actually were.
Nevertheless, there is great probability that at least a few of
these were related as has been surmised. Gosnold's strength in the
colony was great, and it may have depended in part on the
support of the "gentlemen" among those listed above.

John Smith's direct addition to the colonists is more difficult
to assess. He stated that it cost him "many a forgotten pound to
hire men to go; and procrastination [the year-long delay] caused

more to run away than went."[19] But elsewhere he said that he with his "party" prevented attempts to abandon the colony (after Gosnold's death).[20] Clearly, John Smith had no important relatives, and his "party" was probably made up of laborers and soldiers. Yet one gentleman-colonist may be attributed to Smith, Stephen Galthorpe, who died not long after their arrival in Virginia. Stephen may possibly have been a member of the family of that name in Alford, Lincolnshire, where Smith first went to school in the days of the Spanish Armada. This family was far-flung, and included a branch in Suffolk and Norfolk to which Edward Maria Wingfield was connected by inter-family marriages. Stephen and John Smith were apparently close during the voyage out of England.

Wingfield himself claimed credit for the Chaplain, Robert Hunt, a gentle but determined man who died, aged about thirty eight, within a year of his arrival.[21] In addition, he mentioned a friend, with whom he quarrelled bitterly, Richard Crofts, possibly another connection of Gosnold's. Beyond the friendship and the quarrel, nothing certain is known of this gentleman.[22]

Of those not connected in any apparent way with Gosnold or Wingfield there was Captain John Martin, the son of Sir Richard Martin, goldsmith of London and one-time Lord Mayor. Captain John was in his forties and had a career in law and on the sea behind him. He had commanded the *Benjamin* (financed at least in part by his father) under Sir Francis Drake on the voyage that brought back the 1585-1586 Roanoke Colony of Sir Walter Ralegh. Martin's father had been in semi-disgrace over debts — by no means entirely his fault — in 1602 and 1603, and although his name was entirely cleared by 1605, this may have had something to do with the son's determination to go overseas. The deciding factor, however, was undoubtedly the prospect of gain and the fact that he had already visited the coast of America. (Martin's name is a controversial one in early American history.)

Captain George Kendall was another leader in the colony whose identity has been determined only quite recently. He apparently was in some sense in the pay of Spain, went to Vir

inia in some sense as a spy, and was caught. It is known that
e was executed for treason — the first Englishman to have
hat unenviable distinction in North America so far as is known.[23]
Kendall was a continual trouble-brewer, who took advantage
f petty factions among the colonists to promote his own aims,
which might well merit the old-fashioned adjective "sinister."

Last in this list, but first in social standing, was George
Percy, youngest brother of Henry Percy, ninth Earl of Northum-
erland, and scion of one of the most blue-blooded families in
Britain. George was not quite a year younger than John Smith,
nd appears to have joined the expedition for two reasons: his
brother was involved in the Gunpowder Plot and incarcerated
n the Tower since the end of 1605, and George was apparently
red of whatever he himself had been doing in Ireland for some
ittle time. It is likely that, in 1606, he sought independent means
nd some small glory for himself across the seas.

Casting an eye very briefly on the future, we may add almost
parenthetically that a Thomas Sands, "Gentleman", went along,
whose only importance, if any, was that he may possibly have
een a brother of both Sir Edwin Sandys — perhaps second
nly to Sir Thomas Smythe in the London end of the Virginia
enture — and George Sandys, outstanding member of the Vir-
inia Colony in the 1620's.[24]

These, along with a handful of gentlemen whose only reason
or joining the expedition was as ex-adventurers in Ireland or
he Low Countries, or would-be adventurers in America, consti-
uted the company drawn together by the efforts of Gosnold,
is "cousin" Sir Thomas Smythe, his real cousin Wingfield, and
is friend Captain John Smith. It is anyone's guess who the re-
aining unidentified colonists were.

As the preparations neared completion, King James issued
document interminably entitled (as was the custom of the day)
*rticles, Instructions and orders, sett down and established by
s the twentieth day of November* [1606] . . ., and so on, in which
e appointed a group of knights and merchants to form the
he already-mentioned King's Council, or London Council, for

Virginia, and outlined nearly forty basic principles for the func
tioning of the colony.[25]

Three weeks later, on December 10th, the Council in que:
tion issued its first orders, in which the ships for the expeditio
were named, and the powers and responsibilities of Newpor
Gosnold and Ratcliffe outlined.[26] Simultaneously, or very short
thereafter, further *Instructions by way of advice* were issued b
the Council, "to be observed by those Captains and compan
which are sent at this present to plant there."[27] And all was read
Nine days later the fleet sailed.

iii.

It is idle to speculate on the details of embarkation. Samu
Purchas' often quoted marginal note on the subject states tha
71 were aboard the *Susan Constant*, 52 on the *God Speed*, and 2
on the *Discovery*, making a total of 144.[28] There is no more wa
of knowing, however, whether this figure includes sailors as we
as colonists than of determining what passengers were on whic
ship. Nevertheless, it may be surmised that Edward Maria Wing
field sailed on the *Susan Constant*, since he was the only patente
of the company to go on the expedition and, with the exceptio
of George Percy, Esq., the ranking member according to th
strict social scale of the day. And it may be guessed, from wha
happened on the voyage, that Captain John Smith was on th
same ship.

The fleet was grimly detained by contrary winds for nearl
six weeks in the Downs, a part of the North Sea off the coa:
of Kent which is protected by Goodwin Sands. This well-nig
insufferable delay made many of the company ill, and Hur
almost despaired of his life. All of them it made irritable. An
when they at last got away, the seeds of strife were well plante
on all three ships.

Judging by surviving records, trouble broke out most ser:
ously between Edward Maria Wingfield and John Smith. Wing

ield was an "esquire", a gentleman by birth, Smith, a farmer's
boy. Smith, however, had been made a Captain for valor in the
field in Hungary. This made him feel the equal of anybody with
the same or lesser military title, especially since they were all
off on an expedition in which merely social strata might be assumed to be rearranged according to merit or function rather
than birth. Wingfield, unquestionably, was not aware that anything could change the status conferred by the latter. Consequently it was only a matter of time until there were words
between the two which could not be tolerated by the gentleman-
by-birth. By the time the fleet left the Canaries, perhaps toward
the end of the third week in February, 1607, Smith was "restrained as a prisoner" — on fabricated accusations of "concealing an intended mutiny", demonstrably made by Wingfield,
for that born-gentleman was later fined £200 for slander. This
unpleasant situation persisted through the rest of the voyage
and for six and a half weeks thereafter. Smith seems to have
borne his "restraint" with considerable dignity, perhaps sustained
by the thought that George Percy's noble brother was equally
unjustly "restrained" in the Tower at the same time.

When the fleet arrived off Cape Henry on 26 April, the
secret *Instructions* were opened and read, as ordered by the
London Council. According to these, that body had appointed
the following colonists to act as local governing body, or Council,
in Virginia: Captain Christopher Newport (ex officio as Admiral), Master Edward Maria Wingfield, Captain Bartholomew
Gosnold, Captain John Smith, Captain John Ratcliffe, Captain
John Martin, and Captain George Kendall. Wingfield, who ought
to have known that Smith's name was on the list — it can hardly
have been a secret — was patently furious.

The Council promptly held a meeting, as required by the
Instructions, and elected Wingfield its first President, which was
to be expected in view of his age, blue-blood, and dignity.
Wingfield thereupon refused to swear Smith in as a Councillor.
But Newport, from the outset an obedient servant of the London
Company above all and otherwise a fair and moderate arbitrator

211

rather than a commander, delayed all swearing-in, in the hope, perhaps, that hot heads would cool off. He seems to have persuaded the Council to postpone the ceremony until they found a place to settle, and then, when the place was found and Wingfield still refused to administer the oath to Smith, after all the others had been sworn in, he took Smith with him up the James River. His objective was, in obedience to the *Instructions* of course, to see what potential enemies might be lurking above them, as well as what potential food-supplies there might be, mines, and other potentialities. Archer, Percy, and the colony's surgeon — probably also a botanist — went along, but Smith's part in the expedition seems clearly to have some connection with the "intended mutiny" and Wingfield's obduracy. As for that dignitary, he stayed on the admiral's ship, tied close to shore at the new-born colony Jamestown, in company with Gosnold and Ratcliffe and their ships and men.

At first, Wingfield refused to fortify Jamestown, for reasons which may best be labelled "arcane" — a word which may perhaps convey the utter inexplicability of his action. Only with difficulty did Kendall manage to get permission to surround the settlement with "boughs of trees cast together in the forme of a halfe moone", to afford some sort of security. But before Newport, Smith, Percy, and Archer got back, the Indians attacked. This was Wingfield's first serious mistake in "presidential policy."

The attack occurred on Tuesday, May 26th. Newport and his group of explorers returned on Wednesday. Thursday — one wonders if at Newport's insistence — all went to work "palisading" their fort with a strong wooden fence. Friday the Indians came again, but kept out of musket-shot reach. There followed a brief respite until Sunday, when one of the gentlemen, Eustace Clovell, was shot full of arrows, while straggling outside the palisade. He died a week later.

This almost uninterrupted Indian prowling made it clear that, despite Wingfield's stand, the colony was not what could be called at peace with the aborigines, adding this danger to Gosnold's original dislike of the site. (Wingfield had chosen the place and had refused to be budged, causing "some contention" be-ween him and Gosnold two weeks before.)[29] June began with another, minor, attack, followed on June 4th by further skulking and pot-shots with arrows. Clearly the situation demanded radi-cal treatment.

The only strictly military man known to have been among the colonists, if the uncertain and in any case much earlier serv-ces of Wingfield and Martin are excluded, was Captain Smith. At this juncture, those who always supported him, along with some who were perhaps not so steadily friendly, began an ener-getic protest against his continued state of virtual ostracism. Smith undoubtedly was glad to cooperate. By Saturday, June 6th, a petition had been drawn up and presented to the Council for reformation of "certayne preposterous proceedings, and in-convenyent Courses", as the official *Relation* put it. (Gabriel Archer almost certainly was the author.)[30]

The following Wednesday, moved by Admiral Newport, the Council considered the petition and a great stir was made to bring harmony and "uniformity of Consent" back to the Colony. In the end, and on that day, the official account reports: "Cap-taine *Smyth* was . . . sworn one of the Counsell, who was elected in England." Thus John Smith began his true, and loyal, service to America.

By then, Newport had decided that he must return to Eng-land. He had already stayed away longer than the King's Council had wanted — he was supposed to have been back by the end of May, "if God permit" — although part of the delay had been unavoidable from the very outset, due to the North Sea. Never-theless, it behoved him to start back, and about a week after Smith's admission to the Council he called on President Wing-field. He wanted to ask how Wingfield "thought himself settled in government." Wingfield answered "that no disturbance could indaunger him or the Collonye, but it must be wrought eyther by Captaine *Gosnold,* or Master *Archer;* for the one was strong with friendes and followers, and could if he would; and the other was troubled with an ambitious spirit, and would if he could." This indicates that all was not entirely harmonious between Gosnold and Wingfield, as has been said, and it was the first intimation of Archer's potential danger to the peace of Jamestown.

Newport then, curiously, informed both Gosnold and Archer of precisely what the President thought, "and moved them, with many intreatyes, to be myndefull of their dutyes to his Majestie and the Collonye."[31] "Curiously", since Gosnold surely had no intention of overthrowing Wingfield — almost certainly the first man he chose to go with him on the voyage: such a piece of advice would have tended more to arouse suspicion than to allay a feeling that did not exist; while any information given to Archer to the effect that Wingfield was afraid of him would only make matters worse. But Newport was that sort of man, and it was by that very token that the mutual respect which seems to have existed between him and John Smith was doomed, as further evidences of silly, however dutiful, actions became manifest. This is part of Smith's story, however, not of Gosnold's.

The following Monday, June 22nd, Newport sailed on the *Susan Constant*, taking the *God Speed* with him, and leaving only Ratcliffe's pinnace *Discovery* with the colony. On his departure he promised, rather unrealistically, to be back with supplies, and more colonists, within twenty weeks.[32] Considering that it had taken him eighteen weeks to get to Virginia and he would need at least four or five to return to England, the promise was rash, no matter how "unusual" their difficulties had been. Then, no one could predict how long it would take him to "turn around": report to the King's Council — Heaven deliver him from the delays of reporting to the King in person! — load supplies and colonists, and get past the Downs once more. It was not so much that Newport's estimate was unrealistic in this sense, it was worse. It was highly unpolitic, for it encouraged a very large segment of the colonists to rely for supplies on his return, instead of starting off with a will to take care of themselves.

John Smith reported that the day before Newport sailed, the Chief of the Pamunkey tribe sent an emissary to promise

214

the colonists peace, which is an unimportant detail since it cannot be regarded as a sincere gesture — the Chief's record is mute testimony to that. But this item in a very sketchy record serves as a spring-board for Smith to add that the fort was by then properly fortified and all the men in good health, although, because of "some" discontent, "it did not so long continue." Why? Because

. . . the President and Captaine Gosnold, with the rest of the Counsell, being for the moste part discontented with one another, in so much, that things were neither carried out with that discretion [that was demanded] nor any business effected in such good sort as wisdom would, nor our owne good and safetie required.[33]

Nevertheless, the colony settled down to some sort of routine. The only surviving account of what went on, that of Captain John Smith which was so bungled on its way to the press that it is at times almost incomprehensible, has no further word of Indian visits, of attempts at trading with the Indians, or of any rational behavior by anybody. All that emerges is that Newport did have some sort of authority, that Wingfield had none, that he and Gosnold were at odds, and that nearly everybody was sick — mostly from lack of food, but partly from maintaining a continuous watch and ward for attacks by the savages. The only Councillor mentioned for good is Martin, who was too weak and too sick to accomplish much. Thus the stifling July days dragged on, poisoning the colonists morally and physically with its muggy heat, its jungle-bred fear, and its alternate starvation and overeating — the latter when a big sturgeon was caught. Not even Gosnold was a hero then.

Then came August, and on the first or second day of that tragic month, Gosnold's "discontent" and apathy worsened into palpable distemper. In short, he fell seriously sick. A few days later, George Asbie or Ashby died, "of the bloudie flixe" — dysentery. A deadly epidemic had broken out.

The second week of August started with the death of George Flower, probably the Captain Flower of campaigns in

215

Ireland, to be followed the next day by William Bruster, or Brewster, "of a wound given by the Savages." Bruster had just sent a letter to Salisbury, by way of Newport's ship, telling the Secretary that Virginia was "the most statlye, Riche Kingdom in the woorld, nevar posseste by anye Christian prynce."[34] But sickness took a greater toll than the Indians, four, that are known, that week.

The third week was the most tragic yet, perhaps the most tragic of all. Unaided by Indian arrows, Sunday, Monday, Tuesday, and Wednesday each claimed a life, among them that of Captain Martin's son. Then came two days of respite, to bury the dead, and then the blow, from which the colony did not recover for many a month. On Saturday, August 22, 1607, death claimed Captain Bartholomew Gosnold.

Gosnold had been sick for three weeks, as had many others. Scurvy and dysentery were the chief complaints — certainly not malaria, for the symptoms were different. Typhoid fever possibly had its share in pestilence too. And there was hunger, always, made all the more pernicious by unaccustomed diet when there was food, so that George Percy wrote, "For the most part, they [those who died] died of mere famine."[35] The specific cause of Gosnold's lingering death is not known.

During his illness, however, and possibly because he realized that it would be fatal, Gosnold called Edward Maria Wingfield into his tent, along with John Smith. It was an attempt to bring peace between the President and the man who already by then was obviously emerging as the strong man of the colony. While he was alive, Captain Gosnold had been able to maintain a sort of truce between them. With death lurking just around the flap of his tent, he sought to heal the quarrel.

But Wingfield would not, could not, bend. Master Smith, he intoned to the sick Captain, had spread a rumor in the colony, when food was at its scarcest, that he, Wingfield, feasted himself and his servants and associates out of the colony store. This was done, he added — to use his own words — "with intent (as I gathered) to have stirred the discontented company against

216

me." Then he turned to Smith and told him, before Gosnold, "indeed, I had cased half a pinte of pease to be sodden [boiled] with a piece of pork, of my own provision, for a poore old man, which in a sickness (whereof he died) he much desired." And after adding that if Smith "had given it out otherwise", he had lied, the true cause of Wingfield's dislike of Smith burst out. With aristocratic spleen, he charged, "It was proved to his [Smith's] face, that he begged in Ireland like a rogue, without a lycence. To such I would not my name should be a companyon."[36]

Smith seems to have muttered something about their being equal as members of the Council and to have returned the insult by saying that he would disdain to have his serving-man for Wingfield's companion if they were in England.[37] But the account is indeed obscure here and it is difficult to determine who said what and when. Here, in any case, was a social upstart rising in rebellion against the blue-blooded order of things — a man who had fought for his life against all odds, murdering a slave-labor-camp boss to gain freedom, looking down on a man who had always had some sort of protection or preferred treatment because of chance birth into a family that counted many knights and many noble marriages under its broad genealogical branches. Gosnold's appeal for peace between them failed, because of his cousin's unyielding sense of superiority. And within a few days he was gone. Perhaps his own helplessness in the boiling-pot of dissension that was Jamestown contributed to his weakness, his inability to resist disease.

The colony, with proper instinct for the man they had lost, honorably buried Bartholomew Gosnold, shattering the silence of the primeval forest with the crackle of volleys of small shot and the thunder of the discharge of all the ordnance in Jamestown Fort.

Somewhere under the soil of Jamestown, perhaps near the statue of John Smith gazing out over the James River, lies the body of him who failed to plant a bit of England in New England, only to succeed in Virginia. He did not live to see it through its most trying times — John Smith and George Percy did that. But Gosnold's spirit survived, and for many years no one regarded any other man as the prime mover in the establishing of what is now the United States of America than Captain Bartholomew Gosnold.

NOTES

1. WFG refers to Richard Hakluyt's *Divers voyages touching the discoverie of America* (London, 1582), last sheet of Sig. A and beginning of Sig. B. This volume is relatively rare, but the original text, as he mentions, can be found in Hakluyt, *Voyages,* viii, 430-436. The spelling *Verrazzano* has been adopted here, since it is that used in Italian encyclopedias, and by Dr. Lawrence C. Wroth in his study of "The Verrazzano Voyages," now approaching completion under the auspices of the John Pierpont Morgan Library, New York City. (Information obtained personally by the editor from Dr. Wroth.)

2. Verrazzano's latitudes are remarkably accurate for the time. Rome lies in 41° 54' north, Providence, Rhode Island, in 41° 50'. The mouth of the "Haven" (Narragansett Bay) is roughly 41° 30'. As to "half a league broad", this is roughly correct, considering that it is not known whether Verrazzano's "league" was equal to four (probably) or three modern statute miles, or which entrance to the Bay he meant.

3. WFG left a sketch for a note regarding the name *Norumbega,* in which he began an attempt to analyze its meaning. According to Fannie Hardy Eckstorm, *Indian Place-Names of the Penobscot Valley and the Maine Coast* (Orono, Maine, 1941), p. 15, "it is good Indian with several possible meanings." Mrs. Eckstorm's study is so near to being "definitive" that one hardly need search further. Although just what the word meant cannot be determined, it served as a name for the neighborhood of Narragansett for years. As WFG correctly pointed out, we may "assume . . . that these [European] explorers took this to be the name of a large territory, whereas the fact of the matter is, so far as the evidence goes, the eastern Algonquians had no names for territories, beyond the names of the local sachemships." (Gookin *Archives,* "Misc. Notes.") [Note: It should be observed that Sigmund Diamond, in "Norumbega: New England Xanadu", *The American Neptune* XI (1951), pp. 96-97, mentions the conclusions of W. F. Ganong, a thoroughly sound Canadian scholar, that the name Norumbega "in all probability" has some European word as its source. Dr. Ganong had died before Mrs. Eckstorm finished her work, however, and the editor is inclined to accept her statements as against his — much earlier — conclusions.]

4. WFG's treatment of the attitude of the Indians toward gold is a trifle cavalier. According to Dudley T. Easby, Jr., recognized authority on pre-Columbian gold-work: "The Indians of the New World, who had no concept of coinage or monetary value, prized gold for its beauty and rarity, and used it for ornaments and decoration wherever it was readily available in the form of nuggets or dust in stream beds. California seems to be the

only region in which it was plentiful but not used. Gold imported from elsewhere in America was worked by the Indians in Florida. Its use to make beautiful objects all the way from Mexico to Peru is well-known. Indeed, the contrast in attitude toward gold between Indian and European is underlined by the self-evident fact that throughout that region hunger for gold quickly became the *primum mobile* of the Spanish Conquest." (Personal communication to the editor, dated 28 October 1961.)

5. Dr. John Dee (1527-1608), mathematician and geographer (and astrologer!), was a friend of Hakluyt, as WFG pointed out. His map of America, including *Norombega*, (1580) shows Verrazzano's Bay, but no river bearing his own name. For this detail, see Fulmer Mood, "Narragansett Bay and Dee River, 1583," *Rhode Island Historical Society Collections,* XXVIII, No. 4, pp. 97-100, mentioned in Quinn, *Gilbert,* p. 63n, which is the definitive study of Sir Humphrey Gilbert.

6. Hayes' account was, as stated by WFG, reprinted in 1600, and can be found in Hakluyt, *Voyages,* viii, 34-77. [Note that the spelling of *principal* was *principall* in the 1589 edition.]

7. Gosnold's letter to his father is in Purchas, *Pilgrimes,* xviii, 300-302.

8. Christopher Carlile's [*sic*] *Discourse* is in Hakluyt, *Voyages,* viii, 134-147.

9. The relationship can best be shown graphically:

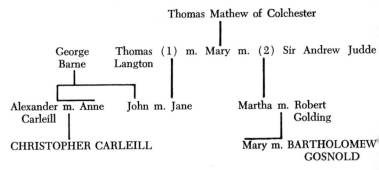

10. Sir George Peckham's *True Report* is in Hakluyt, *Voyages,* viii, 89-131. The quoted passage is on pp. 122-123.

CHAPTER II

1. A. L. Rowse, *The England of Elizabeth* (New York, 1951) p. 21.

2. It would be the sixth generation if the generation of the original purchaser of the site is counted.

3. See *Shakespeare's England* (Oxford, 1917), ii, 77.

4. For the presumed year of Bartholomew's birth, see WFG's *Who Was Bartholomew Gosnold? WMQ*, VI (1949), 400.

5. The relationship, such as it was, is shown below:

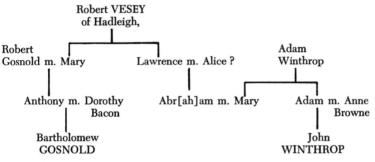

6. Quoted from Collins' *Peerage of England* (London, 1812) in WFG, *Ancestry*, p. 11. It should be noted that 23 Elizabeth comprised the regnal year 17 November 1580 to 16 November 1581. The expedition did not sail until 11 June 1583, or 25 Elizabeth. Cf. Quinn's *Gilbert* (Chapter I, note 5, above), p. 396.

7. For the bed, see WFG's *Ancestry*, p. 11.

8. These involved relationships can be summarized in three tables:

I. Descent of the Earls of Oxford.

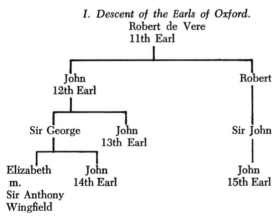

II. Descent of Elizabeth Vere and Her Husband
Sir Anthony Wingfield

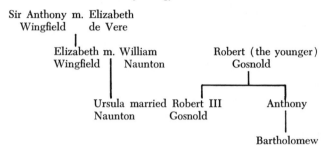

Sir Anthony m. Elizabeth
Wingfield   de Vere

Elizabeth m. William   Robert (the younger)
Wingfield | Naunton   Gosnold

Ursula married Robert III   Anthony
Naunton   Gosnold

Bartholomew

III. Descent of John de Vere, 2nd-Cousin of Elizabeth
and Her Brother, John 14th Earl of Oxford

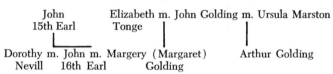

John   Elizabeth m. John Golding m. Ursula Marston
15th Earl   Tonge | |

Dorothy m. John m. Margery (Margaret)   Arthur Golding
Nevill   16th Earl   Golding

Elizabeth Wingfield, the mother of Bartholomew Gosnold's aunt Ursula, was thus the third-cousin of John (de) Vere, 16th Earl of Oxford, who married Margery (or Margaret) Golding. Their son was Edward Vere, 17th Earl of Oxford. Bartholomew Gosnold's wife was Mary Golding, who must have been related to Margery and Arthur Golding (shown above), but the exact relationship has not yet been established. She was probably descended from a cadet branch of the family which was "forgotten" when the Goldings whirled into social prominence through the Golding-Vere marriage.

9. The record reads that Anthony had performed "long and hard service for many years together [in Virginia] in the condition of a Servant [i.e., employee, perhaps a steward of someone's estate], notwithstanding he ought to have been free." Record of a meeting held in Jamestown colony 31 October 1621 (*The Records of the Virginia Company of London*, edited by Susan Myra Kingsbury [Washington, 1906], i, 542).

10. The will provided that he could take possession of the property 21 years after the execution of the will, in 1559 (WFG, *Ancestry*, p. 11).

11. For the tie between the Bacons and the Gosnolds, see WFG, *Ancestry*, pp. 19-20.

12. The Manor of Cleves, like that of Burgh, extended through Burgh and Grundisburgh and other villages. The chief item of interest, not stressed by WFG, would appear to be Bartholomew's association with his father in

the purchase of land at the age of eighteen, and only two years after his matriculation at Cambridge. At the same time a legal item dated 9 February 1592 describes Bartholomew as "late of New Inn", which belonged to the Middle Temple law "school". These are among the very few references to Bartholomew's life which have survived. (See WFG, *Ancestry*, p. 7.) The notation from 1589 is in the *Feet of Fines*, Suffolk, Easter 31 Elizabeth, transcribed for WFG by Miss Lilian J. Redstone, of Woodbridge, Suff. [A *foot of a fine* was one of the parts of a tripartite indenture recording the particulars of a fine, or final agreement, which remained with the court. The *Feet of Fines* book has its modern equivalent in files of carbon copies, duly attested.]

13. This is Miss Redstone's summation of what happened. It is worth adding that the King's Bench Prison was reputed "the most desirable place of incarceration of debtors in England." (Thomas Allen, *History and Antiquities of London* [London, 1827-1828], quoted in *An Encyclopedia of London*, edited by William Kent [London, 1937], p. 528.)

14. East Suffolk County Council, *Deposited Records 51/2/27*, "Court Book of the Manor of Cleeves, No. 1", transcribed by Miss Redstone for WFG.

15. Letter of John More to William Trumbull, 9 November 1609, reporting the return of ships from Virginia. (Historical MSS Commission, *MSS of Marquess of Downshire*, II, p. 126.)

16. See WFG, *Who Was B. Gosnold*, p. 400, and note 8.

17. Personal communication of Mr. Partridge to WFG, of 1949 [?]. Original now apparently lost.

18. Words put by Shakespeare in the mouth of the Duke of Buckingham. *Henry VIII*, Act I, scene i, line 138.

CHAPTER III

1. The text has not been altered, although it is difficult to say just what WFG meant. The Wingfields, for example, who had a strain or two of the blood royal in their veins, would hardly have considered Mary Golding "above" them.

2. The reference is to David Elisha Davy (1769-1851), a noted antiquary who left a great body of manuscripts on Suffolk genealogy, and so on, now in the British Museum. This item is from B.M. Add. MS. 19086, fol. 310 (No. 38), and was communicated to WFG by Miss Lillian J. Redstone.

3. WFG, *Ancestry*, p. 17.

4. All these details are described in WFG, *Ancestry*, pp. 15, 13, 21.

5. The editor has not seen fit to tamper with the text, although there seems to be some doubt as to the exact identity of the John Gosnold who sold the manor. The records are confused, and the text here is in accordance with WFG's analysis of them. (Sources: *Genealogical Gleanings among the English Archives*, by J. Henry Lea, NEHGR lvi (1902), p. 403; Davy's *Notes* to the "Pedigree of the Gosnold Family", B.M. Add. MS. 19133 [see note 2, above]; Davy's *Notes* to the "Manors of Suffolk," Carlford Hundred, Add. MS. 19086, reported to WFG by Miss Redstone; and W. A. Copinger, *Manors of Suffolk* [London, 1905-1911], ii, 283-284 [also see note 7 below].) In any case, the point that the Ungles and Gosnolds were related in Bartholomew's day is correct.

6. This was not the uncle who "was a failure in life", but Bartholomew's father's next-younger brother, born about 1537 or 1538 (WFG *Ancestry*, p. 11). Unfortunately, the background material connecting the story of the first John Gosnold of Coddenham with the second one (Bartholomew's uncle) was set aside, along with other items apparently, for WFG's planned study of "The Gosnolds of Coddenham" (WFG, *Ancestry*, pp. 7 and 11), which was never written, and the notes have not been found. All mention in WFG's printed works of this branch of the family refers to the missing study, not to primary sources consulted.

7. W. A. Copinger, *Manors* (see note 5, above), ii, 284, quoting James Conder, *MS of Suffolk Families*. Copinger says that Robert was not Governor, but chief military officer.

8. Barnabe Riche left a book called *Riche his Farewell to Militarie profession* (London, 1581) which provided Shakespeare and other dramatists with play-material, notably Shakespeare's *Richard III, Romeo and Juliet,* and *Twelfth Night*. See the preface to the modern edition issued by the Shakespeare Society (London, 1846).

9. The basic source for this is in Hist. MSS. Comm., *Salisbury* [or *Hatfield House*] *MSS*, Part XVI (London, 1933), pp. 319-322, 375 and 447, and Part XVIII (London, 1940), p. 190. See also WFG, *Notes*, pp. 313-314.

10. WFG's analysis of the reasons for Scrivener's appointment to posts of authority may be supplemented by reference to the fact that young Matthew (not much over twenty-one in 1607 [WFG, *Notes*, VMHB lvii, 312]) invested £100 in the Virginia Venture — the largest amount paid in by anyone who went in person to Virginia prior to the 1609 Charter. It might well seem that Matthew's large investment had a great deal to do with his position in the infant colony.

11. See WFG, *Ancestry*, p. 13.

12. For further details, see WFG, *Notes*, VMHB lvii, pp. 311-313.

13. Copinger, *Manors*, ii, 283.

14. WFG, *Ancestry*, pp. 16-17. The relationship, including Lady Dorothy Stafford mentioned in Chapter IV, is best shown by the table here given:

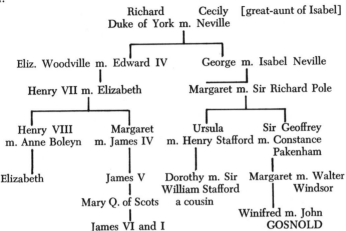

15. WFG, *Ancestry*, pp. 16-17.

16. WFG, *Ancestry*, p. 13.

17. WFG, *Ancestry*, p. 17. (The reference should be corrected, however, to read "King James in 1623", instead of "King Charles in 1623." James did not die until 1625.) The quotation is from the *Calendar of State Papers, Domestic. James I. 1623-1625* (London, 1859), p. 109 (Item 20).

CHAPTER IV

1. WFG's sources for these stories have not yet been found. They read like "modern" interpretations of what went on, and in the case of the threat of the French King (resulting in alarm for Elizabeth) they appear on the surface highly suspect. William Camden's contemporary account of some such doings reads in one place: "The Queen's women . . . wailed, and . . . did so vex her mind with anguish [distress], that she spent the night in doubtfull care without sleepe, amongst her women which did nothing but weepe." (William Camden, *Annales: or The History of . . . Elizabeth*, 3rd ed. London, 1635, p. 235.)

2. This anecdote is recounted by Lytton Strachey, *Elizabeth and Essex* (New York, 1928), p. 143. According to Sir Robert Naunton, Elizabeth's "wonted oath" was *God's death*. That it was considered rather violent in her own time is shown by its appearance, but once, in watered-down form, in Shakespeare's *Coriolanus*, I, i, 221: "And I know not — 'Sdeath!' "

3. On Hakluyt at Oxford, see E. G. R. Taylor, *Late Tudor and Early Stuart Geography, 1583-1650* (London, 1934), p. 3. For further reading regarding Hakluyt, George Bruner Parks' *Richard Hakluyt and the English Voyages* (New York, 1930) is indispensable.

4. See *Letters and Memorials of State*, by Arthur Collins (London, 1746), ii (2), 298.

5. Hakluyt, *Letters*, ii, 366.

6. Hakluyt, *Voyages*, i, xxxii.

7. Hakluyt, *Letters*, ii, 211-326.

8. Hakluyt, *Letters*, ii, 240.

9. Hakluyt, *Letters*, ii, 265.

10. Hakluyt, *Letters*, ii, 313.

11. Hakluyt, *Letters*, ii, 319, and the Italian original, p. 226.

12. Hakluyt, *Life*, p. 248.

13. Copinger, *Manors*, iii, 330-331.

14. *Brockford [cum Wetheringsett] Court Rolls* (East Suffolk County Council), 51/10/14.1, and other transcripts made for WFG by Miss Redstone. (Gookin Archives, "Redstone Reports".)

15. It is perhaps worth adding to WFG's observations the fact that two members of the Cage family, neighbors and connections of the Bacons and the Gosnolds, were interested in Sir Walter Ralegh's Roanoke Colony before Hakluyt moved to Wetheringsett, and one of them died in Virginia with the 1587 expedition. See Quinn, *Roanoke*, i, 194, and ii, 540, and Part III, note 2, below.

16. See Hakluyt, *Life*, pp. 205-206, for a slightly dissenting view. WFG was certain that Hakluyt at one time thought of going to Virginia. George Bruner Parks seems to be of the opinion that he was not expected to go himself, but to send a younger man, the Rev. Robert Hunt, in his place.

CHAPTER V

1. There are four ways to spell the name. This spelling has been preferred because it is the one used in the biography of *Sir Andrew Judde*, by H.S. Vere Hodge (privately printed, 1953, p. 3).

2. The key to all this is found in a letter from F. G. Emmison, County Archivist, County of Essex, to WFG, dated 23 October 1947. (Gookin Archives, "From England".)

3. Gates (spelled Cates) was responsible for publishing the first account of the Drake expedition (London, 1589), which was reprinted by Hakluyt in 1600 (Hakluyt, *Voyages*, x, 97-134 for the account, and x, 98 and 134 for the names). WFG obtained some of his information also from Brown, *Genesis*, "Brief Biographies", under the various names.

4. Charles Wriothesley's *Chronicle*, cited in Fane Lambarde's "Sir Andrew Judde", Archaeologia Cantiana, Vol. XLIII (1931), pp. 99-101.

5. WFG has oversimplified the matter. The sources of the fortune of Thomas Smythe the younger were far more complex than such a statement would indicate. Regrettably no thorough study of Sir Thomas seems to have been published. As for the spelling *Smythe,* it appears on "Mr. Customer's" tomb in Ashford Church, Kent, and appears preferable, although others have it Smith, Smithe, and Smyth. The spelling chosen here has the additional advantage of differentiating this family from other Smiths of contemporary fame — including Captain John Smith.

6. Here WFG seems overhesitant regarding Sir Thomas's position. He was active head of the Virginia Company, with the title of Treasurer, from May 1609 to May 1619, and there can be no doubt that he was virtually that from "very early", if not from the beginning. See Wesley Frank Craven, *The Virginia Company of London 1606-1624* ("Jamestown Booklet", Williamsburg, Virginia, 1957), pp. 3, 18. The reason for his active interest is briefly sketched in the same study, p. 10.

7. H. S. Vere Hodge, *Sir Andrew Judde* p. 82.

8. Alfred B. Beaven, *The Aldermen of the City of London, Temp. Henry III — 1912* (London, 1913), transcripts in Gookin Archives, "From England".

9. P.C.C., 5 Montague, photostat furnished by Somerset House, London, to WFG (Gookin Archives, "Wills".)

10. WFG's picturesque statement is borne out by the fact that Sir Thomas Smythe had apparently forgotten where his grandfather lived less

than fifty years after the old gentleman died — Sir Andrew's house was "rather insignificant for a man of his wealth and position." (Vere Hodge, as above, p. 68).

11. For a fuller exposition, see WFG, *Family Connections*, p. 29.

12. In a personal communication from Francis A. Foster, long associated with WFG in his work, to the editor, it appears that WFG continued to believe in the identification up to the time of his death, but was never able to find substantiating proof.

13. The source of this comparison has not been found, and it seems exaggerated. Sir William Foster, one-time Historiographer to the India Office, does not accord Sir Thomas such pre-eminence. That Sir Thomas had a high opinion of *himself*, however, cannot be doubted — he sent a portrait of himself to Jahangir, Emperor of India, as a mark of his favor! (H. R. Fox Bourne, *English Merchants* [London, 1886], p. 220.)

14. By "all of America" WFG undoubtedly meant "north of Florida." See WFG, *Capawack*, for further details.

CHAPTER VI

1. Daniel Defoe, *A Tour through England and Wales*, Everyman's Library edition, i, 49. Shakespeare, following Holinshed, makes Bury St. Edmunds the scene of one of the last phases of the struggle between King John and the barons (*King John*, IV, iii, 11, and V, iv, 18).

2. The details are to be found in WFG, *Family Connections*, p. 29.

3. This passage is virtually a reprint of WFG, *Family Connections*, pp. 30-31, which see.

4. This is partially supported by Captain John Smith's statement: "The *Captaines* charge is to commaund all, and tell the Maister to what Port he will go . . ." (Smith, *Works*, p. 789). Gosnold, however, had had experience at sea, as has been discovered since WFG wrote this passage. See Part III, footnote 4.

5. This is somewhat exaggerated. Archer is not specifically stated to have been in command of the ship he sailed in (Smith, *Works*, p. xcv); the phrase "graced by the title of . . ." is ambiguous, and may mean that they pretended authority over the passengers because Sir Thomas Gates had

been — temporarily — lost at sea; and Archer may have learned something about navigation when he sailed with Gosnold in 1602.

6. Although this is stated to be "known," it may be questioned whether Essex and Sir Thomas were *friends*. WFG apparently bases his idea on an episode in the Essex affair of February, 1601, which does not necessarily point to any kind of intimacy between the earl and the plutocrat.

7. *STC* [Wing], 1312.

8. Copied from the published copy in WFG, *Family Connections*, pp. 31-32. The photostat of the original will mentioned there has unfortunately disappeared, but the transcript of the registered copy in the Sudbury Archives (Steven, 203) does not differ materially in text. (Gookin Archives, "Golding Wills".)

CHAPTER VII

1. John Smith's *Description* first appeared in 1616. It was reprinted by the Massachusetts Historical Society in 1837 and by Peter Force in the following year. A new "edition" of it was printed by William Veazie in Boston, 1865, and in that same year it was listed in Collier's "Rarest Books in the English Language." Since then it has been published in the editions of Smith's complete *Works* initiated by Edward Arber in 1884, with reprints issued in 1895 and 1910. This relatively "frequent" republishing (to which a few translations must be added) is accounted for by the fact that Smith's was an account of a voyage performed. Hayes' "boost for New England", as Professor Quinn calls it, was a prospectus, a plan of only ten printed pages, not an "eye-witness" account — nor did it have the map or other selling-points that characterized Smith's work. (See note 2 for the reprints of Hayes' booklet.) WFG has apparently not taken into consideration the basic difference between the two accounts.

2. Hayes' *Treatise* (London, 1602), has since been reprinted by Dr. Burrage (from the first edition) and the Massachusetts Historical Society (from the second) as well as in facsimile by L. S. Livingstone in 1902 and George Parker Winship in *Sailors' Narratives of New England Voyages*. See Levermore, *Forerunners*, i, 28 and 41. (On the latter page Levermore excuses his not reprinting Hayes' work on the grounds that it does not "tell the story of any voyage to the New England coast.")

As WFG noted, Brereton's work, although it ran into a second edition doubled in size by added documents, quickly became a rare item. Today only a dozen copies of the first editions exist. Although there are reprints in historical collections, it is small wonder that Captain Edward Hayes and his significant *Treatise* are unknown to most students of American history.

3. For the details, see Edward Hayes' narrative, reprinted in Hakluyt, *Voyages,* viii, 70 seqq., and in Quinn *Gilbert,* ii, 417 seqq.

4. Quinn, *Gilbert,* ii, 342-343.

5. Quinn, *Gilbert,* ii, 435-480.

6. A copy of the pertinent part of the map is in the pocket at the end of Quinn, *Gilbert,* volume ii, while a section of it redrawn on the basis of modern surveys faces p. 343 (same volume).

7. See *Winthrop Papers,* published by the Massachusetts Historical Society (1929-1947), iii, 246.

8. The "mystery" is at least in part explained by Quinn in his *Gilbert,* i, 52-53.

9. The whole subject of Edward Hayes is elaborated so far as known facts permit in David B. Quinn's "Edward Hayes, Liverpool Colonial Pioneer". *Transactions of the Historic Society of Lancashire and Cheshire,* Vol. 111 (1959), 25-45. Portions of WFG's text from here on have been modified in the light of Professor Quinn's somewhat later monograph, the editor's copy of which bears the *simpatico* annotation in Quinn's handwriting, "This should really be dedicated to Warner Gookin."

10. WFG is more concerned than need be about the charge of piracy. The term was loosely used in those days, as was the term "mutiny", although if the offense was serious, so was the punishment. It should be remembered that a sort of piracy called "privateering" was quite legal (it is still sanctioned — though not "permitted" — by Art. I, Sec. 8, paragraph 11 of the Constitution of the United States), and moral stigma was not necessarily attached to coming before a court to answer charges of that sort. These matters, along with many others, must not be regarded in the light of "modern thinking."

11. Quinn, *Hayes,* 33.

12. Brereton, *Relation* (2nd ed. 1602), p. 18.

13. Ibid., p. 20.

14. Ibid., p. 15.

15. Hayes probably passed his fiftieth birthday between 1599 and the time when Gosnold's 1602 plans were formulated, but that was an "advanced age" then to embark on overseas colonizing. (For Hayes' age, see Quinn, *Hayes,* 26.)

16. The relationship here mentioned can best be shown thus:

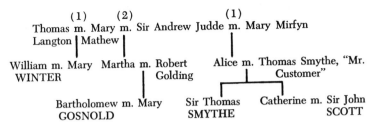

See also Chapter I, footnote 9. (*Note:* Nothing is known about Thomas Hayes beyond the fact of some sort of kinship.)

17. Originally printed in four folio volumes, in 1625. Reprinted in twenty volumes, Glasgow, 1905-1907.

18. John Brereton of Chester was "one of the voyage" with Gosnold. His account was published in 1602. Gabriel Archer, another companion, wrote an independent *Relation* which was not published until 1625 (Purchas, *Pilgrimes*, xviii, 302-313). The passages used in the following comparisons can easily be found in the Brereton volume of 1602, or in Purchas in the case of Archer.

19. It should be noted that Smith wrote that he would not have had so few if he could "have had meanes for more." (Smith, *Works*, p. 218.) The same undoubtedly goes for Gosnold.

20. The last few pages of WFG's manuscript have been considerably shortened because superseded by Professor Quinn's more recent study on Hayes, which see for details. WFG would undoubtedly have altered his manuscript himself had he lived to see the Quinn article.

CHAPTER VIII

1. For a detailed account of Henry Wriothesley, see *The Life of Henry, Third Earl of Southampton, Shakespeare's Patron*, by Charlotte Carmichael Stopes (Cambridge, England, 1922).

2. See Algernon Cecil, *A Life of Robert Cecil* (London, 1915), p. 379.

3. An "aside" by WFG, reworked for basic facts by Professor Quinn, can be introduced here by way of explanatory footnote: "Robert Cecil had acted as one of the Queen's Ministers since 1591, but he did not get the

title of Principal Secretary of State until 1596, at the age of thirty-three. Old Lord Burghley, the Lord Treasurer, died in 1598, and so Robert was the Queen's chief adviser for the last five years of her reign. He was consequently in control of state affairs when the Earls of Essex and Southampton were condemned to death in 1601."

4. Stopes, *Southampton*, pp. 115-116. The squire was by no means blameless himself, but the whole story was much more involved than can properly be explained here.

5. A sidelight is thrown on WFG's account in Stopes, *Southampton*, pp. 318-322, which attributes Southampton's interest in America rather to reading (for which he had plenty of leisure in the Tower!) Hakluyt's new edition, with an entire volume dedicated to America (1600). This same passage (*Southampton*, p. 320) has the following pertinent comment: "The puzzle is, not where he found the interest, but where he found the money."

6. Strachey, *Historie*, pp. 150-151.

7. Brown's *Genesis*, ii, 814. Archer's death is by surmise only – there is no record of the date.

8. Strachey, *Historie*, pp. xxvi-xxx. Note that the 1953 edition, which is used here, was based on the most painstakingly prepared copy of the original manuscript. The Hakluyt Society also issued the last manuscript (of 1618) in 1849, under the title *The Historie of Travaile into Virginia Britannia*, edited by R. H. Major, to which reference is made in the next footnote.

9. The headings for Strachey's "Second Book" are missing in the copy printed in 1953. The reference here is to the 1849 edition, p. 155, corresponding (except for the heading) to the 1953 edition, p. 152.

10. William Foster, *England's Quest of Eastern Trade* (London, 1933), p. 149.

11. Stopes, *Southampton*, p. 360.

12. Smith, *Works*, pp. 696-697.

13. For further details, see WFG, *Capawack*.

14. Smith, *Works*, p. 701.

15. See Richard Arthur Preston, *Gorges of Plymouth Fort* (Toronto, 1953), esp. p. 400, fn. 31.

16. George Chapman, Ben Jonson, and John Marston, *Eastward Hoe* (London, 1605), Act. II, Scene ii, spoken by Security near the end of the scene.

17. *Eastward Hoe,* Act III, Scene iii, spoken by Seagull, in his first long speech. David Ingram's *Relation* and *Reports* are to be found in Quinn, *Gilbert,* ii, 283-307.

CHAPTER IX

1. Hakluyt, *Letters,* ii, 216.

2. These passages can easily be found in the 9-10 small pages of Brereton's *Relation.*

3. Similar misconceptions have plagued Gosnold's friend Captain John Smith even more.

4. Brown, *Genesis,* ii, 814.

5. See Part III of this work.

6. Archer's "penchant" for quaint names helps "prove" that he wrote the account, commonly called "Archer's Relation", of the first voyage of exploration up the James River, in Virginia, in May and June, 1607, as published in Smith, *Works,* pp. xl-lv. In fact, so quaint was his "penchant" that WFG seems to have missed the point in the naming of "Hill's Hap" and "Hap's Hill." Archer named Buzzards Bay "Gosnoll's Hope", not because there was any prospect of anything, but because an old English word "hope" (of Norse origin) survived in the meaning "haven, bay." Another surviving word, apparently of Norse origin also, was "hap", which meant "a covering of any kind." Archer stresses the point that the islet was "full of cedars" — covered with them. Then, with a "quaint" twist, when he saw "another [islet] the like", Archer played on the double meaning of "hap" and wrote that he called this one "Hap's Hill, for that I hope much hap may be expected from it." For this interpretation of Archer's "penchant", see his account in Purchas, xviii, 307-308, and the *Oxford English Dictionary,* under the words: Hope, *sb.*²; Hap, *sb*²; and Hap, *v.*². See also note 20, below.

7. WFG's statement will hold good for Brereton's account, but for Archer's needs a little explaining. Archer's, as appears in the text shortly below, was not printed until five years after the Pilgrims landed at Plymouth Rock. It is the editor's opinion that WFG has regarded the matter of descriptions and apparent omissions with too "modern" an eye. The 1602 expedition after all was not sent out on a 1952 geodetic survey.

8. The 1602 account is in Purchas, *Pilgrimes,* xviii, 302-313; the letter of 1609, in xix, 1-4.

9. Velasco sent the map to Philip III with his letter of 12/22 March 1611 (Brown, *Genesis,* i, 455-457). WFG's surmise is apparently based on Brown, *Genesis,* i, 459. Brown was the "discoverer" (by correspondence) of the letter, the map, and many other valuable documents in the Spanish archives during the years preceding the publication of his *Genesis* in 1890.

10. Alexander Brown was of the opinion that the Velasco map "shows traces of the surveys of Captains Gosnold, Archer, Pring, Weymouth, and probably of the North Virginia colonists [Popham's company of 1607], as well as of Champlain and possibly other foreigners" (*Genesis* i, 459).

11. The brief account by Smith (*Works,* p. 336) was printed in 1624. Purchas's account, printed in 1625 but undoubtedly written down by 1622 or so, is to be found in *Pilgrimes,* xviii, 322-329. The whole matter of Gosnold's and Pring's voyages is discussed with considerable acumen by B. F. De Costa, in "Gosnold and Pring, 1602-3", NEHGR, xxxii (1878), pp. 76-80.

12. See Quinn, *Gilbert,* i, 76-77, and ii, 350-351.

13. Purchas, *Pilgrimes,* xviii, 322.

14. Edward Maria Wingfield's *Discourse,* printed in Smith, *Works,* p. lxxvi.

15. The letter is printed in Edward Edwards, *The Life of Sir Walter Ralegh* (London, 1868), ii, 251-253. That Gilbert was "a complete stranger" is perhaps *implied* in the letter, but it is certainly not *stated.* (See Part III, note 6.)

16. Sir Anthony Ashley was Clerk of the Privy Council, and had been knighted in 1596. The details of Gilbert's troubles with the "great diamond", so far as known, are published in the Publications of the Royal Commission on Historical Manuscripts, Series 9, *Salisbury (Cecil) MSS., at Hatfield* (London, various dates). See volumes for the years 1590-1603, indexes. There are a good many documents.

17. Gosnold's letter to his father is reprinted in full (from Purchas, *Pilgrimes,* xviii, 300-302) in Appendix B.

18. The account of this is in Purchas, *Pilgrimes,* xviii, 329-335.

19. Although not printed until 1602, this "pamphlet" was obviously written in the interest of Ralegh's Roanoke colony.

20. Brown does not agree that there was a man named Hill on the expedition (*Genesis*, i, 26). On the basis of information obtained in England while this volume was in the press, the editor admits that there is a possibility that a Hill was a member of the expedition. Bartholomew Gosnold's aunt Dorothy married Sir John Gilbert, as we know. Sir John's mother was Elizabeth Howe, and her mother was a Hill, of Great Finborough, Suff. Both the Howes and the Hills were also connected with Bartholomew Gilbert. (See Part III, note 6).

21. A "Daniell Tucker, Gent." went to Virginia in 1608, after news of Gosnold's death had reached England, but there is no way of knowing if there was any connection. Daniel Tucker apparently stayed on in Virginia for twenty years or so (Smith, *Works*, pp. 159 and 885, and elsewhere).

CHAPTER X

1. The phrases are taken from Captain John Smith's *Accidence for Young Seamen* (*Works*, p. 798).

2. We know nothing about the *Concord* beyond what Brereton says, unless it was one of Drake's ships, of the same name and size unknown, which sailed with him on his last voyage, in 1596 (Hakluyt, *Voyages*, x, 242).

3. Brereton's estimate (clearly more a guess than a calculation) was remarkably close, since great-circle routes from Falmouth to Portsmouth, New Hampshire, by way of the Canaries and West Indies, as against the route via the Azores, would be roughly 6,000 miles as against roughly 3,200.

4. It is 917 miles from Fayal to Lisbon and 1,134 from Fayal to Gibraltar (as against 2,000 from Boston to Fayal), according to the map of the Atlantic Ocean published by the National Geographic Society, September, 1941.

5. The "run to the Azores" was indeed familiar, since the Azores were the Grand Rendezvous for Spanish treasure fleets on their way home from America — legitimate objects of prey for the English after the undeclared war with Spain broke out in 1584. But the Canaries had previously been used for "setting the course across the Atlantic." For a scholarly study of the question of trans-Atlantic routes, see D. W. Waters, *The Art of Navigation* (New Haven, 1958), pp. 261 seqq., including the chart of winds and currents facing p. 265. Note particularly the importance of two *rutters* (marine guides) first printed by Hakluyt in 1600 (Waters, pp. 262-265), overlooked by WFG, which may well have had decisive influence on the route taken by Gosnold.

6. Irish *Culdees* (monks) had run across Iceland very early — probably in the eighth century (*Facts About Iceland*, Reykjavík, 1953). Whether contact was from western or northern Irish ports is immaterial, the distance to the south-central coast of Iceland (few harbors, but Mount Hvannadalshnúkur can be visible a long way off) is not over 800 statute miles; from western Iceland to south-eastern Greenland is about the same distance, or less; and from the tip of Greenland to Labrador is perhaps 600 miles. In short, by great-circle routes a ship would never be more than 400 miles from land. To what extent Elizabethan mariners could or would follow so accurate a route, however, is open to considerable question. Often, the most experienced sailors had no idea where they were.

7. Note by WFG: "The yellowish color was caused by a vast swarm of minute plankton, a crustacean, *Calanus copepod*, slightly more than a sixteenth of an inch in length, and invisible in a bucket of water." While the specific identification of the plankton may be questioned, and the invisibility of a crustacean 1/16″ in length seriously doubted, WFG was certainly right in attributing the yellowish color of the sea-water to some sort of plankton. *What* sort is unimportant.

8. St. John's Island appeared on many maps. As Professor Quinn has commented in a personal communication to the editor, "a mythical island on a map is as 'real' as a real one!" It is possible, of course, that the French name *Ile Sablon* was misread as *Ile St. John* (often written Jhon). This long, narrow island, known in English as Sable Island, lies off the coast of Nova Scotia, in generally shallow water, and would fit the picture so far as the "schools of fish" are concerned. In any case, no one *saw* the island.

9. As WFG noted, this "phenomenon" was natural to the Gulf Stream, through which most of their voyage lay (and which undoubtedly slowed their passage). The existence of the "Stream" had long since been observed, and Hakluyt had written a marginal note to Frobisher's mention of it in 1577: "Inquire further of this current" (Hakluyt, *Voyages*, vii, 214). But the reference had obviously escaped Master William Strete (and lawyer Archer). No one had "done anything about it" anyway.

10. Note that the reference here is to *land* weeds — a sign that confirmed the "smell of the shore."

11. The entire "Reconstructed Log" is retold from Archer's account, printed in Purchas, *Pilgrimes*, xviii, 302-303.

12. Cape Neddick is near York Beach in extreme southwestern Maine, a dozen miles from Portsmouth, New Hampshire.

13. See Purchas, *Pilgrimes*, xviii, 304.

14. There is no "firm" evidence that the Indians were so obliging. Nevertheless, we know that many Indians were remarkably well-informed geographically — witness the geographical knowledge picked up by Captain

John Smith a few years later, which was instrumental in guiding Henry Hudson to the river that bears his name (Smith, *Works*, pp. xli, xliii, cxix, 413, 427-428, and elsewhere).

15. Brereton, *Relation*, p. 4.

16. With sunset about 7:30 p.m., and a three-day-old moon following the sun an hour and a half later — at most — it was obviously a dark night, even if it was clear. Sometimes the moon was of help on such voyages of exploration.

CHAPTER XI

1. Recent scholarship has cast doubt on the time-honored story of a Cabot voyage down the American coast. The editor has heard that J. A. Williamson has something in preparation on this, but it is not to hand at the time of writing.

2. Diego Ribero, about whom we know very little except that he apparently was Portuguese, was appointed Royal Cosmographer of Spain on 10 July 1523, and died nine and a half years later. His map of 1529 was based on the *Padrón real*, or royal master-map, compiled first sometime before 1511 under the direction of Amerigo ("Américo") Vespucci, then Chief Pilot ("Piloto mayor"). (See Diego Luis Molinari, *El Nacimiento del Nuevo Mundo* [Buenos Aires, 1941], pp. 63-64 and 159, and the biographical article in *Enciclopedia Universal Ilustrada* [Espasa-Calpe, Madrid, 1908-1930], Vol. 51, pp. 349-350.) Vázquez de Ayllón was a wealthy nobleman who accompanied Cortés to Mexico in 1519, but soon took off on his own and began exploring the southeast coast of today's United States as far north, probably, as the North Carolina state line (see brief biography in the Espasa-Calpe *Enciclopedia*, Vol. 67, p. 376). Estevan Gómez was a Portuguese mariner who had sailed with Magellan in 1519 and had himself discovered the straits named after the latter — Gómez merely got there first. He turned back, however, leaving Magellan and others to continue their first circumnavigation of the globe. For this he was criticized, yet was soon made Chief Pilot of Spain. In 1525, Gómez sailed north from Cuba in search of the northwest passage — already believed to exist. According Gonzalo Fernández de Oviedo (properly, Gonzalo Hernández de Oviedo y Valdés), the famous contemporary historian, Gómez got only to 41° or 41° north latitude. Cape Cod projects above 42°, which seems to rule out the equation Cabo de Arenas = Cape Cod. Paul Quattlebaum, in his *Land Called Chicora* (Gainesville, Florida, 1956), however, brings evidence in its support (p. 31). Peter Martyr, available in translation by Francis Augustus MacNutt (1912), is perhaps the best general contemporary source.

3. Purchas, *Pilgrimes,* xiii, 352.

4. Part of Waymouth's story follows immediately in the text. Hudson's story, written by Robert Juet, mariner, of Limehouse, is in Purchas, *Pilgrimes,* xiii, pp. 333-374, especially pp. 350-354 (see note 3, above). John Smith's story is in *Works,* p. 205. As for Captain Jones, see the more "modern" account and interpretation by John A. Goodwin, *The Pilgrim Republic* (Boston [1888], 1920), pp. 59-62, with copious footnotes.

5. Purchas, *Pilgrimes,* xviii, 336-337.

6. See note 3, above.

7. Purchas, *Pilgrimes,* xix, 76.

8. Purchas, *Pilgrimes,* xix, 82.

9. Brown, *Genesis,* ii, 1019.

10. Strachey, *Historie,* p. 50.

11. A sound, and conveniently brief, outline of the Popham Colony is in Levermore, *Forerunners,* i, 352-358. Professor Quinn has suggested the basic sources of the Velasco map in a personal communication to the editor. WFG's manuscript has been slightly condensed here, because of the later publication of evidence invalidating his hypotheses — sound enough when he wrote them.

12. Bradford, *Plymouth,* pp. 93-94.

CHAPTER XII

1. See the facsimile, with notes, published by The John Carter Brown Library, Providence, Rhode Island, 1942.

2. Brereton, *Relation,* p. 4.

3. Purchas, *Pilgrimes,* xviii, 304.

4. The details of setting here were supplied to WFG by Halford R. Houser, Editor, *Cape Cod Standard-Times,* Hyannis, Massachusetts, in a personal letter dated March 10, 1947. (Mr. Houser calls attention to the fact that the range of vision from several hills in the neighborhood is rather greater "on a clear day" than WFG states in his text. Nevertheless, we must consider that Mr. Houser knew what to look for, and Bartholomew Gosnold did not.) The entire "journal" of activities on that day as docu-

mented totals a little over 200 words in Archer's account and some 275 in Brereton's (including a long excursus on Newfoundland). WFG expanded this skeleton to give the reader a clearer picture. All quotations are from Archer's story in Purchas, *Pilgrimes*, xviii, 304-305, or Brereton's *Relation*, pp. 4-5. Specific references to these accounts are therefore omitted for the balance of this chapter.

5. WFG has overlooked the fact that May is not hot in England and that the costume of the period, with leather jerkins in all probability, would underscore the heat. Englishmen were quick to put on more clothes for northern voyages, but were astoundingly recalcitrant about removing any for the sake of warmer climes.

6. Precisely how this was done is not known. See "Notes on a Shallop," by William A. Barker, *The American Neptune*, Vol. XVII (1957), pp. 105-106.

7. Bradford, *Plymouth*, p. 97.

8. WFG has apparently disregarded the *normal* stoicism of the Indians. Only the copper ear-rings could have pointed pretty definitely to some relationship with an Indian of superior social rank.

9. The editor is unable to agree with WFG in his interpretation of this incident. The Indian may have been a chief's son — witness the copper — but the rest of the deductions are a trifle *à la Chateaubriand*. Even the greatest Indian chiefs did what the English considered menial labor, and it was "natural" for the young Indian to help the English. The general picture of the noble (and idle) brave and his laboring squaw is romanticized. On the Algonkians, see Flannery, *Analysis*, pp. 104-106, with many specific references. The whole subject is far too complicated for analysis here.

10. Brereton, *Relation*, p. 5.

11. Although the Eldridge charts are somewhat antiquated, those of the U.S. Geodetic Survey confirm the soundings.

12. Personal communication from Professor Quinn.

13. WFG's original text for this paragraph has been modified to accord with later analyses. The editor is grateful to Professor Quinn for suggestions and for the reference to Hakluyt's editing of the Barlowe journal of 1584 (Quinn, *Roanoke*, i, 91-115) "to fit in with the promotion ventures" of his client, Sir Walter Ralegh.

14. Smith, *Works*, pp. 205-206.

15. Purchas, *Pilgrimes*, xviii, 337.

CHAPTER XIII

1. See Richard Arthur Preston, *Gorges of Plymouth Fort* (Toronto, 1953), pp. 321-322. For a brief outline of the history of the Council, see p. 12 of the same work.

2. *Martha's Vineyard Guide*, p. 13.

3. Martha is spelled *Mortha*. See WFG, *Capawack*, pp. 37 and 50, *fn.* 12.

4. Preston, *Gorges*, pp. 151, 154, and 161.

5. WFG, *Capawack*, p. 16.

6. WFG, *Capawack*, pp. 8-10 and 21-22.

7. WFG, *Capawack*, pp. 31-32, and 54, *fn.* 27.

8. From a deep-water point one league off modern Cape Cod Light (due east by *magnetic compass*), where a ship could be said to begin to "trend southerly", to a deep-water point two leagues off the southern tip of Monomoy Island (again, due east by magnetic compass) is almost exactly twelve leagues — i.e., 36 statute miles.

9. By the route outlined by WFG it is almost 45 miles from the tip of Monomoy Island to Muskeget Island — a very few miles less to Smith Point, at the western tip of Nantucket.

10. For some mention of these alterations in the geography of the region, see *Martha's Vineyard Guide*, p. 15.

11. It should be noted that WFG's explanation here, and in the paragraphs that follow, is based on the assumption that Gosnold was determined to find a bay *opening to the south*, and that he therefore kept to the open sea south from Cape Cod until he had rounded Nantucket Island, passing the *eastern* opening to the Sound without hesitation, or so much as a comment. Since it is not known (1) where Archer's "twelve leagues" were reckoned from, or (2) that Archer's text has not been cut to unintelligibility, it is impossible to do more than hazard "informed guesses." This WFG has done, and his basic assertion regarding the identity of Martha's Vineyard is unquestionably sound — though perhaps not always for his reasons. Under these circumstances, it is idle to quibble over the exact route followed by the *Concord*. WFG's guess, or in this case hypothesis, must not be discounted because it may have a few shortcomings. Those whom he criticizes are basically more patently in error. See the map of Gosnold's course as interpreted by WFG, Frontispiece.

240

12. The general trend of the southern coast of Cape Cod between Chatham and Falmouth is rather west-by-south or west-southwest, than southwest; and it would show almost east-west on a magnetic compass, subject to more than a compass-point magnetic variation west today. That is neither here nor there. Several short stretches of shore-line are northeast-southwest.

13. "East Chop derives its name from an old English term, chops, used to describe the entrance of a harbor or channel (*Martha's Vineyard Guide,* p. 103)."

14. From East Chop Light to a line drawn from Monomoy Point to Great Point on Nantucket is 28 statute miles.

15. From the point of view of mere distance, Cape Poge, on Chappaquiddick Island, fits the requirements better, being some nine and a half miles from Great Neck, just east of Falmouth, As for Noman's land, the distance from the mainland is beside the point — it lies outside of Martha's Vineyard, and both Vineyard Sound and Buzzards Bay must be crossed before reaching the mainland near the Rhode Island-Massachusetts border.

16. Its very *accuracy* makes the figure suspect. As WFG says, correct latitudes were almost unknown then (although European latitudes were pretty accurate). Note that the "epoch-making" *Certaine Errors in Navigation* of Edward Wright had appeared only in 1599, less than three years before Gosnold's voyage.

17. There is evidence that Gay Head once was indeed an island — at least, that the sandy beach was broken by a waterway. See *Martha's Vineyard Guide,* p. 122.

CHAPTER XIV

1. According to the Inca Garcilaso de la Vega, *La Florida del Ynca* (English translation, "The Florida of the Inca," by John and Jeannette Varner [Austin, Texas, 1951], p. 8 and footnote 15), "the fountain that made the old young" was an Indian fable which don Juan Ponce de León heard somewhere. Some modern Spanish authorities consider the "Fountain" a mere detail in a general exploratory trip. In any case, as with Gosnold's voyage, all the details are not known.

2. WFG clearly means the northeastern coast, which is actually *southeastern* Maine. No white-man had so much as approached the impenetrable forests of northern Maine by Gosnold's time — nor would any for some years to come. As for the "useful reports", their real value should not be

241

exaggerated; little concrete information was to be found in them. (See Charles M. Andrews, *The Colonial Period of American History: The Settlements,* Vol. 1 [New Haven, 1934], p. 23.)

3. These are WFG's analyses of the meaning of the names. They seem sound, although we can seldom be certain of the meaning intended by the Indians in 1602. The reference to the "muskeg" of the Arctic, however, is erroneous. A muskeg is a swamp, a bog (Cree *muskak,* to rhyme with "cake"). The name *Muskeget* is from Natick *moskeht,* "grass", plus the locative ending *-et,* "at the place of." (Both Cree and Natick were Algonkian languages, related somewhat as Italian and French. Cree is still spoken, mostly in Canada. Natick was spoken to the east of Narragansett Bay, in Massachusetts.)

4. "Dead reckoning" implies lack of knowledge of latitude, which was not the case here. What WFG undoubtedly means is that Gosnold knew his ship's latitude, but did not know that of the islands — in fact, he was not even certain that they existed. From that point of view, his reckoning was "dead".

5. Tuckernuck Bank, out of which both Tuckernuck Island and Muskeget Island emerge, is a shelf one foot to two fathoms below mean low water and of a fairly uniform three-mile width, which extends northwesterly some six or seven miles from Nantucket. It should be remembered that these measurements are very recent, and do not necessarily correspond with conditions in 1602. Since WFG's basic reasoning is sound, the details are not of too great concern.

6. Muskeget Channel today is half a mile wide at its narrowest, and fourteen to sixteen miles long — from deep water to deep water. There are shoals at both ends, however, with soundings of little more than three fathoms. The eastern entrance to the Sound provides a deeper, if narrower, channel just off Monomoy Point (Pollock Rip Channel), and a broader one to the south (Great Round Shoal Channel). In any case, the eastern entrance, as WFG notes, is well protected by shoals, rips and breakers far out to sea. The *Rose and Crown* and *Great Rip* shoals, for instance, are well out of sight of land, twelve to fourteen miles east of Nantucket Island.

7. The editor is far from convinced that the latitude recorded by Archer here was the latitude taken at the time. Gosnold must have known that his calculations were only approximations, although he also must have known that they were a vast improvement on the calculations which Verrazzano could have made, nearly eighty years before. The editor regards Archer's statement as to the latitude of Gilbert's Point as merely a roundabout way of saying that Gosnold was convinced, on the basis of his calculations, that he had reached the goal set him, three generations before, by Verrazzano. (Who knows, indeed, but what Samuel Purchas' goose-quill was responsible for the exact correspondence in latitude?)

242

8. See complete text of Gosnold's *Letter* to his father in Appendix B.

9. Archer does not specify what kind of canoes, but WFG may well be right. It should be noted, however, that canoes of bark were used by the southern New England Indians (see Flannery, *Analysis*, pp. 58-60). Still, it is likely that a softer wood than oak was used — in Virginia it was usually pine or cedar.

10. WFG extracted the details of this story from *New England Judged, by the Spirit of the Lord*. Formerly published by George Bishop, and now somewhat Abreviated (London, 1703), pp. 161-162. Bishop adds, dryly: "[the Indian] shewed himself more Hospitable (as did the rest of the *Indians*) and supplied them freely with all Necessaries, according to what the *Indians* had, during the space of those three Days they stay'd there, waiting for a calm Season, and refused to take any Consideration; he who had them in custody, saying, — *That they were Strangers, and Jehovah taught him to Love Strangers.*" This account does not seem to appear in the original edition, of 1661.

11. The word *pawwaw* or *powwow* basically means "he dreams, he derives his art from his dreams", hence "priest, medicine-man." The meaning (noisy) ceremonial rite, or (finally) any noisy meeting is secondary, although that is the meaning best understood and most used today.

12. The great auk is also known as the gare-fowl. Charles Kingsley, in his *Water Babies*, describes poetically how the gare-fowl came to be extinct. (Everyman's Library edition, pp. 156-160.)

13. The *Oxford English Dictionary* does not record the word "chop" in this sense until the end of the century.

14. Note by WFG: One of these not far from the head of the shore cliffs has been called Telegraph Hill; so named because it was a semaphore station for the transmission of news of whaling ships and East India traders to the mainland.

15. From the scant mention, it is impossible to identify this island.

16. In those days, the word "vine" to all practical purposes meant "grape-vine".

17. According to *Martha's Vineyard Guide* (p. 115), the lake was originally known as Onkokemmy pond, but was re-named for James, Duke of York, afterwards King James II.

18. The latter half of this paragraph, it should be noted, is a mere guess. See note 3 above.

19. WFG seems to be mistaken here. Brereton's list of commodities (*Relation,* p. 13) says: "Sorrell, and many other herbs wherewith they made sallets." The reference here seems rather to be to the Englishmen than to the Indians. The editor does not recall any reference to Indian use of such herbs other than as *cooked* food, and in any case the picture of the Indians bringing a meal of boiled fish with "salad" is misleading. For the America of 1602, it is an anachronism. Again, WFG is looking at the Indians with Chateaubriand's romantic eye.

20. *Nobility* is rather strong. John Smith divided the Indians into "the common sort" and "the better sort." The latter, he wrote, "use large mantels of deare skins not much differing in fashion from the Irish mantels" (Smith, *Works,* p. 66). It may be added that the Indians quite conceivably had trade rather than honors in mind. Kings, nobles, honors, supreme gods — these and many other terms are inapplicable *in their European sense* to any phase of Indian culture along the Atlantic coast north of Mexico.

CHAPTER XV

1. Hugging the shore around the two islands, and discounting the 1½ mile SW extension of *Sow and Pigs Reef,* the circuit measures about 14½ miles today.

2. Note by WFG: It was on this reef that at night, in the dead of winter, 1884, a carelessly-navigated coastwise passenger ship, the *City of Columbus,* was wrecked a half mile off-shore, with a loss of one hundred and twenty-five passengers and crew members, and with only a score of survivors.

3. It may well be questioned to what extent the play on words was in the minds of the company.

4. First printed in the second edition of Brereton's *Relation* (London, 1602), p. 32.

5. The U.S. Geodetic Survey indicates a tank at 154', practically in the middle of the island.

6. One wonders if George Percy was "inspired" by Brereton when he wrote of the shores of Chesapeake Bay, five years later, "I was almost ravished at the first sight thereof" (Smith, *Works,* p. lxi). This extravagant use of *ravish* is not over-common in Shakespeare, or even Spenser.

7. Note by WFG: Personally, and I may be wrong, I think Brereton is describing a tree-studded area of salt-marshes which I have often seen

rom a train skirting this shore of Buzzards Bay. Beautiful from a distance,
t is a useless bit of landscape, good only for the gathering of salt-marsh
grasses for cattle, and therefore it has remained to our day about as
Brereton saw it.

8. Purchas, *Pilgrimes*, xviii, 308. The many quotations from Archer in
the text that follows are taken from pages 307 to 313 of that book, and are
not specified further in the notes.

9. Brereton, *Relation*, p. 7. The quotations from Brereton which follow
are taken from the 1602 edition, pages 7 to 12, and are not further specified
in the notes.

10. Archer's is apparently the first mention of these nuts in printed
English literature (though not in the *OED*, which gives 1636 as the first
recorded use of the word). They are the roots of the wild bean, *Apios
tuberosa*, and have nothing to do with peanuts, which are sometimes given
the same name. The editor has not run across any basis for WFG's claim
that ground-nuts were eaten only when other foods failed, and it is hardly
borne out by *Bradford's Journal*, which mentions a gift of ground-nuts and
tobacco from Massasoit in 1621 (in *Mourt's Relation* [London, 1622], reprinted in Edward Arber's *The Story of the Pilgrim Fathers* [London, 1897],
p. 460).

11. WFG observed that Tilney was a recognized, if distant, kinsman
of the Queen, to which Professor Quinn adds, "I think the 'sister's name'
theory is plausible, but it does not rule out the 'Queen' theory. After all, the
post was to be one *Elizabeth's Isle*, a royal outpost. If Elizabeth liked it,
fine; if not, it could be Gosnold's sister's name (*that* seems more likely)."
(Personal communication.)

12. The concept of *ownership* of real estate was hardly developed
among these Indians. WFG is once more treating the Indians much too
"Europeanly". Individual hunting-grounds and agricultural plots were
recognized among the eastern Algonkians, and trespass was resented — but
ownership in a modern sense was no more present than were any "nobles".
See such works as Flannery, *Analysis*, pp. 76-78, and various monographs
by Frank G. Speck on *Family Hunting Territories*, and so on, in such publications as the *American Anthropologist*, the *Notes and Monographs* of the
Heye Foundation, and the like.

13. A tendency toward despotism was developing among the Coastal
Algonkians generally, although it had not yet produced a New England
equivalent to Powhatan of Virginia. It is probable that this tendency was
spreading northwards from the non-Algonkian tribes of the Southeast. See,
inter alia, Flannery's *Analysis*, p. 116.

14. This is again romanticizing. We do not know enough about Indian

245

life in the 16th century to make any clear-cut assertions. It seems on the whole that these tribes were only beginning to emerge from the state of improvident food-gatherers and -hunters; and it is to be surmised that the first real change in their totally unplanned economy (only the chiefs showed vague signs of planning) came with the catastrophic arrival of the Europeans. (Be it remembered that *catastrophe* means a [sudden] overturning!)

15. According to Dermer, the suspicion fell most strongly on "an English man"; although he added "it may be douted" whether they [the culprits] were English or French. See Bradford, *Plymouth*, p. 117.

16. For a fuller picture, see John A. Goodwin, *The Pilgrim Republic* (Boston, 1920), pp. 122, 130-135, 164, and 168.

17. See James Hammond Trumbull, *Natick Dictionary* (Washington, Smithsonian Institution, 1903), p. 25, s.v. *chokquog*.

18. Dog-fish (small sharks) were eaten by some Indians, but the Englishman who gorged himself on dogfish-belly was more likely indulging a taste acquired at home.

19. This sort of naive disobedience or wilfulness cost the English many lives. The story is repeated elsewhere and with other details for a good quarter of a century in the tiny English colonies of Massachusetts and Virginia, and later in others.

20. John Smith may have heard about the Patent granted to representatives of the Pilgrims in 1619, although 1620 seems more likely. (See Goodwin, *Pilgrim Republic,* p. 43f.) That he "applied for a job" is too direct a statement in any case; he would undoubtedly have wanted to lead the Pilgrims' expedition, but providing a number of well-nigh impossibilities were removed. That the Pilgrims knew they needed a vigorous military leader is evidenced by their taking Miles Standish, a "stranger" (i.e., not a Pilgrim), with them. But that Smith could not have been chosen for the post, despite his personal knowledge of the problems they were about to face, is obvious from his attitude toward Pilgrim non-conformity in religious matters. For a fuller discussion, see Part III of the editor's forthcoming study of *John Smith.*

21. One cannot but wonder, in the light of Archer's "optimistic" remarks about the streams flowing into Buzzards Bay, if he and Gosnold (and perhaps others) were not trying to make the bay they found correspond with, and actually be, the bay of Verrazzano's *Norumbega.* After all, seventy-eight years had elapsed, and who knew how accurate the Florentine's observations had been?

22. As in the case of the so-called "Powhatan Confederacy", the word summons up a picture of a primitive Switzerland, which is hardly what it

was. The editor has called Powhatan's realm a despotate — which is closer to what it was — but that term is probably too strong for the Pokonocket scheme of things. As long, however, as the reader understands that the "confederacy" was highly primitive, that it depended in some measure on force and repression, and that the Great Chief exacted tribute, the term may stand.

23. The suggestion as to previous trade, probably with the French exploring Canada, was made in a personal communication from Professor Quinn.

24. The Algonkian languages, to which WFG refers, naturally were not complicated to the people who spoke them, and quite possibly would not have seemed "complicated" to a Greek of Pericles' time. It is a matter not of a difference of *degree* in complexity, but of *kind*.

CHAPTER XVI

1. Bartholomew Gilbert is mentioned by Archer but three times, and by Brereton not at all — unless his name on the title page of Brereton's *Relation* constitutes "mention". Archer reports that Gilbert "almost never went ashore" (Purchas, *Pilgrimes*, p. 310), that "the victuals . . . by Captaine Gilberts allowance could be but six weekes for [instead of?] sixe moneths" (*ibid.*, p. 311), and that Captain Gilbert had "a purpose . . . not to returne" with relief supplies (same place, three lines below). These are hints that Gilbert had some sort of control of the supplies and that he stayed on ship-board either to protect or perhaps to conceal (the shortness of) the supplies. He may have been the purveyor for the ship, rather than the commissary, with private profit realizable by insufficient purchases made with quite sufficient sums at his disposal. As will appear in Part III, Gilbert seems to have been a goldsmith by trade, and had a record of apparent financial dishonesty. Just what his position on the *Concord* was, however, is not accurately known. Certainly, he would hardly have been *called* the "commissary" — in those days primarily an officer in charge of food, stores, and so on, for a body of soldiers.

2. WFG's comparison falls short of aptness. In Gosnold's case, the tiny settlement would have been left with quite inadequate supplies by an apparently disloyal co-captain; Ralegh's colony was more than five times as numerous, was organized specifically to plant a colony, and was at least sufficiently if not elaborately provisioned. That colony was lost, *despite* Ralegh's efforts to relieve it, by overriding circumstances — which included the threat of Spain that reached the climax of the *Armada* in July 1588, less than eleven months after John White sailed from Roanoke to England for supplies.

3. WFG overlooks the fact that the Englishmen were ignorant of corn-planting methods, that the Indian economy was hardly suited to English needs, and that the exploring parties still operated *mentally* from an English base. There is a modern parallel in the tendency of most Americans to go abroad, taking all the supplies possible from home and carefully looking for hospital-clean restaurants "approved" by some self-appointed American "approving" agency. They operate mentally from an American base. They do not "live as the Europeans live", as WFG expects of the English coming here in 1602.

4. The southern New England Indians are reported (by Bradford) to have gotten fish and planted their corn with it for fertilizer, but this seems to be an exceptional case among the Algonkians. William Wood (1634) remarked that the Indians there "were too lazy to catch fish [for that purpose]". See Flannery, *Analysis,* pp. 10-11.

5. It should be remembered that these hundreds of bushels of corn were available the early summer following the death of no less than seven hundred Narragansetts from an epidemic of a malignant sort of small-pox during the winter of 1633-1634. See John A. Goodwin, *The Pilgrim Republic* (Boston, 1920), pp. 372-373. The quotation is from *The History of New England from 1630 to 1649,* by John Winthrop (otherwise known as his *Journal*), Boston, 1825, i, 147, with a variant reading of '100' for 'one thousand'. The date of this entry is 5 November, 1634; the plague is reported on 20 January, 1634. No connection between the two is intimated by Governor Winthrop.

6. Most of this reconstruction partakes more of *possibility* than of *probability.* There is no way of knowing the food-storing habits of the Indians Gosnold met — although an additional twenty mouths would hardly have been too great a burden on the Indians providing they were filled from other sources by winter. There is in any case no reason for assuming that Gosnold would not have found out about Indian food supplies if he had been interested. John Smith did, in Virginia, with no greater knowledge of Algonkian. Something besides food surely took Gosnold back to England. (Parenthetically, there is no evidence that clam chowder was known to Indian or white-man in 1602.) M. K. Bennett's study, "The Food Economy of the New England Indians, 1605-1675" (*The Journal of Political Economy,* lxiii 1955, pp. 369-397), shows that some corn was stored, but this "does not in itself suggest the importance of stored grain in the total food supply or indicate whether enough was generally stored to last from harvest in the autumn to the new crop of green corn in the following summer" (p. 377).

7. Brereton's *Relation,* p. 41.

8. Hakluyt, *Letters,* pp. 223-224.

248

9. As WFG says, Archer gives the precise name for copper or "every metall whatsoever" which was recorded by Ralph Lane in North Carolina in 1585-1586: *Wassador*. (See Quinn, *Roanoke*, i, 268.) This word appears merely to be common Algonkian for "it shines, it is bright" (Cree *wasitao*, Natick *wôsittáe, wôósuppáe*, etc.), *pace* Professor James A. Geary's more involved derivation (Quinn, *Roanoke*, ii, 898). If Archer pointed at a bit of gold and said "Wassador?" to the Indians, quoting Lane, the Indians would most likely have nodded (regardless of minor differences of pronunciation), for Archer was merely saying "It's bright, it's shiny, isn't it?" Archer's premise was of course wrong, for there was no gold, and no people has a name for a thing that does not exist (for them). English, for instance, had no words for tomato or chocolate until those plants were found in Mexico, and the Spaniards provided us with the *Aztec* names. This is a phenomenon common to all languages — although new words are often made up to replace the original name, as in the case of pine-apple (*ananas*).

10. Brereton, *Relation*, p. 47.

11. The Hayes quotation is to be found in Brereton's *Relation*, p. 16; that from Hakluyt, *ibid.*, p. 33.

12. Archer's statement is less emphatic: "Whereupon the planters diminishing, all was given over" (Purchas, *Pilgrimes*, xviii, 313).

13. Brereton, *Relation*, p. 11.

14. See complete text of letter in Appendix B.

15. There does not seem to be any documentary evidence for or against WFG's picture of fresh food from the Gosnold acres, but Brereton mentions the herbs "wherewith they made sallets [salads]" (*Relation*, p. 13).

16. See complete text of letter in Appendix B.

CHAPTER XVII

1. How "close" Cobham and Ralegh were is hinted at by the latter during his trial: "[My Lord Cobham] hath dispositions of such violence, which his best friends could never temper [control, curb]. But it is very strange that I, at this time, should be thought to plot with the Lord Cobham, *knowing him a man who hath neither love nor following*" (editor's underlining). See Edward Edwards, *The Life of Sir Walter Ralegh* (London, 1868), i, 397-398.

2. It is conceivable that Gilbert, with Cobham's backing, particularly wanted such an excuse as this letter to be admitted to Secretary Cecil's "office", for reasons not unconnected with the famous "diamond" matter.

3. Professor Quinn writes that there is no evidence in the Court records that any such action was taken. He has further supplemented WFG's analysis by sending latest analyses to the editor. This additional material has merely been incorporated in the text, as being consistent with WFG's own habits in such matters.

4. See Quinn, *Roanoke*, references in Index under *Howard, Lord Charles, Baron of Effingham, Lord High Admiral*.

5. Brereton, *Relation*, p. 3.

6. The apt description is quoted from Catherine Drinker Bowen, *The Lion and the Throne* (London, 1957), p. 165. (Added by the editor.)

7. Although there is little in Ralegh's known character to support WFG's assumption that he was glad to take such credit as he could, there is no evidence to the contrary and the assumption cannot be invalidated. While disagreeing in detail, the editor concurs in principle: that Ralegh in a sense was glad to cooperate. Professor Quinn has put the whole matter appropriately and succinctly: Ralegh was "half angry and half glad" over Gosnold's voyage. (See D. B. Quinn, *Raleigh and the British Empire* [London, 1947], pp. 214-215.)

8. Purchas, *Pilgrimes*, xviii, 322-323.

9. See Quinn, *Gilbert*, ii, 418. Gilbert's words are more vague than WFG's statement would indicate.

CHAPTER XVIII

1. Hakluyt, *Life*, p. 255.

2. First printed in Brereton, *Relation*, p. 14. Reprinted in Purchas, *Pilgrimes*, xviii, 321, with some printing errors corrected and new ones made. The editor has corrected one error and modernized the text here and there for facility in reading.

3. Hakluyt, *Voyages*, viii, 346-347.

4. The second version of the *Inducements* is shorter than the one

printed in Brereton's *Relation,* and "embodies material taken (sometimes verbatim) from the longer tract by the elder Hakluyt, and from the younger man's *Discourse* [of 1584]" (E. G. R. Taylor, in her preface to Hakluyt, *Letters,* p. 39). See Hakluyt, *Letters,* ii, 327-338 and 339-343, for the texts of the two *Inducements.*

5. See: Elvas, Gentleman of, *Virginia richly valued . . ., out . . . of Don Ferdinando de Soto . . . Written by a Portugall gentleman of Elvas . . . and translated . . . by Richard Hakluyt* (London, 1609). Chapter XLIV, including the material mentioned, covers pp. 177-179.

6. See: Laudonnière, René de, *A notable historie containing foure voyages . . .* Translated by Richard Hakluyt (London, 1587), and reprinted in Hakluyt, *Voyages,* viii, pp. 451-452 and pp. 455 and 456.

7. The full detail about the commodities, from which this list was taken, is to be found in Hakluyt, *Voyages,* viii, 353-371.

8. These references to the *Voyages* are in the following numbered paragraphs:
>   3. Laudonnière, in *Voyages,* ix, 88.
>   4. Espejo, in *Voyages,* ix, 169-185 (in Spanish) and 186-204 (in English). ["Paginis 303, &c." should read "paginis 383, &c."] The reference to Francisco Sánchez Xamuscado and his map is in *Voyages,* ix, 187. [Xamuscado, modern Chamuscado, is obviously a nickname. It means "depraved, addicted to vice," etc.]
>   5. Lane, in *Voyages,* viii, 328-329.
>   7. Verrazzano, in *Voyages,* viii, 430-434; and scattered references to Cabot, for which see Index, *Voyages.*

As to Hakluyt's scholarly accuracy and care, Parks writes that Hakluyt painstakingly gave "chapter and verse" for all his notes (Hakluyt, *Life,* p. 156).

9. *Virginia Richly Valued, By the description . . . of Don Ferdinando de Soto . . . Written by a Portugall gentleman of Elvas* ["hum fidalgo Delvas"], translated by Richard Hakluyt (London, 1609). The name of the "Gentleman of Elvas" is still unknown.

10. It was called *Terra sigillata* (sealed earth) because it was a kind of "earth" or clay, from the island of Lemnos, then part of the Turkish Empire, each small "loaf" (or brick) of which bore the seal of the Grand Signior. It was used also as an antidote for poison.

11. For a full note on the "Beades", see Quinn, *Roanoke,* i, 347.

12. Purchas, *Pilgrimes,* xviii, 322.

13. Brereton, *Relation,* p. 15.

PART III

1. With regard to this see, for example, Quinn, *Hayes* (see Chapter VII, note 9), pp. 39-41; and Hakluyt, *Letters*, i, 60-61 and footnote.

2. There was a Cage family, for instance, resident in Pakenham (5 miles ENE of Bury St. Edmunds, where Bartholomew Gosnold lived in the late 1590's), one of whom married Bartholomew's great-grandfather's brother. Another Cage, of the same village but a later generation, had five sons all of whose given names correspond with the names of Cages interested in Virginia — two of them with members of the Ralegh expeditions of 1585 and 1587. From such neighbors (even relatives of a remote kind) as these, Gosnold would have heard intriguing stories of unknown lands that blocked the way westwards to the Orient.

3. The Rev. Warner F. Gookin in his long studies of Bartholomew Gosnold reached the conclusion that he was born in 1571, on the basis that he was matriculated at Cambridge University in 1587 and that he was mentioned in his great-grandfather's will, dated 20 October 1572. (See, e.g., Gookin's "Who Was Bartholomew Gosnold?" *William and Mary Quarterly*, 3rd, ser., Vol. VI [1949], p. 400.) WFG failed to note that among the Gosnolds and affiliated families there is no one named Bartholomew prior to our "hero", so far as very extensive records show. Roberts, Johns, Williams and Edwards there were, and an Anthony or two, but not a single Bartholomew. We therefore venture to suggest that this name was inspired by the frightful massacre of Protestants on St. Bartholomew's Day in France, 24 August, 1572. News of this reached England within the week. It is not unlikely that the Protestant Gosnold-Bacon alliance named their first son in commemoration of the event, and that Bartholomew Gosnold consequently was baptized between the end of August and 20 October, 1572, the date on which Robert Gosnold the elder signed his will (in which Bartholomew is mentioned). This suggestion does not conflict with WFG's guess of 1571, but rather sharpens the focus.

4. Cf. Gookin, *Who Was Bartholomew Gosnold?*, pp. 400-401, which was written before the record of Gosnold's privateering voyage was found. As for the record, WFG gave the details to the *Boston Daily Globe*, Boston, Massachusetts (24 July 1952, page 24), on the basis of information obtained directly from Dr. Kenneth R. Andrews, editor of *English Privateering Voyages to the West Indies* (Hakluyt Society, 2nd ser., cxi, 1959.)

5. *Purchas His Pilgrimes* (Glasgow, 1905-1907), xviii, 324.

6. Bartholomew Gilbert is still somewhat a mystery. When the great Portuguese carrack *Madre de Dios* was captured early in August, 1592, the treasure aboard was such that it was impossible to estimate its value, not to mention protect it from pilfering. Much of this treasure fell into un-

scrupulous hands, vast quantities of diamonds and pearls trickling through the captors' fingers into the London market, and elsewhere. At that time Bartholomew Gilbert was a (young?) goldsmith in London. He may have been a son, nephew or cousin of a Gilbert, also a goldsmith, who settled near Bury St. Edmunds in 1572. Whoever he was, he turns up in history in June, 1594, asking to be let out of Wood Street Counter (prison) "because of a diamond that cost him £500 and more" (Historical MSS Commission, *Salisbury Papers*, iv, 549). This diamond, of 26½ carats uncut, was apparently part of the *Madre de Dios* booty, and Gilbert attempted to sell it at an exorbitant price to the Queen. The story is a long and involved one, but after much watching, questioning, and so on, Gilbert was obviously eventually exonerated — or served out a short prison term. Captain Christopher Newport of Virginia fame was in the fight that took the carrack, and such names as Lord Cobham, Sir Richard Martin (father of Captain John, who went to Virginia with Gosnold in 1606), a William Hamor (another Hamor went to Virginia), and so forth, turn up in reports on the case. What does not turn up is the connection between Bartholomew Gilbert and Bartholomew Gosnold. [*Note*: During research in the East Suffolk County Archives, while this volume was already in the press, the editor succeeded in identifying Bartholomew Gilbert as the son of a first cousin of Bartholomew Gosnold's aunt, Dorothy Gilbert. This fact, coupled with other details gathered in England, throws further light on Gilbert's career.]

7. Richard Arthur Preston, *Gorges of Plymouth Fort* (Toronto, 1953), pp. 138-139.

8. Smith, *Works*, p. 830, and J. Franz Pichler, "Captain John Smith in the Light of Styrian Sources", *Virginia Magazine of History and Biography*, Vol. 65 (1957), pp. 335 and 349.

9. For further details, see Part II of my forthcoming study of Captain John Smith.

10. Smith, *Works*, pp. 89-90. Although the passage is part of the chapters signed by Thomas Studley, the style seems to betray Smith as the author. WFG's *First Leaders* is primarily an elaboration of the information supplied in Smith, *Works*, but without the benefit of a vast amount of information that has been brought to the fore since that article was written. Significantly, it was only in 1953 that Bradford Smith, in his *Captain John Smith: His Life and Legend* (Philadelphia, 1953), began to apply modern historical research to the details of the beginnings of Jamestown — a year after the lamented death of Mr. Gookin. Bradford Smith and his associate Dr. Laura Polanyi Striker (since deceased) have been followed by the author of Part III.

11. *Aubrey's Brief Lives*, edited by Oliver Lawson Dick (London, 1950), p. 246.

12. Preston, *Gorges,* p. 140 (cf. Chapter XIII, note 1).

13. *Eastward Hoe,* by George Chapman, Ben Jonson and John Marston (London, 1605), particularly in Act III, Scene iii (in a Billingsgate Tavern).

14. Based on *The Records of The Virginia Company of London,* edited by Susan Myra Kingsbury (Washington, 1906-1935), i, 11-21, with side-lights from Preston, *Gorges,* pp. 139-140, D. B. Quinn, *Raleigh and the British Empire* (London, 1947), pp. 228-229, Wesley Frank Craven, *The Virginia Company Of London* ("Jamestown Booklet", Williamsburg, Virginia, 1957), pp. 2-3, and Alexander Brown, *The Genesis of the United States* (Boston, 1890), i, 36-42.

15. For details, see Charles W. F. Smith, "Chaplain Robert Hunt and His Parish in Kent", *Historical Magazine of the Protestant Episcopal Church,* Vol XXVI (1957), pp. 15-33.

16. Smith, *Works,* p. 90.

17. Most of what is known about Christopher Newport is contained in K. R. Andrews, "Christopher Newport of Limehouse, Mariner", *William and Mary Quarterly,* 3rd. ser., Vol. XI (1954), pp. 28-41.

18. While it is still impossible to identify Sicklemore/Ratcliffe, there are indications that he may have been a Sicklemore of Ipswich (in which case he was vaguely connected with the Gosnold family by marriage) who had chosen to take the name of his home port or residence of Ratcliffe (near London) as his *nom de plume,* or better *nom de mer.* (In the only [?] surviving document bearing his own signature he writes: *John RadClyeffe./ S comenly called.* His writing, in an age of elaborate and illiterate hand-writing, is like a pile of thread-ends in a tailor-shop, in strong contrast with the simple, clear handwriting of John Smith.) It is also possible that he married a Ratcliffe (or Radcliffe) and took his wife's name — the Radcliffes were a distinguished family, which included the Earl of Sussex. (Alexander Brown thinks he was a soldier. See *Genesis,* ii, 977-978.) Whoever he was, we cannot tell whether Newport chose him, or Gosnold, or who; or precisely why he was chosen at all.

19. Smith, *Works,* p. 263.

20. Smith, *Works,* p. 931.

21. See note 15, above.

22. See Wingfield's *Discourse,* in Smith, *Works,* pp. lxxxii-lxxxiii and lxxxviii.

23. See my article, "Captain George Kendall: Mutineer or Intelligencer?", *VMHB,* Vol. 70 (1962), pp. 297-313.

24. See Richard Beale Davis, *George Sandys: Poet-Adventurer* (London, 1955), p. 93, 94 and various references to be found in the Index.

25. The best modern reprint is in *The Three Charters Of The Virginia Company Of London*, edited by Samuel M. Bemiss ("Jamestown Booklet", Williamsburg, Virginia, 1957), pp. 13-22.

26. See Brown, *Genesis*, i, 75-79.

27. In Smith, *Works*, pp. xxxiii-xxxvii.

28. Purchas, *Pilgrimes*, xviii, 460. The Jamestown Foundation, Williamsburg, Virginia, has made a thorough study of the three ships, the numbers aboard each, and the like, a copy of which was kindly supplied to the author. He has followed this analysis with the insignificant change of spelling *God Speed* as two words rather than one.

29. Smith, *Works*, p. 6.

30. Smith, *Works*, p. liii.

31. This is Wingfield's own account, in Smith, *Works*, p. lxxv.

32. George Percy, in Smith, *Works*, p. lxx. Raleigh had also estimated twenty weeks for a round-trip.

33. Smith, *Works*, p. 8.

34. Alexander Brown, *The First Republic in America* (Boston, Massachusetts, 1898), pp. 33-34.

35. Smith, *Works*, p. lxxii.

36. Smith, *Works*, p. lxxxix.

37. Smith, *Works*, p. lxxx.

BIBLIOGRAPHY

A selective bibliography, extending beyond the works referred to in the footnotes, would be of little use to the casual reader, and of none at all to the specialist. A full bibliography lies beyond the scope of practicality. Readers, casual or specialized, are therefore referred for further sidelights on Gosnold and the earliest history of English-speaking America to the bibliographical details contained in such works as these:

> On Bartholomew Gosnold — the brief biography by Fulmer Mood, in the Dictionary of American Biography.

> On pre-Gosnold voyages — the extended bibliography in Quinn, Roanoke (as listed below), Appendix IV, Sources, pp. 911-946.

> On post-Gosnold developments — the "Selective Bibliography" in George F. Willison, Saints and Strangers (New York, 1945), pp. 487-494.

While there are many other bibliographies, both large and small, these three have been chosen for mention because of their convenience and general accessibility.

BIBLIOGRAPHICAL ABBREVIATIONS USED IN FOOTNOTES:

Bradford, Plymouth — Bradford's History "Of Plimoth Plantation," printed under the direction of the Secretary of the Commonwealth [of Massachusetts]. Boston, 1899.

Brereton, Relation — A Briefe and true Relation of the Discoverie of the North part of Virginia . . . by M. John Brereton. 2nd ed., London, 1602.

Brown, Genesis — Alexander Brown, The Genesis of the United States. 2 vols. Boston, Massachusetts, 1890.

Flannery, Analysis — Regina Flannery, An Analysis of Coastal Algonquian Culture. (The Catholic University of America, Anthropological Studies, No. 7.) Washington, D.C., 1939.

Hakluyt, Letters — The Original Writings & Correspondence of the Two Richard Hakluyts, ed. by Eva G. R. Taylor. (Hakluyt Society, 2nd ser., LXXVI-LXXVII.) 2 vols., 1935.

Hakluyt, Life — George Bruner Parks, Richard Hakluyt and the English Voyages. (American Geographical Society, Special Publication No. 10.) New York, 1930.

Hakluyt, *Voyages* — The Glasgow reprint (1903-1905) of Richard Hakluyt's *Principal Navigations Voyages Traffiques & Discoveries of the English Nation.* 3 vols., London, 1598-1600.

"Jamestown Booklet" — refers to the series of 23 monographs by various authors called *Jamestown 350th Anniversary Historical Booklets,* ed. by E. G. Swem (Williamsburg, Virginia, 1957).

Levermore, *Forerunners* — *Forerunners and Competitors of the Pilgrims and Puritans,* ed. by Charles Herbert Levermore. 2 vols., Brooklyn, New York, 1912.

Martha's Vineyard Guide — *Martha's Vineyard: A Short History by Various Hands, together with A Guide to Points of Interest,* ed. by Eleanor R. Mayhew. Edgartown, Massachusetts, 1956.

NEHGR — *The New England Historical and Genealogical Register.*

OED — *The Oxford English Dictionary,* Oxford, 1933. 12 vols. plus Supplement. (Sometimes abbreviated in older reference works as *NED,* for *New English Dictionary . . .*)

PCC — Prerogative Court of Canterbury; the office where probated wills were registered. References are to the names of bound volumes of transcripts housed in Somerset House, London.

Purchas, Pilgrimes — The Glasgow reprint (1905-1907) of Samuel Purchas' *Hakluytus Posthumus or Purchas His Pilgrimes.* 4 vols., London, 1625. (The occasional "5th volume" is a reprint of an earlier, different work.)

Quinn, *Gilbert* — *The Voyages and Colonizing Enterprises of Sir Humphrey Gilbert,* ed. by David Beers Quinn. (Hakluyt Society, 2nd ser., LXXXIII-LXXXIV.) 2 vols., 1940.

Quinn, *Roanoke* — *The Roanoke Voyages 1584-1590,* ed. by David Beers Quinn. (Hakluyt Society, 2nd. ser., CIV-CV.) 2 vols., 1955.

Smith, *Works* — *Capt. John Smith, . . . Works,* ed. by Edward Arber. (The English Scholar's Library, No. 16.) Birmingham, England, 1884. [Note: A reissue of this with a new introduction by A. G. Bradley was published under the title *Travels and Works of Captain John Smith,* in 2 vols., with identical, continuous pagination, Edinburgh, 1910.]

STC [Wing] — *Short-Title Catalogue of Books Printed . . . 1641-1700,* compiled by Donald Wing. 3 vols., New York, 1945-1951.

Strachey, *Historie* — *The Historie of Travell into Virginia Britania; By*

William Strachey, gent., ed. by Louis B. Wright and Virginia Freund. (Hakluyt Society, 2nd ser., CIII.) 1953.

VMHB — The Virginia Magazine of History and Biography.

WMQ — The William and Mary Quarterly, third series.

WFG — The Reverend Warner F. Gookin.

GOOKIN ARCHIVES. These are located in the Library of the Dukes County Historical Society, Edgartown, Massachusetts. The titles in quotation marks here used for reference may be only temporary, but will serve in any case as a guide to the location of correspondence, documents, etc.

Ancestry — "The Ancestry of Bartholomew Gosnold," *NEHGR,* cv (1951), pp. 5-22.

Capawack — Capawack, alias Martha's Vineyard, Edgartown Massachusetts, 1947.

Family Connections — "Family Connections of Bartholomew Gosnold," *NEHGR,* civ (1950), pp. 27-36.

First Leaders — "The First Leaders at Jamestown," *VMHB,* 58 (1950), pp. 181-193.

Norumbega — A Voyage of Discovery to the Southern Parts of Norumbega, Edgartown, Massachusetts, 1950.

Notes — "Notes on the Gosnold Family," *VMHB,* 57 (1949), pp. 307-315.

"Who Was Bartholomew Gosnold?" *WMQ,* vi (1949), pp. 398-415.

APPENDICES

A. Genealogical Table
B. Gosnold's letter to his father

This genealogical chart is based on studies made for Mr. Gookin.

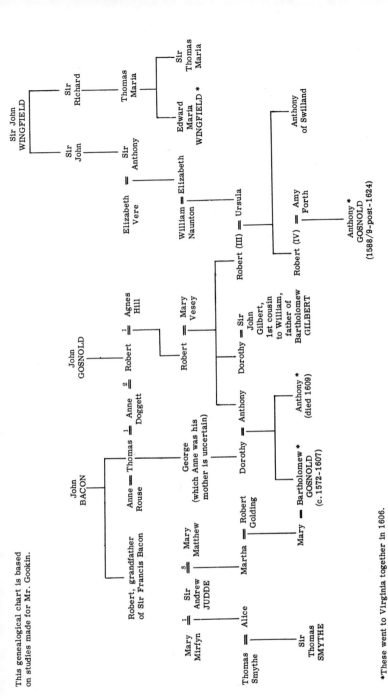

*These went to Virginia together in 1606.

APPENDIX A

Master BARTHOLOMEVV GOSNOLDS *Letter to his Father, touching his first Voyage to* Virginia, 1602.

20

M*Y dutetie remembred, &c. Sir, I was in good hope that my occasions would haue allowed mee so much libertie, as to haue come vnto you before this time; otherwise I would haue written more at large concerning the Countrie from whence we lately came, then I did: but not well remembring what I haue already written (though I am assured that there is nothing set downe disagreeing with the truth) I thought it fittest not to goe about to adde any thing in writing, but rather to leaue the report of the rest till I come my selfe; which now I hope shall be shortly, and so soone as with conueniency I may. In the meane time, notwithstanding whereas you seeme not to be satisfied by that which I haue already written, concerning some especiall matters. I haue here briefely (and as well as I can) added these few lines for* 30 *your further satisfaction: and first as touching that place where we were most resident, it is in the Latitude of 41.degrees, and one third part; which albeit it be so much to the Southward, yet is it more cold then those parts of* Europe, *which are scituated vnder the same paralell: but one thing is worth the noting, that notwithstanding the place is not so much subiect to cold as* England *is, yet did we finde the Spring to be later there, then it is with vs here, by almost a moneth: this whether it hapned accidentally this last Spring to be so, or whether it be so of course, I am not very certaine; the latter seemes most likely, whereof also there may be giuen some sufficient reason, which now I omit: as for the Acornes we saw gathered on heapes, they were of the last yeare, but doubtlesse their Summer continues longer then ours. We cannot gather by any thing we could obserue in the people, or by any triall we had thereof our selues; but that it is as healthfull a Climate as any can be. The Inhabitants there, as I wrote before, being of tall* 40 *stature, comely proportion, strong, actiue, and some of good yeares, and as it should seeme very healthfull, are sufficient proofe of the healthfulnesse of the place. First, for our selues (thankes be to God) we had not a man sicke two dayes together in all our Voyage; whereas others that went out with vs, or about that time on other Voyages (especially such as went vpon reprisall) were most of them infected with sicknesse, whereof they lost some of their men, and brought home a many sicke, returning notwithstanding long before vs. But* Verazzano, *and others (at I take it, you may reade in the Booke of Discoueries) doe more particularly intreate of the Age of the people in that coast. The Sassafras which we brought we had vpon the Ilands: where though we had little disturbance, and reasonable plenty: yet for that the greatest part of our people were imployed about the fitting of our house, and such like affaires, and a few (and those but easie labourers) vndertooke this worke, the rather because we were informed before our going forth, that* 50 *a tunne was sufficient to cloy* England) *and further, for that we had resolued vpon our returne, and taken view of our victuall, we iudged it then needefull to vse expedition; which afterward we had more certaine proofe of for when we came to an anker before* Portsmouth, *which was some foure dayes after we made the land, we had not one Cake of Bread, nor any drinke, but a little Vinegar, left: for these and other reasons, we returned no otherwise laden then you haue heard. And thus much I hope shall suffice till I can my selfe come to giue you further notice, which though it be not so soone as I could haue wisht, yet I hope it shall be in conuenient time. In the meane time crauing your pardon, for which the vrgent occasions of my stay will pleade, I humbly take my leaue.* 7.Septemb. 1602.

Your dutifull Sonne,   63

BARTH. GOSNOLD.

CHAP.

APPENDIX B

INDEX OF PERSONS,
AND PLACES IN THE NEW WORLD,
MENTIONED IN THE TEXT

270